TURKEY AND RUSSIA.

The latest and best Works published.

A YEAR WITH THE TURKS:

OR, SKETCHES OF TRAVEL IN THE EUROPEAN AND ASIATIC DOMINIONS OF THE SULTAN. By Warington W. Smyth, M. A. With a colored Ethnological Map of the Empire. 12mo., cloth 75 cents. *Second Edition now ready.*

"Wallachia, the Danube, and other places now so prominent, are made familiar by the plain, easy style of our author, while a flood of light is shed upon the Turks as a people, their system of government, the policy of their rulers, and the whole internal arrangement of the Ottoman Empire."—*Phila. National Argus.*

"We advise all those who wish for clear information with regard to the condition of the Empire, and the various races that make up the population, to get this book and read it."—*Boston Commonwealth.*

"This is a plain and simple history of a region invested just now with peculiar interest. The geography of the country is minutely set down, the character, habits, idiosyncrasies of its inhabitants thoroughly portrayed, its resources, wealth and wants pointedly referred to, its government, laws and provisions clearly defined."—*Buffalo Express.*

"Mr. Smyth traveled in Turkey in the fall of last year, and his descriptions of the country are therefore more recent than can be obtained elsewhere."—*Troy Daily Times.*

"Mr. Smyth is just the right sort of man for a pleasant and useful traveling companion; good-humored, shrewd, intelligent, observant, and blessed with a good stock of common sense; and he has given us in this small volume a graphic, attractive and instructive account of what he saw and heard and experienced during twelve months of travel through the wide-spread dominions of Sultan Mahmoud."—*Boston Traveller.*

ALSO, THE THIRD EDITION OF

THE RUSSIAN SHORES OF THE BLACK SEA:

WITH A VOYAGE DOWN THE VOLGA, AND A TOUR THROUGH THE COUNTRY OF THE DON COSSACKS. By Laurence Oliphant, Author of a "Journey to Nepaul." From the Third London edition. 12mo., cloth, two maps and eighteen cuts. 75 cents.

Seven hundred copies of this work are advertised by one English Circulating Library.

"The volume is adorned by a number of wood-cuts and by two useful maps. It is a valuable contribution to our knowledge of Russia, and should be read by all who desire to be well informed."—*N. Y. Commercial Advertiser.*

"His book is full of exceedingly valuable information, and is written in an attractive style."—*Cincinnati Christian Herald.*

"Mr. Oliphant is a fluent, easy, companionable writer, who tells us a great deal we want to know, without a particle either of pedantry or bombast. This neat little book, with its maps and illustrations, will prove a most acceptable informant to the general reader, and at the same time prove highly entertaining."—*Boston Transcript.*

"Mr. Oliphant is an acute observer, a shrewd and intelligent man, a clear, vigorous and distinct writer, and his book embodies the best account of Southern Russia that has ever appeared. His account of Sebastopol will find many interested readers."—*Boston Atlas.*

"This book reminds us more of Stephen's delightful Incidents of Travel than any other book with which we are acquainted. It is an extremely interesting and valuable book."—*Boston Traveller.*

THE WAR IN THE EAST.

THE

RUSSO-TURKISH CAMPAIGNS

OF

1828 AND 1829;

WITH A VIEW OF THE PRESENT STATE OF AFFAIRS IN THE EAST.

BY COLONEL CHESNEY, R. A., D. C. L., F. R. S.

AUTHOR OF THE EXPEDITION FOR THE SURVEY OF THE RIVERS EUPHRATES AND TIGRIS.

With an Appendix, containing the Diplomatic Correspondence and the Secret Correspondence between the Russian and English Governments. 1 vol., 12mo., Cloth; Maps. $1.

AMONG the many works at present appearing on the Russian and Turkish affairs, this volume demands special attention, from the high reputation of its author. Colonel Chesney, of the Royal Artillery, proceeded to the seat of the last war, in 1828, with military stores—intending to give his assistance to the Turks, in their resistance to the Russian invasion. He arrived too late for active service, but he had opportunity of collecting materials on the spot for a narrative of the campaigns, and he became well acquainted with the countries which are again the theatre of warlike operations. The account of the war of 1828–1829 is a valuable record of the events of that period, and has fresh interest from the light it throws on passing events. * * * The narrative of the Campaigns of 1828 and 1829 is a valuable contribution to military history. It is an important and well-timed publication.—*Literary Gazette.*

COLONEL CHESNEY has peculiar claims on our notice. Few men possess more extensive knowledge, personal and other, of the geography and statistics of the East. * * * His work is written throughout in a fine, manly spirit. We cordially recommend it to our readers as the best historical companion they can possess during the campaigns which are about to open.—*Athenæum.*

COLONEL CHESNEY here supplies us with full information respecting this important period of European History, and with an accurate description, from a military point of view, of the countries which form at the present moment the theatre of war.—*Examiner.*

A CONDENSED detail of facts, and the results of personal observation, it is replete with instructive matter; a record of one of the most striking events in modern history; a guide to the formation of correct judgment on the future. Good maps, and minute descriptions of the principal seats of the past and present war; a statistical account of the military resources of Turkey; its present state and prospects; its political and commercial value—occupy an interesting portion of the work, which we heartily recommend to the attention of our readers.—*Lond. Critic.*

THE

RUSSO-TURKISH CAMPAIGNS

OF 1828 AND 1829.

THE

RUSSO-TURKISH CAMPAIGNS

OF 1828 AND 1829

WITH A VIEW OF THE

PRESENT STATE OF AFFAIRS IN THE EAST

BY

COLONEL CHESNEY, R.A., D.C.L., F.R.S.

AUTHOR OF "THE EXPEDITION FOR THE SURVEY OF THE RIVERS EUPHRATES AND TIGRIS"

WITH AN APPENDIX

CONTAINING THE DIPLOMATIC CORRESPONDENCE BETWEEN THE FOUR POWERS, AND THE SECRET CORRESPONDENCE BETWEEN THE RUSSIAN AND ENGLISH GOVERNMENTS

With Maps

REDFIELD

110 AND 112 NASSAU STREET, NEW YORK

1854

TO

HIS IMPERIAL MAJESTY

THE SULTAN ABDUL MEDJID KHAN,

EMPEROR OF THE OTTOMANS,

&c. &c. &c.

SIRE,

The belief entertained by Namik Pasha, your Majesty's Ambassador Extraordinary at the Court of St. James's, that such a request would not be quite unacceptable, if there were time under present circumstances to make it, induces me to venture to solicit your Majesty to be graciously pleased to accept the present dedication of my work on the invasions of the Ottoman dominions by Russia in 1828 and 1829.

I feel the more anxious to be permitted to do myself this honour, since it affords me an opportunity of expressing my grateful acknowledgments for the uniform kindness I received, when journeying as a traveller through your Majesty's dominions in Europe and Asia; as well as the furtherance experienced at a later period by me, in a public capacity.

I allude to the expedition, carried out under my command, to survey the rivers Euphrates and Tigris; which undertaking, as I expected then and still expect, must ultimately be the means of extending the commerce of Turkey with the rest of Europe, and also of uniting more closely, by the bonds of mutual advantage, the Turkish and British Empires.

Nearly seven years have been passed by me in your Majesty's dominions, partly at the head of the preceding undertaking, and partly as an ordinary traveller to gain information; and a high estimate has been formed in consequence, of the fidelity and straightforward character of the Turkish people. Nor can I doubt for a moment, that increasing intercourse will at length remove existing prejudices, and produce throughout Europe, the same impressions of the loyal character of the Turk, which are now entertained by

Your Majesty's most obedient

and very humble servant,

F. R. CHESNEY, *Colonel*,

Royal Artillery.

Packolet,
near Kilkeel,
Ireland.
31*st Jan*. 1854.

PREFACE.

A visit which I made to the seat of the Russo-Turkish war in European Turkey towards the close of 1829, and to that in Asia shortly afterwards, has furnished the principal part of the materials for the following account of the campaigns of that and the preceding year. Although not personally present during the whole of the campaigns, I had the advantage of collecting materials on the spots where the struggle had taken place between the Russian and Turkish forces, and also of conversing with officers of both sides, fresh from the scenes of action, and full of reminiscences of the contest, which was then drawing towards its close.

The narrative of the campaigns of 1828–29, both in European and Asiatic Turkey, will be found in the first nine chapters of this work. In Chapter X., some notice has been given of the principal circumstances which have occurred lately in connection with the Eastern question, so as to present a connected view of the interval between the past and present wars of Russia against Turkey.

A mere abstract of these occurrences, which have been so recently before the public as to have been read of by almost every individual, might have been more acceptable in some respects to the generality of readers. But since a very condensed view of these important negotiations might have raised a question as to its impartiality, it seemed to me the preferable course to go at some length into the transactions that have taken place, chiefly in Constantinople, during the last twelve months, and to give the leading documents *in extenso.* These will be found in the Appendix, as taken from "La Question d'Orient devant l'Europe," par M. A. Ubicini.

In the concluding chapter I have endeavoured to give some account of the present state of Turkey, and to show what may be done by her, *single-handed*, against Russia. If the opinion of the Turks there given should appear to some too favourable, the reader may feel assured that I formed this opinion quite independently of the late successes at Oltenitza and Citate, and irrespectively of the now universally acknowledged bravery of the Turks at Sinope, and elsewhere. Whether it be considered a just and fair, or an overcharged appreciation of the Turkish character, it has been long entertained by me, and is founded upon what was done by this people under the most adverse circumstances; and it is known to many that I expressed a similar opinion in 1829, when there was still a question of renewing the war with Russia rather than ratifying the oppressive treaty of Adrianople.

Having alluded thus briefly to the contents of the present work, a few words will show the cause of its publication in its present form.

The noble defence that Turkey continued to make against her invaders in 1829, was too powerful a temptation for me to resist, and I determined to proceed to the seat of war. It may be asked, how a simple individual could have served the Turkish cause at the period in question? Two openings at least presented themselves. I was the bearer of a strong letter, from a very distinguished admiral, the late Sir Sydney Smith, G. C. B., to the Turkish Government, which was calculated to inspire such confidence as was necessary to enable me to be useful to the Sultan.

The then growing power of steam had particularly attracted my attention, and I conceived that by the purchase of a certain number of steam vessels, the naval superiority of the Sultan in the Euxine might be partly, if not wholly, recovered. With reference to this all-important object, I ascertained the number of steam vessels that might be purchased, and took with me to Constantinople a paper showing the expense of each, and the means of manning and equipping them for the intended service.

The other proposed means of utility was connected with the artillery; and I prepared a similar estimate of the various kinds of guns and ordnance stores which could be purchased at different establishments in Great Britain: these included Congreve rockets.

It so happened that the house of Niven, Kerr, Black and Co., had just received orders to ship some rockets for the Sultan's service; and, after the necessary arrangements had been made for this purpose, I embarked with these missiles in a fast sailing clipper, the *Premier*. My object was, with the assistance of a man who had served with that arm in the battle of Leipsic, to form a rocket corps, for the special defence of the more elevated passes of the Balkan.

But whilst the *Premier* was running through the Russian blockading squadron into the Dardanelles, General Diebitsch was scaling those mountains—and the steamers and rockets (with which, it should in justice be added, the Government had nothing to do) were almost rendered unavailable by the arrival of the Russians in Adrianople.

Subsequently I proceeded to the seat of war; and, accompanied by a youthful traveller, W. N. Peach, Esq., visited the different fortresses described in this work, as well as the various posts occupied by the Russian and Turkish troops in Wallachia and Bulgaria, previously to the ratification of peace.

After all idea of renewing the war was ultimately abandoned, my journeyings to Egypt, Syria, Arabia, &c., led to the Euphrates expedition, of which it was afterwards decided by the Government that an account should be given to the public; and the contents of the first nine chapters of the present small volume were to have appeared, in a more condensed form, as a part of this larger work.

A few words of explanation as to the cause of this change of plan, may not be unacceptable to those friends and that portion of the public who have continued to feel an interest in the appearance of the narrative of the Euphrates expedition.

In consequence of the great expense necessarily attendant on the publication of fourteen sheet-maps, and a large number of drawings, the Government of the day (Lord Melbourne's) decided that the Treasury should give £1,500, the India Board £600, and the Court of Directors another £600, in order to cover the anticipated loss. Owing, however, to departmental difficulties, I only received ultimately the Treasury grant, and was therefore unable to complete more than the two introductory volumes of the work; which, deducting all receipts, left me with the heavy loss of £3,382 8s. 11d. as the result of my labours.

My position in this respect, as well as with regard to travelling expenses and other expectations held out by Government, was brought before Lord John Russell by three members of the House of Commons. His Lordship, after making all proper inquiries and references, is understood to have replied, that "his only difficulty was how to make good the promises of a former Government."

In consequence of the loss of the various departmental references at the time of the next change of ministry, some difficulty was found in bringing the case before Lord Derby's government. That part of it, however, which related to the publication of the narrative of the Euphrates expedition, now took another phase. A distinguished Member of Parliament, whose indefatigable services are about to be lost to the nation as well as to the University of Oxford, proposed, in a letter to the Government, on the 31st of January, 1853, that the third and fourth volumes, or Narrative of the Expedition, should be executed at the Stationery office; the author giving his time for this purpose gratuitously, and the country to receive the proceeds of the work.

So far as is known to me, this application has not led to any result; and it is under these circumstances that a part of the work in question appears in its present form.

But, however painful it may be to me to find myself still unable to fulfil my engagement to the public of laying before them the Narrative of the Euphrates Expedition, I cannot but rejoice at being enabled, by the liberality of my present publishers, to publish this account of the campaigns of 1828 and 1829, at a moment when the subject has become one of no common interest, and when I trust it may, in some degree, serve the cause of those for whose benefit it was originally written, and for whom the author must ever feel sincere admiration and deep interest.

F. R. CHESNEY, *Colonel*,
Royal Artillery.

Packolet,
near Kilkeel,
Ireland.
31*st Jan.* 1854.

CONTENTS.

CHAPTER I.

POLITICAL RELATIONS OF TURKEY PREVIOUS TO THE WAR OF 1828 AND 1829.

CHAPTER II.

SKETCH OF THE SEAT OF WAR IN EUROPEAN AND ASIATIC TURKEY.

CHAPTER III.

PLANS FOR THE INVASION OF TURKEY AND COMMENCEMENT OF THE CAMPAIGN OF 1828.

CHAPTER IV.

FAILURE OF THE ATTACKS UPON SCHUMLA, AND CONCLUSION OF THE CAMPAIGN OF 1828.

CHAPTER V.

CONTINUATION OF THE OPERATIONS OF 1828, AND CLOSE OF THE CAMPAIGN.

CHAPTER VI.

THE CAMPAIGN OF 1828 IN ASIATIC TURKEY.

CHAPTER VII.

FIRST PART OF THE EUROPEAN CAMPAIGN IN 1829.

CHAPTER VIII.

FALL OF SILISTRIA AND CONCLUSION OF THE CAMPAIGN OF 1829.

CHAPTER IX.

ASIATIC CAMPAIGN OF 1829.

CHAPTER X.

CAUSES OF THE PRESENT WAR BETWEEN TURKEY AND RUSSIA.

CHAPTER XI.

ON THE PRESENT RESISTANCE OF TURKEY TO RUSSIA, AND THE MEANS OF DEFENDING THE EMPIRE.

THE RUSSO-TURKISH CAMPAIGNS

OF 1828 AND 1829.

CHAPTER I.

POLITICAL RELATIONS OF TURKEY PREVIOUS TO THE WAR OF 1828 AND 1829.

Cause of Russian aggression—Acquisition of Georgia—Persian and Turkish hostilities up to 1812—Treaties of Gulistan and Bucharest—Persian war of 1826—The Greek insurrection—Tripartite treaty of London in 1826—Battle of Navarino—Tahir Pasha's history—State of Constantinople, and dignified conduct of the Divan—Progress of negotiations—Cogent reasons of the Divan—The ambassadors at length quit Constantinople—Europeans are taken under the protection of the Porte—Peace urged upon Russia by the Porte—The injudicious Hatti Scheriff of the Sultan is made the ground of war by Russia—Alleged grievances of Russia answered by the Porte—Manifesto of the Emperor of Russia—The Sultan declines to make it a religious war.

ALTHOUGH the struggle carried on by the Greeks to obtain their independence, and its climax in the bay of Navarino—which has been so expressively termed, "le crime politique de l'Europe"—appeared to be the immediate causes of the Russo-Turkish campaigns of 1828 and 1829 in Europe and Asia, the real origin of this war dates much farther back: it was in fact the result of the previous extension of the Russian territory along both sides of the Euxine.

2

A few words will suffice to show the gradual progress of this power previous to the treaty of Adrianople in 1829, by which Russia obtained the pashalik of Akhaltsikh, with the castle, and some districts she had hitherto retained contrary to the treaty of Akkerman in 1826.

In 1724 the territory south of the Caucasus was invaded by Peter the Great in person. This prince, having taken Derbend, entered into a treaty with Persia, by which, in return for the provinces of Daghestan, Shervan, Ghilan, Mazanderan, and Aster-abad, he was to recover from the Affghans the dominions of Shah Tamas. These conditions were not fulfilled, and the provinces in question continued to be held by Russia, till Nadir Shah recovered them from the Empress Anne in 1735, when the Georgian territory reverted to the government of its own princes.

After the death of Shah Tamas in 1783, the then reigning sovereign of Georgia, Heraclius, in consideration of his dominions being guaranteed to himself and his successors, declared himself a vassal of Russia ; by this fatal step he undermined the foundation of his dynasty, and of the previous independence of his country. This consummation took place soon after the demise of George XIII., the son and successor of Heraclius, when Georgia was declared to be a province of Russia by ukase of the Emperor Alexander, September 12th, 1801. This annexation led to very important consequences.

In order to secure a communication with the country

thus obtained on the southern slopes of the Caucasus, it became necessary for the Russians to overcome the Lesgis and other warlike inhabitants, who occupy the gorges and narrow defiles of those mountains; and also to be prepared for the wars with Persia and Turkey, which were the necessary consequences of thus approaching the territory of the former power situated on the shores of the Caspian, and that of the latter bordering upon the Euxine.

Persia became the first object of encroachment; and Russia having claimed Gandja as a former dependency of Georgia, a force advanced from this territory, and carried by storm what is now the fortress of Elizabethpol. This success caused the Chans of Derbent, Baku, Karabagh, Karaikaïtakh, and the Sultan of the Avares, to take the oath of fidelity to Russia. This invasion brought on a war with Persia, and subsequently with Turkey, the consequences of which were a succession of contests up to 1807. By the armistice of the 2nd September of that year, several advantages were gained by Russia. On the renewal of hostilities in 1809, Poti was taken by the Russians; but an attempt to take Akhaltsikh in the following year failed. It was, however, carried in 1811; and the Russians, in following up this success, defeated the Persian army on the Araxes, with severe loss, on the 19th October, 1812. The capture of Lenkoran by assault in January, 1813, was followed by the possession of the Khanat of Talisch. The treaty signed at Gulistan on the 12th October, 1813, ex tended the Russian possessions to the river Araxes; whilst by that of Bucharest with Turkey in 1812, her limits stretched to the mountains of Akhaltsikh: with the exception, however, of the fortresses of Anapa and Poti.*

The peace thus obtained continued until 1826, when the Prince Royal of Persia, Abbas Mirza, actuated by the hope of recovering his favourite hunting ground in the Karabagh, penetrated into Russia with a force of twenty-four battallions of infantry, 12,000 cavalry, 8,000 irregular troops, and twenty-four guns. He was, it would seem, encouraged to take this step by the expectation of hostilities in Europe, to which the aspect of affairs in Poland gave rise at that period.

The Greek insurrection, which had continued without intermission since 1820, began about this time to assume a more favourable aspect as regarded this people. Lord Cochrane, now Lord Dundonald, a skilful and daring seaman, assumed the command of the Greek fleet, and a well-known officer, General Church, that of their army.

Amongst other means, great efforts were made to induce the Albanians also to take arms against the Sultan; and liberal assistance having been sent to Greece by well-wishers to the cause of France and England especially, success would ere long have crowned the efforts of the

* Expedition to the Euphrates and Tigris, by Col. Chesney, R.A. DCL. FRS. vol. i., pp. 129, 130, and vol. ii., p. 503: Longman, London, 1851. La Russie dans l'Asie Mineure et Tableau du Caucase, par Felix Fonton, pp. 98, 103, 104, 105: Paris, 1840.

Greeks, if the Sultan had not summoned Ibrahim Pasha to his assistance. The presence of the Turco-Egyptian army soon changed the aspect of affairs, and everything promised the restoration of the Turkish authority over Greece, when the treaty of the 6th July, 1826, was signed in London—avowedly, to stop the effusion of blood.

The very unusual course of thus asserting the right of interfering between a sovereign and his subjects, which may one day be a precedent for momentous changes in other countries, was followed by more active measures. The Russian fleet proceeded from the Baltic to the Mediterranean; and the blockade, established principally by the latter power against the Turks, was immediately followed by that "untoward event," the battle of Navarino.

With the proverbial speed of bad news, the intelligence of this engagement was carried to the Porte by one of the admirals, Tahir Pasha. The history of this individual previously to his distinguishing himself in this unexpected conflict, is so characteristic of occasional life in Turkey, that a brief sketch of his progress will not be out of place.

Some years before this period, Tahir went to Egypt as reis (or captain) of a small vessel. In this capacity he visited Múhammed Ali, who at that time was very accessible to common people; and being pleased with Tahir's quickness and intelligence, the Pasha sent him in one of his vessels to dispose of her cargo in France. He proceeded accordingly to Marseilles, where he sold the cargo on his own account, and spent the money, partly at Marseilles, and the remainder at Paris. After this, he sailed with the Pasha's vessel for Turkey, where he sold her, and enjoyed himself at Constantinople with the proceeds. In the meantime, Múhammed Ali, after making inquiries over different parts of Europe, learned that Tahir was at Constantinople, and made a request that he should be given up; but the culprit learned this in sufficient time to enable him to enlist in a corps then being raised for Algiers, and thus evaded the Pasha. Arrived at Algiers, he persuaded the Dey that he was no common person, but had merely enlisted for the moment from necessity, and the Dey appointed him in consequence to the command of a large vessel. But Tahir had scarcely entered on his new position, when a firmán of search for him arrived from Constantinople, and he was immediately thrown into prison, until an opportunity should occur of sending him thither. His good fortune, however, did not desert him.

It happened that at this moment a letter arrived at Algiers from Sardinia, with some presents for the Dey. The letter was as usual written in French, and, fortunately for Tahir, the dragoman happened to be confined to his house by illness; no one could be found to make known the contents of the despatch, until the Dey was informed that one of the Turkish prisoners professed to be able to speak French and English. Tahir was immediately sent for from his dungeon, and translated the letter so satisfactorily, giving so admirable a turn to the different phrases, that the Dey professed his readiness to do whatever he might ask. Tahir requested his liberty ; this, however, the Dey could not grant without offending his master the Sultan ; but Tahir, ever fertile in expedients, overcame this difficulty by suggesting that he might be allowed to escape ! This was *not refused*, and our hero made his way to Constantinople, where, with the assistance of some friends, he obtained the command of a man-of-war brig, with a crew composed chiefly of Greeks, with only about a dozen Turks.

At the breaking out of the Greek revolution, the crew murdered all the Turks, excepting Tahir, whom they reserved to be ransomed. But on one occasion, when all hands had left the ship, leaving Tahir locked up, while they were carousing on shore, he managed to extricate himself from his place of confinement, and with great presence of mind and ingenuity got the brig under weigh. Not having power to set a sail by himself, he managed to work a gun overboard with a halyard attached to it, which, added to his own strength, enabled him to hoist some sail; and, having cut the cable, he scudded before the wind, until the vessel struck on the rocks. He then jumped overboard, swam to shore, and demanded of the Agha horses and a Tartar to Constantinople, where he arrived with the news of the Greek revolution. He was immediately appointed to the command of a frigate, and after distinguishing himself at Navarino, he was the first to reach Constantinople with the news of the battle; and thus upset the whole fabric of explanations and justifications which the ambassadors had been building. Tahir went subsequently to Algiers, and at length attained the rank of Capitan Pasha; in which position he died.

The intelligence that the combined fleets of England, France, and Russia, had overpowered and almost annihilated that of the Sultan, on 20th October, 1827, cut short the labours of the three ambassadors, and fell like a thunderbolt upon the Divan, as well as upon the European inhabitants of Turkey; those of the capital especially. The character hitherto so generally given to the Muslim—which in fact seems to have been drawn from accounts of the atrocities committed by Algerine pirates in the middle ages, rather than from anything that even the excesses of Turkish conquest might have justified—was well calculated to cause the greatest alarm amongst the European residents in Constantinople. But whatever may have been the severities practised by the Turks in former times, in common with other people belonging to the same semi-barbarous period, it soon became evident that the mercantile community had nothing to fear, and were not destined to suffer anything in consequence of the calamity inflicted on Turkey by the fleets of the three powers. The proceedings of the Divan were calm, dignified, and, as will presently be seen, eminently peaceable.

The termination of the Greek rebellion, even by coercive means if necessary, had been the object of the tripartite treaty; and as such a preponderating naval force was employed on this service, as would apparently have put an end to anything like resistance, the unexpected intelligence of the battle of Navarino, naturally caused almost as much surprise in London and Paris as in Constantinople itself. The destruction of the Sultan's fleet was therefore, as it was so expressively termed by the Duke of Wellington, "an untoward event;"* especially as the preservation of the Ottoman empire is most essential to the balance of power in Europe.

But since, in a time of peaceful economy, funds were not likely to be forthcoming to make good the injury inflicted, while it was impossible to recall either the event or the false step which had been taken by coercing Turkey, the Divan, as before, was pressed on the 8th and 10th, and again on the 22nd of November, 1827, to carry out the treaty of London without further delay.

The Reis Effendi replied, "that it was not a case of differences or hostilities between two independent powers, which might be arranged by the interference of a third power; nor was it that of an armistice or treaty of peace, which in fact can only be concluded with a recognised power." "How, then," he forcibly asked, "can there be

* Reply of the Duke of Wellington to Lord Holland's speech.

a reciprocal treaty with turbulent subjects who have revolted? and must not the Ottoman Government attribute to those powers who advance such a proposition, views tending to give importance to a troop of brigands?"

"A Greek government is, as it would seem," added the Reis Effendi, "to be recognised by the three powers, in case the Sublime Porte does not consent to the proposed arrangement; and a treaty is even proposed with rebels, who have, moreover, been improperly encouraged by warlike assistance of every kind, instead of any disapproval of their acts. It should, on the contrary, have been borne in mind, that, agreeably to the laws of nations, every independent power has a right to govern its own subjects without permitting the interference of any power whatever. Has not, then, the Sublime Porte great reason to be struck with astonishment at hearing such language from friendly powers? History," continued the Reis Effendi, "presents no example of conduct so opposed to the reciprocal duties of governments, as that of the present interference in the internal concerns of another state, followed, as this has been, by succours given almost openly to an insurgent people, as the means of prolonging their rebellion against their sovereign."

Such were the reasons so conclusively given for refusing to affix the Sultan's seal to the intended encroachments on the integrity of Turkey. But, in refusing to be a party to the treaty of the 6th of July, the Divan used its best efforts to induce the ambassadors to continue at their posts, till they should receive special orders from their sovereigns respecting those ameliorations of policy towards Greece, which Turkey was prepared to carry out. These were, in substance:—the remission of six years' taxes already due, as well as of the customs for the ensuing year; to grant a complete amnesty for the past; to restore confiscated property; to re-establish the rights formerly enjoyed by the Greeks; and, finally, to establish a milder government in Greece. More than this, as it was justly alleged, could not be done for the Hellenic race, without preparing the way for the dissolution of the Ottoman empire.

But as the ambassadors declined remaining on any other terms than the fulfilment of the treaty of the 6th July, 1826, the Europeans belonging to the then contracting powers were placed by the Porte under its own immediate protection, with the understanding that they should communicate their wants to the Reis Effendi; their pecuniary affairs, and matters of litigation generally, being left to the decision of a special commission. These arrangements were made on the 8th of December, 1827, immediately on the departure of the British and French ambassadors for Greece, and that of Russia on his way to St. Petersburgh.

Whether the same magnanimity would have been shown by two of the contracting parties while smarting under the destruction of their fleets in time of peace, may be a question; but it cannot be forgotten that the third had not hesitated, under a much slighter provocation, to retaliate by seizing those British subjects who happened to be residing in France, when hostilities were about to be commenced by England against that power in 1802.

On the final departure of the Russian ambassador, Monsieur de Ribeaupierre, after his detention at Buyuk-Dereh till the 13th of December by contrary winds, a particular note was again addressed by the Reis Effendi to Count Nesselrode, in which he complained that the ambassadors of the allied powers had hastily broken off friendly relations, notwithstanding the anxious desire which had at all times been manifested by the Porte for the maintenance of peace.

No answer having been received to this appeal, the Porte, with reference to the necessary preparations for the impending hostilities, issued a Hatti Scheriff on the 1st of Djemazuil Akhir, 1243 (20 December, 1827), which was sent to the Pashas and Ayans of the provinces, in order to prepare them for this event. One part of this remarkable document was so incautiously worded that it seemed to impugn the well-known fidelity of the Turks to their engagements; for amongst other alleged grievances against Russia, it was stated, "That the treaty of Akherman having been unjustly extorted, ought not to be considered binding;" and that, "as the object of the enemy was to annihilate Islamism and to tread Muhammedanism under foot, the faithful, rich and poor, high and low, should recollect that it is a duty to fight for their religion, and even willingly to sacrifice property and life in this vital struggle." It is not surprising that such a document should have had a prominent place amongst the justificatory reasons set forth by Russia for declaring war upon Turkey; which took place accordingly, without any reference to the other contracting powers.

Count Nesselrode, in his replies of the 13th and 25th of April to the Reis Effendi's letter stating that no explanation had been asked, nor any redress of grievances sought, previously to the departure of Monsieur de Ribeaupierre, said: "that everything regarding the affairs of Greece had the authority of the Emperor; that the propositions were for the real benefit of Turkey, and that having been so frequently urged, the Russian envoy was not bound to state them again at the request of the Porte; and as further delay would have been superfluous, he had no alternative but to maintain the dignity of his country by quitting Constantinople, after giving the Porte a salutary hint and leaving it time to reflect upon the dangers that surrounded it."

The letter next complains "that this very friendly policy was met by proceedings which virtually annulled the existing treaties with Russia. The trade of the Black Sea was impeded by searching the vessels so employed; Russian subjects were attacked, and Turkey even went so far as to announce to all Muslims her determination to return evil for good, war for peace, and not to fulfil solemn conventions." Count Nesselrode's letter concludes by saying: "that since so many hostile measures had been pursued, notwithstanding the representations and endeavours of the Courts allied with Russia, your Excellency cannot be surprised to learn that I am ordered to reply to your letter of the 27th December by the annexed declaratory statement; which will be immediately followed up by the march of an army into the Sultan's dominions, in order to obtain satisfaction for his just complaints."

But, according to the Turkish minister, the grievances were quite the other way. Russia had, he stated, blockaded the Turkish ports, and cut off the supplies of the Turkish armies: She would not allow Turkish vessels to quit the ports of the Morea, and yet denied to Turkey the right of preventing Russian vessels from passing the Dardanelles. Russia did not allow the Sultan's subjects to pass from one part of his dominions to another; and yet complained that a peaceful abode at Constantinople was not continued to Russian subjects. She had, moreover, equipped a fleet for the express purpose of acting hostilely against that of the Sultan; and, having assisted in the destruction of the latter, her ambassador quitted Constantinople, on the alleged grounds that Turkey would not go on in the strict observance of peaceable conventions: as if the relations of amity had not been in any way disturbed, even by blowing the Turkish fleet out of the water with the avowed intention of despoiling her of one of the fairest provinces of her empire.

In explanation of that part of the Hatti Scheriff which attributed hostile designs to Russia, it was affirmed that war had evidently been contemplated by that power for several years; with which view an army had been for some time assembled in Bessarabia, ready to cross the Pruth. Finally, the Porte declared every one of the alleged causes of war to be untrue and unjust, and merely a cover for that love of conquest which had never ceased to actuate the Russian Cabinet. Russia had violated the treaty of Bucharest by retaining certain Asiatic fortresses; and when asked to restore them, her only answer was, that as she had held them so long, she might as well keep them altogether.

This statement of the Turks seems to be borne out by a paper attributed to the pen of Pozzo di Borgo, in which that celebrated minister appears to justify an attack by saying, "how formidable should we have found the Sultan had he had time to give his organization more solidity, and render that barrier impenetrable which we find so much difficulty in surmounting, although art has hitherto done so little to assist nature."*

Without attaching too much importance to this document on the one hand, or to the supposed expulsion of the

* Extract from a secret despatch of Count Pozzo di Borgo, 28th Nov., 1828. Portfolio, vol. 1, p. 349.

Armenians from Constantinople and the rest of the alleged grievances of Russia against the Turks on the other, it must be admitted that the contrast afforded by the proceedings of the two nations immediately before the rupture, was very striking. The Grand Vizier's letter of the 27th Dec. 1827, invites negotiation and explanation. Russia, on the contrary, as if dreading the possibility of an adjustment, allows this letter to remain without any reply being sent, until the 25th of April, 1828. The manifesto then despatched reached Constantinople on the 15th of May, and the Sultan had already heard on the 12th of the advance of the Russians from the Governor of Brailow. Not a single complaint was made by Russia during this interval, nor any explanation demanded; until at length she embodied her grievances in a declaration of war, at the very moment that a powerful army was marching in Europe, and another preparing in Asia, to obtain redress for grievances not previously complained of by her. The preparation of the Asiatic army was a still stronger proof than any of the proceedings in Europe of the intentions of Russia. The historian of Marshal Paskewitch states, that a campaign was undertaken in the midst of winter in Persia, with the express object of leaving the army disposable for another service; and by the *end of February*, 1827, the Marshal had received orders to prepare to invade Asiatic Turkey.*

* La Russie dans l'Asie Mineure, ou Campagnes du Maréchal Paskewitch en 1828 et 1829. Par Felix Fonton, pp. 117, 233, 235, 241. Paris, 1840.

It can scarcely be questioned, therefore, that Russia had previously determined to make war upon Turkey, and the firm belief prevailed throughout the Divan, that on this, as well as on previous occasions, the extension of her territory at the expense of Turkey, was the real object of the manifesto of the Emperor Nicholas. Some of the leading men in Constantinople were of opinion that, under these circumstances, the coming struggle ought not to be met, or even to be regarded as an ordinary misunderstanding between two nations; nor simply as a question of provinces that might be lost; but as one which, in addition to the acquisition of territory, was intended to compass the destruction of Islamism itself.

Such an idea, if inculcated, could not have failed to produce most alarming consequences. The Turkish people were only beginning to depart from that exclusive system which had caused the Muslim to wish to be left to himself, without the existence of treaties of commerce, or the presence of ambassadors in his capital. The more enlightened Sultan did not, however, hesitate to reject the advice given to him to adopt an extreme course; and instead of making use of the powerful lever at his command, had he placed himself at the head of his people in the field and interdicted all communication with Christians, he determined simply to make the best of the limited means at his disposal, without awakening the religious enthusiasm of the nation.

CHAPTER II.

SKETCH OF THE SEAT OF WAR IN EUROPEAN AND ASIATIC TURKEY.

Description of Moldavia and Wallachia—Course of the Danube, from the western side of Wallachia to the Dobrudscha—Obstinate defence of fortresses by the Turks—Description of Adá Kalá, Widdin, Khalafat, Nicopoli, Sistchof, Rustchuk, Giurgevo, Silistria, Hirsova, Brailow, Matschin—Proposed canal to turn the lower Danube—Second line of defence behind the Danube—Tirnova—Varna and Schumla—Description of the Balkan—Various passes of the mountains—General observations on the passes—Positions of Buyuk Chekmedgó, Kuchuk Chekmedgé, and Ramid Chifflick—Proposed additions to the defences of Constantinople.

THE Russian invasion of the Turkish territory was to embrace both sides of the Black Sea; and it will be seen by a glance at the map, that, in each case, the seat of war forms an irregular triangle. The one in Asia has the trans-Caucasian provinces for a base, and Erzerúm, or rather the sources of the Euphrates, at its apex, with a mountainous and otherwise very difficult country intervening. That of Europe has Bulgaria, *i. e.*, the river Danube, with its fortresses, for a base, and Constantinople as the apex. Nearly midway between the extreme points, the noble range of the Balkan runs from side to side of the triangle, almost parallel to the base, having on its northern slopes, Tirnova, Schumla, Pravadi, and Varna. These strongholds are so situated as to serve the double purpose of advanced posts of the great mountain barrier in their rear, as well as points d'appui of the fortresses on the Danube; and it might reasonably be expected that some intimation of the enemy's intentions against the latter, would have been the consequence of a previous occupation of Moldavia and Wallachia by cavalry and light troops

Since, by the treaty of Bucharest, Bessarabia ceased to be a part of Moldavia, this province only extends to the Pruth, which separates it on the eastern side from Bessarabia; the latter having been Russian territory ever since the peace in question was concluded in 1812. The principality of Moldavia now extends nearly 200 miles, from the Danube bordering Wallachia to the borders of Gallicia; and it has a breadth of about 120 miles, from the banks of the Pruth on the east to the Carpathian mountains and Transylvania on the west. The Danube washes the south-eastern extremity of this territory for the distance of about twenty-four miles, and during this portion of its course, receives the rivers Pruth and Sereth. The Pruth has a south-eastern course of about 500 miles to the Danube, from its sources in the Carpathian mountains in the circle of Stanislawow, and is navigable almost throughout the whole extent of Moldavia. The Sereth, in the upper part of its course, receives the Bistritz and the Moldava, which gives its name to the territory; and almost at its termination, the Birlat. These streams and their affluents divide almost equally, and completely water the principality, which has an area of nearly 17,000 square miles. The country is covered in part with extensive forests, producing every kind of timber; and the remainder, which is agricultural or pastoral, is very fertile in wines, as well as in every kind of grain and vegetable. Vast numbers of horses, cattle, and sheep, are grazed on its rich meadows. Rock-salt, asphaltum, saltpetre, and even gold, are found in this principality.

Jassy, the capital, is situated on the Bachlei, a muddy stream, one of the affluents of the Pruth. It contains numerous churches and convents, in addition to about 4,000 houses, chiefly of wood. Owing principally to fires, the population has diminished of late years. Previous to 1827 there were about 40,000 inhabitants.

Galatz, the only port of Moldavia, is situated on the Danube, between the rivers Pruth and Sereth. Having been made a free port in 1834, it has become a very important place, being the seat of imports and exports for the whole of this extensive province, as well as a dépôt for Austrian merchandize passing up and down the Danube. Its trade, especially in grain, is very considerable, and the vessels coming thither from various countries are very numerous. The mixed population of Moldavians, Jews, Armenians, and gypsies, is about half a million.

Wallachia, the other principality, belongs more particularly to the present geographical limits of Turkey, being washed by the Danube on its southern side, and again on its eastern by the bend of this river, as it flows northward to the extremity of this province opposite to Galatz. From its eastern limits on the left bank of the Lower Danube, Wallachia extends about 276 miles to the Upper Danube and Hungary on the west, and again 127 miles northward from the left bank of the Danube to Moldavia, and nearly the same distance to Transylvania. It is abundantly watered by various rivers and streams, which traverse the country from the Carpathians to the Danube. The principal of these are the Schyl, which terminates opposite to Rachova; the Aluta, which enters the Danube at Turna; the Argisch, which ends its course opposite to Turtokai; and the Yanolitza, which debouches at Hirsova. According to Balbi, Wallachia has an area of 21,600 square geographical miles. A broad level tract stretches northward from the Danube, that part near the river consisting of marshes and meadow pastures, which are subject to its inundations. The ground becomes hilly and more elevated as it approaches Moldavia, and the western side of the country is mountainous, or hilly. Like Moldavia, this principality is covered in places with extensive forests; but it is still richer in mineral, pastoral, and agricultural products. Iron, copper, lead, silver, and gold, are found. Horses and cattle abound; and according to Wilkinson's account of the principalities, the number of sheep amounts to 2,500,000; while besides barley, rye, hemp, tobacco, and

Indian corn, there is seldom less than 1,250,000 quarters of wheat produced annually.

The principal towns are Tergovist on the Yanolitza, containing 5,000 inhabitants; the port of Brailow; Giurgevo, a town of 3,500 inhabitants; and Crajova, the capital of Little Wallachia, a thriving town of about 9,000 inhabitants. Bucharest, the capital, contains about 60,000 inhabitants. Owing to the gardens within the town, it covers a very large space, and is on the whole a very fine city. Transverse logs of wood across the streets supply the place of the usual pavement. The metropolitan Greek church is a handsome edifice, and many of the houses of the Boyards are fine buildings. The Bazars are extensive and well supplied, as might be expected in the centre of a productive and populous country. This district is supposed to contain 100,000 gypsies, 20,000 Jews, 5,000 Armenians, and only 3,000 Greeks; the remainder being Wallachians, who increase the aggregate to about a million.

The inhabitants of these principalities are a quiet passive race, of Sclavonian origin, but claiming descent from the Romans of the lower empire; which is partly supported by the fact of their speaking a doggrel Latin. The origin of the Bohemians is not known; but they are, as usual, a migratory people. The rest of the Wallachians are partly so; and, their pursuits being chiefly pastoral, their huts, which are half buried in the earth, are easily changed from place to place; so that, unless there should be either a convent or a church, whole villages frequently disappear from the places marked on the maps.

The tribute paid directly by these provinces to the Porte was by no means oppressive; but a heavy contribution was drawn from them indirectly, in the shape of wheat, timber, and cattle, which were sent to Constantinople at fixed prices, much below the market value. This was, however, a small disadvantage compared to that of being in the van of the Turkish territory, and consequently the first to suffer from an invading enemy.

In approaching the confines of Bulgaria, the river Danube breaks through a mass of chalk, which, added to a narrow rocky bed, and the eddies, causes some difficulty in the navigation, both at Gladova and Demir-Kapu. Below these so-called "Iron gates," the river and valley gradually widen as far as the fortified town of Widdin, which is seated on the right bank. Below this place the banks are higher on the Bulgarian than on the opposite side of the river, which has a current of about two miles per hour, and a width varying between 300 and 500 yards, as far as Nicopoli. At this place, the ancient Nicopolis ad Istrum, the stream widens to nearly three miles, and so continues, interspersed with islands, and passing with an east and north-easterly course Rustchuk, Turtokai, and Silistria, to Boghazkoi.

At the latter place—from whence the celebrated wall of Trajan crosses to the Euxine, a distance of only thirty-eight miles—the Danube makes a northerly course along the Dobrudscha, by Hirsova, in three principal branches; which, after uniting at Brailow, continue a northerly course to Galatz. Here it again turns to the east, and at the distance of about ninety miles, falls into the Black Sea by the several arms of the Delta. Below Brailow and Galatz—where the more active commerce, chiefly in corn, commences—the streams, as they wind through a flat country, display quite a forest of masts, which appear to be moving in different directions through the fields. Vessels, however, make their way up to Widdin, and even higher; the depth of water mid-stream being seldom under seventy feet.

With some difficulty, the Danube may be passed a little above Widdin, and again at Oltenitza, or rather Turtokai, below that fortress; also at the island near Silistria, and again at Hirsova: which, in descending thus far, is the first suitable place for the passage of an army. Saturnovo and Tuldcha, in the Delta, are, however, preferable points; particularly the latter, at which a bar with only fourteen feet water would facilitate the construction of a bridge: although in this part of the Delta, as well as higher up the main stream, the right bank usually gives to the defenders the advantage of higher and more difficult ground, to assist in disputing the passage.

The difficulty which must be experienced in crossing a deep and somewhat rapid stream, even with the assistance of one of the islands, ceases during the severity of a Bulgarian winter. On the 19th, and again on the 25th of December, 1829, the writer crossed the Danube with horses; and it was evident that the ice had been for some days sufficiently solid for that purpose, the frost having been severe since the 7th of the month.

In addition to the ordinary difficulties in crossing when the river is not frozen, even where there is no kind of resistance, may be added the strongholds on the banks of the Danube. These deserve a brief description; the more so that the defence of a fortress by the Turks may, in one sense, be said only to begin with them where it usually ends in more scientific warfare: namely, after a breach has been effected in the body of the place.

Ada-Kalá, the most westerly post of the Turks, and originally an Austrian work, contains bomb-proofs for about 2,000 men. It is situated on an island, and is well calculated to defend the passage, as well as to resist any attack made from this part of Wallachia.

Widdin, the next fortress in descending the river, stands on its right bank, towards which it presents revetted lines *en crémaillère*. On the land side there are seven bastioned fronts, with ravelins of tolerably regular construction, and the place is surrounded by a deep and wide ditch, which is either wet or dry at pleasure. The revetment is nearly forty feet high, and there is a covert way and glacis. Towards the west, there is also an ancient castle, which serves as a citadel, and a well provided arsenal. The suburbs of Widdin extend along the river, and are defended by permanent lines, flanked at intervals by tower bastions. The parapets are of earth, faced with and retained by hurdles; which are frequently used for this purpose by the Turks, agreeably to a practice originally borrowed, it is said, from the Poles.

On the left bank, opposite to Widdin, is the *tête de pont* of Khalafat, a revetted work of but moderate strength, until the recently added entrenchments.

About ten miles below Widdin is the town of Lom, defended by lines similar to those of the suburbs of Widdin, with the addition of loopholed parapets, constructed with gabions.

Again, at nearly the same distance lower down, two inferior forts have been constructed to defend the river at Oreava or Rachova; which, with this exception is an open town.

Forty-five miles lower, and nearly opposite to the river Schyl, the ancient Tiarantus, Nicopoli occupies two steep hills on the right bank of the Danube. The town is defended by irregular lines which are revetted, and have hurdle-faced earthen parapets. The works are surrounded by a deep ditch, flanked by flat bastions. On the left bank of the river, and immediately opposite, are the forts of Yeni-Kala and Eski-Kala, both of which are commanded and protected, at the distance of about 900 yards, by the guns of the town. A garrison of 8,000 men was destined by the Sultan for the defence of this place.

The position of the commercial town of Sistchof, the next place in descending the Danube, closely resembles that of Nicopoli. It stands on the right bank, and occupies two hills, which are divided by a deep valley. The crest of the eastern hill is crowned by a turreted castle, said to have been built by the Genoese ; and intrenchments were hastily thrown up by the Pasha to defend the western hill and its acclivity. These works, which are a fair specimen of Turkish science, consist of long curtains flanked by semicircular bastions, having earthen parapets faced with hurdles, and surrounded by a deep and narrow ditch. With the intended allotment of a garrison of 3,000 men, Sistchof was capable of a respectable defence.

Some distance lower is Rustchuk and its *tête de pont*. The former, which is rather commanded by higher ground on the south-west side, played an important part in previous wars. It is defended by eight bastioned demi-revetted fronts on the land side, with a ditch and counter-scarp of masonry, without ravelins or other outworks ; but having, at the eastern part of the town, the additional protection of a bastioned work, which serves as a citadel. Six very irregular fronts, and the bastion of Kalá Alik Tabia projecting into the river, protect the town on the side of the latter.

Nearly opposite to Rustchuk, but beyond the range of

artillery, are the three separate works at Giurgevo. The first is an ancient castle on an island, which, with the addition of the second work—a pentagonal stone-work, and rather strong—forms a kind of harbour. Adjoining the latter fort is the town, which had been recently fortified by the Pasha, with a chain of works, forming nearly a semicircular sweep, of which the Danube is the chord.

Silistria occupies the right bank of the Danube, nearly at the commencement of its delta, and had nearly 24,000 inhabitants in 1828.

The town is but imperfectly fortified, and it is commanded from the exterior: more particularly on the south-western side. There are ten fronts, each of which has an extremely long curtain and two small bastions; which, as is commonly the case in Turkish works, give an imperfect flanking fire to the ditch. The scarp and counterscarp have scarcely a relief of fifteen feet. The former is surmounted by a hurdle parapet, with a strong row of palisades rising above its crest on the interior side. There is a low and very imperfect glacis, but no covert way or outworks of the usual construction; the place of the latter being partly supplied by three exterior redoubts enclosed to the rear. A fourth, outside the western angle of the town, and a fifth, similarly situated near the eastern extremity, flank the works towards the river, and protect the trading vessels when anchored under the walls.

The next place of any consequence is Hirsova, a town

containing about 4,000 inhabitants, and seated on the right bank, nearly midway between Silistria and Brailow. The fortifications form an irregular parallelogram, with rocky ground on three of the sides, and the river Danube on the fourth.

There are five bastioned revetted fronts, surrounded by a ditch defended by ten guns : an old castle on the western side of the town serves as a kind of citadel.

As the Russians had a bridge at this place in 1809, the Turks bestowed some pains on its defences. The contour is, however, defective, having several dead points, with the additional disadvantage of some ground outside commanding the works : particularly the island below the town.

At nearly the same distance below Hirsova, the town of Brailow stands on the left bank. It is defended by eight fronts of fortification with revetted scarps and counterscarps, a glacis, a deep ditch, and a castellated citadel within the works at the western flank of the town ; but there are no outworks to assist in its defence. This place is nearly opposite the centre of the alluvial track of the Dobrudscha, in which are several small fortified places, which, when supported by an army in the field, might be defensible.

Matschin, though at some distance from Brailow, may be considered its *tête-de-pont.* It is on the right bank, and has a population of 1,000 or 1,500 souls. It is surrounded by seven bastioned revetted fronts of fortification, and has a kind of citadel, which being placed on some elevated ground on the side of the Danube, commands the town from thence.

The town of Tuldscha stands on the right bank of the river, and is defended by a detached, hexagonal work, without ravelins or other outworks. This was formerly the *tête-de-pont* of what is now the Russian fortress of Ismaïl. There is also a work serving as a kind of keep or citadel; but the ground is unfavourable to defence, since it offers many dead points to assist an enemy's approaches.

Nearly at the eastern side of the Dobrudscha, about the spot where the Danube would have entered the Black Sea had it continued an easterly course from Boghaz-koi, near Tchernowoda, is the small port and town of Kustendji. It occupies a bluff peninsula, three sides of which are washed by the Euxine, and the fourth is defended by a line of works. The latter, however, are scarcely defensible, being commanded by a chain of limestone hills outside, from which the celebrated walls of Trajan run across to the banks of the Danube. If a navigable cut were to be made to this point, a distance scarcely exceeding forty miles, the body of the river would ere long take this direction; thus, at a very trifling expense, by resuming its ancient bed, it would secure the Turkish and European commerce, and give, besides, in a military point of view, an important accession to the means of defending Bulgaria.

In the comparatively level portion of this country which

intervenes between the Danube and the Balkan, at about sixty miles from and nearly parallel to the Danube, is the second line of defence. Of this Schumla may be considered the centre, with Pravadi and Varna at its right or eastern, and Tirnova, the ancient capital of Bulgaria, at its other extremity.

Tirnova, the most western place d'armes, is situated about fifty miles from the Danube, at nearly an equal distance from Nicopoli, Sistchof, and Rustchuk; all on that river. The town is singularly placed in a basaltic mountain basin of 800 feet, or even occasionally 1,000 feet in depth. The houses are built on a plateau, as well as on both sides of a precipitous tongue of land, which runs into and nearly bisects the basin in question.

Near the southern extremity of this projection, but connected with it by means of a bridge, there is an otherwise isolated and more elevated portion of rock, on which stands the citadel, a work originally constructed by the Genoese. Tirnova, therefore, with the rapid river Jantra flowing round it, may, even with reference to the power of modern warfare, be considered a very defensible position.

At the opposite or eastern extremity of the line are the port and fortress of Varna. The town occupies a spreading valley at the head of Lake Devna, and has the shape of a truncated pyramid, the base of which is towards the interior, with its apex on the Euxine. The third side faces the north, and the fourth is washed partly by the anchorage and partly by the river Devna. The places contain about 25,000 inhabitants, but although better fortified than most of the Turkish towns, it cannot, in a scientific point of view, be considered strong. Towards the sea, as well as towards the river Devna, are high loop-holed walls imperfectly flanked; ten flat bastions connected by long curtains, and surrounded by a ditch with a cunette, form the rest of the enceinte. The scarp and counterscarp are revetted, and the former has a parapet faced with wicker-work hurdles to retain the earth. In the interior, a Byzantine castle with high square turrets at the angles, serves at once as a citadel and magazine. Since the seige of 1828, a hornwork and some lines have been erected by the Turks, to occupy the commanding ground on the western side of the fortifications; but it is doubtful whether the means of defence have been much strengthened in consequence.

The ancient Hœmus runs from west to east: that is, from the shores of the Adriatic to those of the Black Sea; with, however, an unequal degree of elevation, which varies from 5,000 feet at the pass of Gabrova to a little more than 3,000 feet at that of the Kamtchik, about ten miles south of Schumla. The mountains are chiefly conical, and generally clothed with oak and beech trees of a large size; the valleys are very bold and rocky, and usually covered with evergreens. The abutments of the southern side, which are higher than those of the northern, have the effect of lessening to the eye the great height of the range itself; from which they also differ in character, being of limestone, with precipitous sides, terminating in walls of rock from ten to two hundred feet in height. Numerous streams and thick underwood abound in the northern slopes, and owing to these impediments, the plateaux above these outlying hills cannot be reached without much difficulty.

The principal range of the Balkan, exclusive of its abutments, is twenty-one miles across at its greatest width, and about fifteen from side to side at its narrowest points, including the windings.

The Turkish historian, Von Hammer, states that there are only eight defiles by which the Balkan can be crossed; that from Chamaderé to Chenga, on the Nadirderbend, being the most eastern. General Jochmus, however, mentions five other passes, including mere pathways, between Nadirderbend and the sea at Cape Emineh, viz. :—

1. From Misivri by Erikly-Kilisi and Dervish Jowan to Varna.

2. From Misivri by Bana to Varna.

3. From Aschli by Aiwadschiki to Varna.

4. From Aschli by Kaldumatch and Shrikus-Hissar to Pravadi; and again,

5. From Sudshiderabad and Kiuprikoï to Pravadi.

But the principal routes which are more or less practicable for the passage of troops across the Balkan, are the following. That farthest towards the west, and at the same time one of the most difficult, is the road which quits the Danube at Rachova, and proceeds by way of Sophia to Phillippopoli. For the greatest part of this distance it is little more than a bridle path, chiefly winding round the crests of the mountains.

The next points of approach are made from the Danube, about Nicopoli and Rustchuk. Several of these routes from the Danube converge on Tirnova ; from thence there are three roads across the mountains. The First passes by the castle of Tirnova, and thence along the Jantra. A narrow, steep, but not rocky saddle, which might be forced by tirailleurs, is passed in proceeding towards Tuncha, and after a mile of very steep ascent we roach Shipka. The mountains resemble those of the Hartz, and the country is rich in fruit trees, corn, pasture, and wood, with luxuriant fields of roses, from which the attar is made.

The Second route leads from Tirnova to Demir Kapu, and from thence to Selimno ; passing the range at a great elevation, and by a track scarcely known.

The Third route leads from Tirnova to Stararecka, from whence it ascends to the summit of Binar-dagh. Here it meets the road from Osman Bazar, and passes thence between high and naked rocks to Kasan and Demir Kapu. South of the pass of the Iron Gates—which could scarcely be forced, and could only be turned by a narrow footway to the right—the road separates ; one branch going to the left by Karnabat and Dobrol, while the other goes from thence to the right towards Selimno, over a succession of wooded and difficult ascents and descents. The latter part of this road, which is steep and winding, brings the traveller to the fresh climate of Selimno, with its cotton, vines, olives, and rich vegetation, interspersed with meadow land.

A Fourth route proceeds from Schumla to Tschalikewak, from whence—by means of difficult ascents, and by subsequently winding through deep ravines and precipitous rocky passes, particularly the defiles of the Derbent—the Delli Kamtschik is reached, which is only fordable at certain places. After crossing this river, the road ascends over precipitous and wooded mountains, until it eventually descends through an open country to Dobrol; from whence a tract covered with brushwood and intersected with numerous streams, leads to the considerable town of Karnabat. In advancing onwards towards Adrianople, the difficult defile of Buyuk Derbend occurs: the remainder of the march thither would be comparatively easy.

The Fifth road leads from Kosludscha to Pravadi, where it separates. One branch proceeds onwards by Kiuprikoï to Kirk-Getschid or the Forty Fords; where it enters a critical defile of fifteen miles in extent, which at Gokbehuet-arakdsche narrows to about fifty paces in width, with high and precipitous rocks on each side. The difficulties from thence towards Aidos are comparatively moderate.

The other branch, which proceeds by Jenikoi from Pravadi, is less difficult; because the Kamtschik may be crossed in summer at several places by fording, and subsequently the Delli Kamtschik can be crossed anywhere about Tchenga. Beyond this place, however, the road is so precipitous that it might be closed entirely without difficulty. The plateau above Tchenga is a mile and a quarter in extent, and troops might be advantageously intrenched at this spot, which offers the defensive advantage of ground falling rapidly towards the Delli Kamtschik on one side, and the Dellidschedereh on the other. On the neighbouring open space at Bairam Ovo a considerable encampment might be formed; and, as a practicable road leads from thence to Varna, a force concentrated on this spot could either debouche on that fortress, or towards Pravadi, at pleasure.

Passing through the marshy country south of Varna, the Sixth route crosses the Kamtschik by a bridge of boats at Podbaschi; where the banks are precipitous, and from six to twelve feet high. But in order to obstruct the passage of the marsh (which is about 5,000 paces in extent) before reaching this point, entrenchments have been thrown up on some rising ground beyond it, at a spot from whence two narrow but passable roads lead westward. Encountering moderate ascents through beautiful but almost impenetrable woods, these routes lead to Dervish Jowan and Misivri, passing through the deep valleys of the Kip-Dereh. The latter consist of an almost continuous succession of defiles; nor are there, here or elsewhere, any means of cross communications between the various roads of the Balkan: excepting those at the southern declivity of the chain, where one such intercommunication leads from Misivri to Aidos, and another from Burgos to the same place, from whence a single line is continued to Karnabat and Selimno.

The Fourth, Fifth, and Sixth passages, being the most practicable for an enemy, an army placed at Aidos might defend the country with great advantage; since it could *debouche* from the mountains either towards Schumla or Varna, with every prospect of overhelming the advancing columns: whose passage across the Balkan may be considered to be impracticable, so long as both, or even one, of those places should be maintained and strongly garrisoned by the Sultan's forces.

These passes are not in themselves more difficult than some of those in the Alps and in Spain, and far less formidable than those of the Taurus and the Eastern side of Persia. The routes by which they are traversed wind through the valleys, and along the sides of the mountains when ascending; nor are the latter either so steep or so rugged as to prevent an advancing body from securing its flanks by means of light infantry: nor even occasionally from employing the latter to endeavour to turn some of those defensive positions.

This description of the passes of the Balkan is the

result of personal observations, made during two journeys across that range in 1829, compared with the accounts given by Moltke, General Jochmus, and others.

It is not, however, so much the physical impediments presented by rugged valleys and lofty mountains, as the accessories connected with these difficulties in a country like Turkey—such as the want of practicable roads, and the deficiency of supplies consequent on a thinly scattered population—which present the greatest obstacles. Under these circumstances, and with ordinary precautions on the part of the Turks, it is difficult to imagine how the barrier of the Balkan could be forced; unless, indeed, the invaders should be in a position to bring forward, and (what is far more difficult) to support, an overwhelming force in this part of the country.

There is but little to obstruct an enemy between the southern slopes of the Balkan and that formidable position, about twenty miles from the capital, so celebrated in history,—where, owing to the nature of the ground, Attila was stayed in his march to conquer the eastern empire; and where, at a later period, the Huns were signally defeated by Belisarius.

This natural barrier is formed by a chain of steep hills, which, running almost continuously from the inlet of Kara Bournu on the Euxine to the sea of Marmora, separates, as it were, Constantinople and the extremity of the Peninsula from the rest of European Turkey. The northern side of these hills is washed almost throughout their whole length by the Kará-su, which in certain places forms a difficult marsh, and ultimately a lake, flowing into the sea below Buyuk Chekmedgé, or the great drawbridge. In addition to the latter, which is about 500 paces long, there are three other bridges leading to the capital: one from Midia, passing along the shores of the Black Sea to the mouth of the Bosphorus; a second, crossing the marsh between Tsjalatalatje and Tasjalik; and the third, at Kastanakoï. By constructing *têtes-de-pont* at these passages, and scarping some of the hills, as well as strengthening other weak points, these defences might become a second Torres Vedras, and one of the strongest positions in Europe.

Even in its present state, if defended by an organized force, assisted by an armed population, it would prove a serious if not an insuperable impediment; since an enemy must either endeavour to turn it by landing, at great risk, close to the Bosphorus, or attempt to carry it by an attack in front: which in all probability would be attended with serious loss, independently of that still to be experienced in attacking another position six miles from thence.

This position consists of a somewhat similar range of hills, running also nearly parallel to those just described, almost from sea to sea. But not being altogether continuous, it is scarcely so defensible towards the eastern as it is at the western side; where an enemy would have to cross six different streams in approaching the lake formed by them in front of the hills, both above and below Kuchuk-Chekmedgé, or the lesser drawbridge. It is scarcely necessary to remark that, as the left of this position as well as that more in advance are particularly strong, their defenders would be enabled to mass their troops towards the centre and right of the space to be defended.

After mastering successively these two very defensible lines, the heights of Ramid Chifflik, just outside Constantinople, would be the last means of endeavouring to cover its dilapidated walls, which have been totally neglected since the conquest of the city in 1453.

The exposure which has been the consequence of this neglect, might, however, be easily remedied. By the ordinary repairs of the towers, walls, counterscarp, &c., with the addition of a line of martello towers, or a stronger description of works, constructed at certain intervals parallel to the contour, so as to prevent an enemy from bombarding the place until they are mastered, Constantinople could be rendered capable of a more protracted defence. In its present state, however, there is not anything to impede an enemy, beyond desultory resistance from house to house; until a terrible conflagration, which must be the result of the bombardment of wooden structures, should end the struggle in the capital.

CHAPTER III.

PLANS FOR THE INVASION OF TURKEY AND COMMENCEMENT OF THE CAMPAIGN OF 1828.

Russian officers reconnoitre the passes of the Balkan—Plans of attack by General Geismar and Baron Valentini—Troops assembled by Russia for the invasion—Strength of the army—Commencement of the campaign—Critical state of Turkey at that moment—Nizam, and means of taking the field—Various attempts made by Russia to conquer Turkey—The Russians cross the Pruth—The Sultan sends troops towards the Danube—First combats in Wallachia—The plague attacks the Russian troops—Siege of Brailow—How the passage of the Danube was effected—Fall of Isaktschi and other places in the Dobrudscha—Turkish forces assembled at Schumla—Description of its intrenched camp—Movements of the hostile forces up to Schumla.

It was generally understood in Constantinople, at the time that the war was about to commence, that the actual state of the passes of the Balkan, as well as the means of defence in Turkey generally, had been well known for some time to the Russian Government.

It would appear that about two years previously to the rupture, Colonel Berg and some other officers, who had been sent as attachés of the mission to the Porte, took the opportunity of returning from Constantinople to Russia through the principal passes of the Balkan. Detailed notes and sketches of these were made, and in consequence a plan was submitted to the Emperor for marching upon Constantinople, without, as heretofore, the delay of securing the line of the Danube.

It does not, however, quite follow that the Imperial Government itself actually took such steps as to reconnoitre, in time of peace, the routes leading to the Bosphorus ; since the hope of preferment and desire of distinction are of themselves sufficient inducements to enterprising officers, not only to seek such information, but also to devise plans instigated by those undefined hopes of advancement which influence the actions of mankind so powerfully. But be this as it may, the strong belief which for some time prevailed in the Russian army that Turkey would be invaded ere long, was quite sufficient to give rise to numerous projects.

One of these was submitted by General Geismar in 1826, the basis of which was, either to carry Schumla by a *coup-de-main*, or mask that place. After taking either of these steps, whichever might prove most feasible with reference to the defensive preparations of the Turks, a rapid march across the Balkan was to follow. The Russian troops were to be joined by another corps d'armée coming by sea to Domos Dereh ; and the united force was to seize the reservoirs at Belgrade, in order that the want of water might cause the surrender of the capital.

The merits of this and other plans, all more or less

similar to that of Baron Valentini,* were freely discussed with the author, by Russian officers in Bucharest, at the close of the campaign in 1829.

The one ultimately adopted was based on the project of Colonels Berg and Rüdiger, making the fall of Varna, Silistria, and Schumla, precede the grand operation. When, in accordance with this project, the frontiers were suddenly passed, it was believed that Turkey—owing to the state of transition in her army, through the substitution of an organized force for that of the Janissaries—would be comparatively helpless.

Had the reorganization of the Turkish forces been more advanced, so as to have enabled the Sultan to concentrate a respectable army on the banks of the Danube, with cavalry and light troops pushed on to the Pruth, it would have been easy not only to retard the march of the enemy, but also to deprive him of those supplies so abundantly furnished by the principalities. And after disputing the passage of this difficult river, as well as subsequently covering the fortresses on its banks for a time, the Turkish army could have fallen back on its second line of defence at Schumla, and ultimately could have occupied the formidable passes of the Balkan itself. But even if the Sultan's means had permitted such combinations, there

* Traité sur la guerre contre les Turcs, traduit de l'Allemand du Lieut.-Général Prussien Valentini, par L. Blesson. Berlin, 1830, p. 49–60, and p. 182.

would not have been time to march from the more distant parts of his Asiatic territory to the scene of operations; for, as has been seen, the declaration of war and the passage of the Pruth were nearly consentaneous.

Nor was this the only disadvantage. The daring winter march of General Paskevitch to the Kaflan-Ku, had just forced the Shah of Persia to conclude a peace at Turkman Chaï; and the Russian General had, consequently, already commenced operations, with the double object of diverting the Sultan's forces from the defence of European Turkey, and of securing additional territory in Asia.

The troops which had been for some time accumulating on the southern frontier of Russia amounted to about 216,000 men; of which, however, only a part could be considered available against Turkey. The course pursued by Russia could scarcely have been satisfactory to those allies from whom she had suddenly separated herself; and the position of Austria, then the steady friend of the Sultan, on the flank of a long line of operations, gave great importance to any representation she might choose to make. It was, doubtless, with reference to some political contingency, that about one half of the force remained in reserve to watch the course of events; and that, as an additional precaution, a levy of one man in every 500 was ordered throughout the Russian empire.

It was under these circumstances that, according to information obtained by the author in Wallachia, 120,000 men,* with upwards of 300 guns, were put in motion, and commenced operations under the command of an experienced general, Count Wittgenstein. The projected campaign embraced in the first instance the capture of Brailow, Silistria, and Varna; and in the second, a march upon Constantinople, after either capturing or masking the intrenched camp at Schumla. Any serious resistance on the part of the Turks seems to have been entirely excluded from these calculations; and, under their peculiar circumstances, it was certainly scarcely to be anticipated.

The despatch of the Pasha of Brailow, announcing the commencement of hostilities, placed the Sultan in a most critical position. The Greeks, who had been aided by the moral as well as the effective support of a large section of the European people, were rapidly gaining ground; and the destruction of the Ottoman fleet at Navarino had transferred the command of the Euxine to Russia, at the moment when the troops destined to oppose an invasion were in a most inefficient state. The officers and privates of the Nizam, which is the active or regular army, were, for the most part, mere lads, without any military experience; and this force presented altogether a most singular spectacle. The infantry appeared in Turkish trowsers, and close-fitting Russian jackets, with the red Fez or Arab cap.

* Imanitschew makes the force 180,000; Witzleben, in his account of the campaign, states that there were 95,000 men; and Moltke gives the effective strength at 100,000 men, although he states it to have been nominally 120,000.

The cavalry had Tartar saddles, French stirrups, and English sabres. The musket and bayonet of the infantry were of French or Belgian manufacture; and a French system of organisation had been recently commenced, by means of instructors brought for this purpose from various parts of Europe, without reference to anything like uniformity. It should be added, by way of completing this sketch of the Sultan's position, that the destruction of the Janissaries had caused discontent to prevail in almost every Muslim family.

Undaunted, however, by these difficulties, and hoping eventually to carry out those enlarged reforms to which the mass of the people were obstinately opposed, Sultan Mahmoud met the approaching dangers both at home and abroad, with a firm but calm determination to maintain his crown, and, if possible, preserve his territories intact. And, in making for this purpose a touching appeal to the Faithful of every age, he expressed his fixed purpose to maintain with the sword what his ancestors had gained by the sword. Nor was he disappointed in this hope; for it will be seen that the inherent bravery of the people, aided by the natural and artificial defences of the country, were sufficient to resist the forces of the Emperor Nicholas during two protracted campaigns.

With regard to the Sultan's actual means of defence, the aggregate of the Nizam was far below the nominal strength of 80,000 men. Moreover, the soldiers were totally unaccustomed to everything connected with war, for, owing to the early age which had been selected as the most promising for instruction, they were physically unequal to the fatigues of actual service. But, on the other hand, these recruits possessed three most valuable qualities—implicit obedience, enthusiasm in the cause of their Sultan, and abstinence from the use of fermented liquors; which, in fact, led to the best results.

The artillery was very inferior in number to that of the Russians, and incapable of any rapid movements, being drawn by bullocks instead of horses. The guns were, however, well served in the field, and, with better appointments, would have been the most efficient part of the Turkish army.

In addition to the preceding, the Dellis and other irregulars answered the call of the Chief of the Faithful; bringing, as usual, into the field, their arms, and when mounted, their horses also; together with that kind of bravery in desultory warfare which at one time carried the Turkish hordes triumphantly over the plains of Asia Minor and those of Europe, to the very gates of Vienna. But things have long been changed in this respect; the tide of conquest was completely reversed when the loss of Azoff and Choten was followed by the retreat of the Turks to Bender, in 1769.

This was succeeded by the invasion of Turkey, and the campaigns of 1770, 1771, and 1772, by Romanoff's army; with, however, but little ultimate advantage. In 1773, the

Russians failed against Silistria; but in the following campaign, Romanoff drove the Grand Vizier into Schumla, and a treaty was signed in consequence, at Kuchuk Kainardji, on the 10th of January, 1775, by which Russia acquired the protectorship of Crimea, as well as that of Moldavia and Wallachia.

With a view to the conquest of Turkey, a joint attack was made by the armies of Catherine and Joseph of Austria, in 1787; but the defeat of the Emperor's army brought about a peace with Austria in 1789. Russia, however, continued the conquest till the peace of Jassy in 1792, when the Crimea was incorporated in her territory. The interference of the Emperor Alexander in the domestic affairs of Moldavia and Wallachia, produced a war with Turkey in 1806, in which Great Britain took part, and the fleet, commanded by Admiral Duckworth, proceeded against Constantinople. After peace was concluded with England in 1809, Russia continued the war with partial success. In 1810, the Russian army appeared before Schumla, under Count Kaminski. He was, however, unable to make any impression, and retired to the Danube. The succeeding campaign was favourable to the Turks, with the exception of the fall of Rustchuk, after a very protracted siege; and by the peace of Bucharest, which put an end to the war in 1812, the Russian forces became available to oppose the invasion of Napoleon during the ensuing winter.

Serious difficulties between Russia and Turkey were for the moment arranged by the treaty of Akkerman, in 1826, which gave Turkey a short respite, until the troops of the Czar again prepared to invade her territory.

On the 7th and 8th of May, 1828, the 16th, 17th, 18th, and 19th divisions of infantry, with six regiments of Cossacks and the Hulans of the Bug, composing the 6th and 7th corps, passed the Pruth, on bridges which had been previously prepared, leaving the 3rd corps for the moment on the other side of the river. The 7th corps marched at once against Brailow, under General Woinoff. The 6th, under General Kleist, took another direction, and reached Bucharest on the 16th; from whence General Geismar advanced to Aluta, and his Cossacks reached Crajova, the capital of Little Wallachia, without opposition, on the 21st.

It was only at this period that the fear of a rising in Constantinople had so far passed away as to allow some troops to be spared from the capital to meet the invading army. But now, 800 artillerymen, under Kara-Djehennem, reached Schumla, on the 17th of May, and 2,000 cavalry, under Osman Pashá, followed on the 22nd. These were succeeded on the 27th by 8,000 cavalry, and 19,000 infantry, under the Seraskier (Generalissimo) Hussein Pasha.

The Sultan reviewed these troops at the time of their departure from the capital, and encouraged their commander by saying,—"Behave bravely: I shall speedily follow." With 3,000 Dellis, in addition to those just enumerated, the Pasha had only, on the 2nd of June, a force of 13,000 cavalry, and 19,800 infantry, to cover the fortresses on the Danube, and defend Roumelia from invasion. On the same day some Turkish irregulars from Rustchuk, in conjunction with others from Giurgevo, moved forward, and had the first, but as it proved unimportant, affair with the Russian advance.

On the 3rd of July, a more important combined movement was made from those places by a Turkish force, consisting of 2,000 cavalry and 1,000 infantry with seven field pieces; and an attack was also made on General Geismar by the Pasha of Widdin, at the head of 4,000 infantry and 5,000 cavalry, with ten guns. In each of these affairs, both parties claimed the victory; but as the Turks regained their former positions with their guns, it may be inferred that the usual activity of the Turkish horse in desultory operations, had gained some advantage. As the Turks seemed to be disposed to dispute the passage of the Danube at Oltenitza, as well as other points above and below Widdin, and as there was little probability of effecting a passage so as to co-operate, as had been intended, with the 3rd and 7th corps in Bulgaria, the Russian operations were for the present confined to watching the fortresses on the right bank, and at the same time accomplishing the all-important object of securing supplies.

Extensive requisitions had previously been made on the

principalities by the Turkish Government; but as only 500 head of cattle and 1,000 sheep were received in consequence from Wallachia, and nothing whatever from Moldavia, it is clear that the inhabitants of those districts did not suffer materially by the Sultan's requisitions. The Russian declaration of war, however, was accompanied by a demand for 250,000 loads of corn, 400,000 tons of hay, 50,000 barrels of brandy, and 23,000 oxen; in addition to the forced labour of 16,000 peasants, who were to be employed in making hay on the banks of the Danube. The loss occasioned by the payment for these requisitions in bills instead of cash, was not the only disadvantage to which these unfortunate people were immediately exposed; for, as the local supplies were soon exhausted by such an army, it became necessary to transport provisions from Bessarabia by means of forced labour. The peasants also soon exhausted their own supplies, and were reduced to such extreme want in consequence that they died in great numbers on the road; as did also their cattle, in consequence of a murrain. The serious extent of this disease covered the roads with carcasses, which, by their putrefaction, coupled with the want of cleanliness in the Russian soldier, gave rise to typhus fever in its very worst form: that of the plague. This fearful scourge first appeared at Bucharest; and it continued to afflict the Russian army, as well as the inhabitants, during the whole of this and the succeeding campaign.

With regard to field operations, a period of comparative inactivity for the 3rd corps followed in Wallachia, during which interval the other two corps were employed; the one in besieging Brailow, and the other in effecting the passage of the Danube.

The siege was entrusted to the 7th corps, under General Woinoff, who crossed the Pruth and advanced to the Lower Danube, taking with him a battering train of 100 pieces of ordnance. On their arrival at Galatz, a small body of Turks retired hastily; who, first burning their boats to delay the enemy, entered Brailow with the loss of about forty men, taken prisoners.

Brailow, which is also called Ibraïl, stands on the left bank of the Danube, and is defended by eight bastioned fronts with revetted scarps and counterscarps; both of which are higher, in point of relief, than those of most other places in Turkey. A castellated citadel, flanked by round towers, defends the western front of the town; but there are no outworks to strengthen this fortress, nor any casemates to defend the garrison from shells, &c. Being armed with 278 guns, and mortars of various calibres, with (including the inhabitants) about 8,000 men under arms and amply provisioned, Brailow was sufficiently prepared for a siege; although labouring under the serious disadvantage of some cover outside the works, particularly in the ruined suburbs, which was calculated to facilitate the enemy's approaches

On the 8th of May, 4,000 cavalry and 6,000 infantry commenced the investment. On the 11th, the besieging force was increased to 18,000 men; and on the 16th, operations were commenced in form, under the Archduke Michael; while on the 19th, the Emperor Nicholas himself joined the army.

The strongest of the three *corps d'armée*, the 3rd—which was composed of the 7th, 8th, 9th, and 10th divisions of infantry, the 3rd division of Hussars, the 4th corps of cavalry, the 2nd Mounted Chasseurs, and two regiments of Cossacks—had remained in Bessarabia, to give time to collect materials for the bridge, and the dike which was to lead to it through the marshes. These being at length prepared, those troops to whom the principal operations of the campaign were to be entrusted, moved onwards in two divisions, under the immediate command of General Radovitch; and on taking post at Saturnovo, nearly opposite to Isaktschi, a battery of twelve guns was constructed to facilitate the passage of the Danube.

The Turks, who anticipated the enemy's intention of passing at this point, appeared on the opposite bank on the 7th of June, where they constructed a battery of fifteen heavy guns in a suitable position; and as the soft alluvial soil increased the difficulties of the enemy very seriously in approaching the left bank, the attempt to cross at this spot would in all probability have failed, had it not been for some unexpected and very opportune assistance. In addition to sending up the Jäger brigade in the gun-boats from Ismaïl, General Tutzkow, the governor of that fortress, had rendered a still more important service to the Russians, by inducing Ossip-Michailowitsch-Gladkoy, and his people, the Zaporoga Cossacks, to join the invaders and desert the cause of the Sultan; to whom they had been faithful since their settlement in that part of the country in the time of the Empress Catherine.

On the 8th of June these Cossacks succeeded, by means of their light fishing-boats, in conveying some 1,500 Jägers, without being perceived, to a wood on the opposite bank; and one of those important results which occasionally occur in warfare, was the consequence of the judicious employment of this small force. The Turks, who were numbered by the Russians at 12,000, but probably scarcely exceeded 6,000 men, were so exclusively occupied with the position of the Russian flotilla and troops in their front, that they totally overlooked what was taking place on their right flank; and on finding themselves suddenly attacked in rear by the Jägers, they were seized with panic and fled; a part taking the route of Bazarjik, and the remainder hurrying into the neighbouring fortress of Isaktschi. But instead of being of any assistance to the latter place, and endeavouring in conjunction with the garrison to dispute the passage of the river, their alarm was communicated to the others; thus, a place still capable of a respectable defence was shamefully abandoned to the enemy, together with eighty-five pieces of cannon.

Twenty-three hours' work now completed a bridge over the Danube, of 900 paces in length; and the remainder of the 3rd corps defiled along it, in presence of the Emperor, to the right bank, in order to commence operations in the Dobrudscha.

For this purpose four battalions and two squadrons were detached against Tuldscha; two battalions against Matschin; four battalions and two squadrons against Hirsova; four battalions and eight squadrons against Kustendji; and four battalions with seven squadrons against Bazarjik:* making in all 14,000 men. Thus there were about 2,000 men and ten guns allotted for the reduction of each place: a task which was the less difficult since not one of them was provided with a regular garrison. These arrangements being made, the main body—which, with the addition of some Hulans, exceeded 18,000 men—now advanced through the Dobrudscha towards Trajan's wall; proceeding thither by very slow marches, in order to give time to the troops employed elsewhere to complete their operations; more particularly the siege of Brailow.

Eleven days of great activity had enabled the Archduke Michael to open five batteries against the north-eastern side of the works of Brailow; but, as these works had

* Der Rüssisch-türkishe Feld-züg in der eüropaïschen Türkei, 1828 ünd 1829, von Freiherrn von Molkte. Berlin, 1848, pp. 79, 80.

been injudiciously placed, it became necessary to construct others; this was effected under the cover of the suburbs at the south-western side of the town. It was not, however, till the night of the 25th of May that the first parallel was completed; the right portion of this work being 500 paces, and its left about 800 paces from the counterscarp. Between the 26th and 29th of the month some additional batteries, for guns as well as mortars, were constructed. The besieged endeavoured to ascertain what was doing in the trenches at night, by lighting immense fires on the ramparts; and it is stated that from ten to fifteen men of the besiegers were killed each day. But notwithstanding the activity of the garrison, additional batteries were constructed by the 1st of June; and between the 4th and 6th of the month the 3rd parallel was completed. The latter was only 150 feet from the counterscarp; and it was not only of sufficient depth to cover the besiegers, but wide enough, also, to transport guns along it.

Since the usual ricochet batteries had not been brought into play, it became necessary for the besiegers to employ mines, to destroy the defences and breach the walls. For this purpose a gallery, which had been commenced on the 7th of June, was carried below the foot of the counterscarp, and thence under the cunette to the body of the place: globes of compression being occasionally used to facilitate the work. During these mining operations, the besiegers were constantly exposed to shells, shot, and small arms; in addition to repeated sallies, which were made with the most determined bravery, in the following manner:—Small bodies of from 50 to 100 men suddenly rushed across the ditch to attack the trenches; every man holding a loaded pistol in each hand, and a dagger between his teeth: for use after having discharged his fire-arms.

By the 15th of June four powerful mines were prepared by the besiegers, which, on the discharge of three rockets as a signal, were to be sprung simultaneously on that morning; when two columns, each accompanied by a body of Sappers, were instantly to storm the place.

Two of these mines proved quite successful, and a practicable breach was opened in the body of the place; but the other two failed, in consequence of the officer who had charge of the operation being struck down by the previous explosion. Unconscious of the failure of one part of the combination, the left column advanced at the given signal; but not finding the expected opening in the bastion, they were all killed: with the exception of a single man, a non-commissioned officer, who jumped into the Danube and escaped by swimming. The other column found a moderately practicable breach more to the right; but some of the guns in the flank of the adjoining bastion being still serviceable, and the Turks prepared to dispute the breach, a desperate struggle was maintained hand-to-hand, until the Archduke Michael at length ordered those who could not advance, and who scorned to retreat, to abandon the attempt. According to the Russian account, this abortive, and it may fairly be added injudicious attack, was attended with the loss of four generals, 118 officers, and 2,251 men killed and wounded.*

On the following day the other two mines were sprung, and with partial success; but during a truce which ensued for the purpose of burying the dead, a negotiation was commenced, which, after having been carried on sixteen hours, terminated by a capitulation and evacuation of the place. The garrison reserved to themselves the right to continue to serve, and the greater part retired to Silistria: they thus tarnished their previous brilliant defence of twenty-seven days with open trenches, by putting the enemy in possession of a fortress that was still defensible, and had 278 guns and mortars, with a sufficient supply of ammunition and provisions.

The ordnance mounted on the walls of Brailow was of mixed calibre, from 36-pounder guns downwards, and mortars throwing shells of 200 lbs., 150 lbs., and 7 lbs. weight; but the greatest execution was by the small mortars and wall pieces. The powder was stored in temporary excavations, chiefly under the ramparts; from whence, as was the case in the very infancy of artillery, it was carried loose to the pieces. The *résumé* of the attack shows that 1,700 workmen were employed each day in the trenches,

* Ibid, p. 92–96.

or 45,900 men in all, during the siege, and 14,789 guns were fired into the place. The Russians admitted a loss of about 4,000 officers and men, but the Turkish accounts, with more probability, make it exceed 5,000.

Great praise was bestowed on General Count Suchtelen, who, owing, as it is stated, to the advantage derived from *his previous experience*, was enabled to terminate the siege by negotiation. It may, however, be mentioned with reference to its premature conclusion, that Kuchuk Hamed told the author that the Russian Commander in Wallachia, in endeavouring to induce him to surrender Giurgevo, stated, as a reason for such a proposal, *that a golden key had opened the gates of Brailow:* and it must be admitted that Solyman Pasha's conduct is not free from suspicion, since he forgot his own spirited answer to the first summons to surrender: "When the rampart is destroyed, we shall form a living one of our bodies." The evil resulting from this surrender was not confined to the loss of one of the strongest places in Turkey, for every day that Brailow held out would have been so much additional time gained for the Sultan's defensive preparations.

On the capitulation of this fortress, the Russian flotilla, which had latterly taken a very active part in the siege, immediately commenced the bombardment of the *tête-de-pont* of Brailow; the surrender of which soon followed, as did that of Hirsova, Isaktschi, and Matschin. Tuldscha and Kustendje held out for a time; but after referring to Solyman Pasha, and receiving the promise of a free exit for their garrisons to proceed to Varna or Silistria, these small places were also evacuated. Thus, a moderate force, with some field pieces, and probably the use a little gold also, made the invaders masters of the country as far as Trajan's wall.

On the 5th of July a forward movement was commenced with reference to the concentration of the Russian forces at Bazarjik. Seven squadrons of cavalry, 100 Cossacks, and four battalions of infantry, formed the advance of the right wing under General Akinfief, and twelve squadrons of cavalry, with 200 Cossacks, and four battalions of infantry, that of the left wing under General Rüdiger; whilst General Benkendorff, with four battalions and some cavalry, took the route of Kousgoun and Silistria, followed by some of the 6th corps from Wallachia.

During the siege of Brailow, the Turks had done a great deal towards the defence of their country. Besides the artillery despatched to reinforce the garrison of Varna, 8,000 regular infantry, and 4,000 Albanians, reached Schumla on the 30th of June; thus, including the troops previously assembled, there was a force of 13,000 cavalry and 31,800 infantry at that place, under the Seraskier. Hussein Pasha, from the moment of assuming the command, had employed his wonted energy and no mean talent in improving the defences of this position; which, being the pivot of the Turkish main line of defence, claims more particular notice.

The town occupies a deep mountain basin formed by two abutments of the Balkan, which project north-eastward from that chain nearly in the form of a horse-shoe, the heel or extremities of which are towards the exterior; where, however, they are connected by a low range of hills running across the space. The road from Varna by Pravadi, and those from Silistria, Widdin, and other passages of the Danube, converge upon the side of the town; on which the best efforts of Turkish art and science have been expended. The rest of the contour of this position is well protected by the rocky sides of an almost inaccessible chain of hills, covered with brushwood, and rising in places to 600 feet or more.

Feeling the paramount importance of a position of this kind, as the grand pivot of a line of defence on the Danube, the Turks, for more than a century, have endeavoured to protect its weak point by a line of almost continuous field-works, extending from the heights of Strandscha on the north-west, to those of Tschengel on the south-south-east; both of which completely flank these works, and would, if fairly defended, be inaccessible to an enemy.

Though not by any means such works as would under other circumstances be considered sufficient, these intrenchments resisted the Russians successfully on several occasions; more particularly Marshal Romanoff, in 1774, and Marshal Kaminski, in 1810.

Instead, however, of confining himself to the renovation of the old defences, the Seraskier determined to construct a new line of works, a little in advance of the old intrenchments; so as to secure additional space, and at the same time, by means of a better trace, an improved line of defence. With these objects in view, 4,000 Turks, and as many Christians, were employed without intermission for forty days constructing fresh intrenchments.

These works have the shape of a grand front of fortification, which runs along the crests of the hills already mentioned, from side to side of the basin, a distance of nearly two miles and a half. In addition to eighteen bastioned projections at intervals, to give a flanking fire, there is a strong redoubt constructed at each extremity, on the crests of the higher hills; which in this way were made to flank the new lines artificially as well as naturally. Instead of outworks, a chain of redoubts was constructed at 300 yards, and another at 500 yards in advance of the lines, all countermined, and most of them enclosed towards the rear. Other detached works were also erected to defend the approaches to Schumla on the western and southern sides, so that in case of being turned by an enterprising enemy, it would be no longer an open town towards the Balkan.

The improvement of the defences of Schumla was no doubt an important object; but if the Seraskier had ventured either to postpone these works for a time, or to have entrusted their execution to another, Kara-Djehennem for instance, his presence, and that of the force he might have collected on the Danube, would in all probability not only have saved Brailow, but would also have prevented the passage of the Russian army across the river, and have put a stop to the operations subsequently carried on in the Dobrudscha by isolated corps. But on the other hand it should be borne in mind that Schumla has always claimed the peculiar care of the Turks, and it is therefore probable that the Seraskier had precise orders from the Sultan to make its safety a paramount object. But, be this as it may, Hussein Pasha having, with more prudence than skill and daring, made this place his first consideration, was enabled by the 7th of July to commence a Fabian system of warfare in advance of the position which has just been described. For this purpose some cavalry had been pushed on to Bazarjik.

Two Russian columns were now moving towards that place. The advance of the right under General Akinfief was composed of four squadrons of Hussars, three squadrons of four battalions of infantry, and some Cossacks. That of the left under Lieutenant-General Rüdiger consisted of twelve squadrons of Hussars, four battalions of infantry, and 200 Cossacks.

At the same time the advance of the Seraskier's force was moving to meet the enemy by way of Kosludsche, and the skirmishers had entered Bazarjik. The latter retired on the appearance of General Akinfief's corps, and, under the impression that the Turks had retreated, he proceed to take possession of that place without awaiting the arrival of General Rüdiger. The Dellis appeared in force next morning, the 8th of July, and led by a well-known artilleryman, whose success with his own arm had gained the Turkish *soubriquet* of Kara-Djehennem (black hell) speedily drove the Russians out of the town with considerable loss.

Colonel Reid, one of the Emperor's aides-de-camp, endeavoured to recover the town by making a determined charge with two squadrons of Hulans of the Bug; he was, however, repulsed, and two squadrons of Hussars which had hastened to his support, were also overcome by the impetuosity of the Turks, who took a horse artillery gun. But the brigade of Chasseurs, and the tenth division of infantry, partly recovered the day by the opportune discharge of a shower of canister from a battery of artillery. The Dellis now rushed with fury upon the guns, and one individual who had placed himself astride on one of them, in proof of its capture, was bayoneted in that position. The Turks eventually retired, leaving 200 men dead on the spot. On this occasion it was stated in the Russian bulletin that forty men were killed, but that from 8,000 to

10,000 Turks had been repulsed and driven from the heights towards Schumla!

Thus far the Russian movement had been directed against Varna, and General Roth had received orders to prepare the requisite materials for a bridge, which he was to throw across the Danube at Turtokai, between Rustchuk and Silistria, in order that he might advance to co-operate with the invading army in Bulgaria. But as the failure of his attempt to cross the Danube would not only have exposed the right flank, but also the rear of the Russian army, if the advance were to be continued along the coast, it became necessary to change the line of march towards Schumla, so as to be directly in front of the Turkish army with a concentrated force.

Under these circumstances, part of the 6th corps remained in Wallachia to keep Widdin, Rustchuk, &c., in check, and General Roth made a detour with the remainder to join the field force. He marched accordingly along the left bank of the Danube, as far as Hirsova, where he crossed in boats, and ascended the right bank to Kousgoun. This movement enabled the divisions of Benkendorff and Matadow to push on to Bazarjik, whither they were followed by the 7th corps from Brailow. The main body now diverged from the road to Varna, and taking that of Schumla, passed Kosludsche, which had been abandoned, and reached Jeni Bazar. Here the second affair of the campaign took place, on the 12th of July, when the

Russian advance was attacked and roughly handled by the Turkish cavalry, which drove it for some distance beyond the town, notwithstanding the arrival of General Rüdiger with a reinforcement of cavalry and infantry, to cover the retreat.

By the 16th of July, the arrival of the various corps employed against Kustendje and the other places in the Dobrudscha, had augmented the operating force to 41,000 men; in addition to 24,000 men employed in the rear, according to one account,* or even 85,000 men according to others.† Now commenced simultaneous movements against Varna, Schumla, and the intermediate position of Pravadi. General Benkendorff, at the head of four battalions of the 10th division, and some Hulans, &c., advanced from Kosludsche, and occupied Pravadi; which, notwithstanding its importance in maintaining the communications between Varna and Schumla, had been neglected by the Seraskier. The left wing, under General Count Suchtelen, marched to the coast; but instead of being able to commence operations against Varna, he encountered a vigorous sortie; a bloody engagement followed, in which he lost 300 men, and being driven back, reinforcements were thrown into the place by the Turks. The Emperor Nicholas himself directed the principal operations on the other line, by moving against Schumla.

* Der Russisch-türkische Feldzug in 1828, 1829, von Freihern von Molkte, p. 109.

† Imanitschew-Geschichte des Russisch-Turkischen Kruges, von 1828, p. 196. Ilmenau, 1829.

Before the beginning of the campaign, a very low estimate had been formed of the Nizám, and of the Turkish forces generally; but the defence of Brailow, and the encounters near Bazarjik, had produced a great change in this respect. The heavily-equipped Russian cavalry, mounted on large horses, were found unequal to cope with the more active Dellis, who were expert swordsmen as well as excellent horsemen; and this difference was perceptible even in the early part of the campaign, when the cavalry was in its most efficient state. But although the morale and enduring courage of the Russian infantry were as yet unshaken, it was thought necessary to take extreme care to avoid unnecessary exposure to the determined attacks of the Turkish cavalry; to which at all times the advancing enemy would otherwise have found himself exposed.

The next affair began a mile and a half from Yassi-Tepe. Here the advance fell in with some Turkish cavalry, which retired on its appearance, towards the village. On reaching the neighbourhood of Yassi-Tepe, the Russians discovered that their right was suddenly surrounded, and a fire was opened upon it by the Turks, with such tremendous effect, that but for the arrival of a body of Hussars, the whole force must have been sacrificed. As it was, they were not extricated from their perilous position without serious loss.

On the 16th, the Russian head-quarters reached Shamly, and the advance was pushed on to Yeni Bazar; which was occupied, after a slight skirmish, and a junction of the grand army with General Rüdiger was thus effected. Count Suchtelen with his force was already under the walls of Varna, and General Benkendorff, with the 10th division, a portion of cavalry, and some Cossacks, was sent towards Pravadi to cover the left of the army, while the advance was continued by the main body upon Schumla. In accordance with the orders of the Emperor Nicholas, this advance was made in two columns, observing, at the same time, the greatest caution. General Rudovitch, with three brigades of the 9th division, and their complement of artillery, ready to form a square, was in advance of the right column, which was accompanied by the Emperor himself, and consisted of the 15th and 16th Jäger regiments, with twelve guns. The right flank was covered by twelve squadrons of cavalry; the whole prepared to form squares.

The 7th corps, under General Woinov, assisted by General Diebitsch, formed the left column. It was covered by Hussars on each flank, and was also prepared to form squares on the appearance of the enemy. Four battalions of the 8th division, with the reserve artillery of 108 guns, covered by Count Orloff with a division of mounted Jägers, formed the rear.

On the 20th of July, a Turkish force was discovered occupying the heights between Kisjila and Boulanlik, behind the Pravadi river, with eighteen guns; part of the troops being concealed by brushwood. In the expectation that the Seraskier's whole army was prepared to prevent the advance upon Schumla, the Emperor immediately arranged the following order of battle; by which his force, at the lowest estimate about 45,000 men, outflanked that of the Turks, both on the right and left.

The 3rd corps was to form in front of the enemy, in separate brigades. Each of these had two battalions formed in squares in the first line, with twelve guns in the interval; and two other battalions formed in squares in the second line, about a hundred paces behind the first and covering the intervals; twenty-eight squadrons of cavalry, 1,000 Cossacks, and twenty-four light guns, were on the right, and forty-eight guns were kept in reserve by the Emperor. Whilst forming in this order, the 7th corps, with four squadrons of the Orange Hussars, and four light guns, advanced on the left of the 3rd corps, with the intention of attacking and outflanking the enemy; but the moment the head of the column appeared, it was fiercely charged by a swarm of Turkish horse; these were, however, repulsed by a battery of artillery judiciously opened upon them, which caused them to retreat, pursued by the Orange Hussars and the 7th corps. The latter was in turn exposed to the fire of the Turkish guns, and was driven back with heavy loss; Colonel Read, the Emperor's aide-de-camp, being amongst the slain. Some of the Dellis who had crossed the stream, were at this moment engaged hand to hand with the Cossacks on the right of the 3rd corps, nearer to Boulanlik.

The Emperor Nicholas had only awaited the result of his preliminary operations before making a general attack upon what he still believed to be the whole Turkish army. It proved, however, to be a force of only about 6,000 cavalry, which, as had been previously arranged, retired within the lines of Schumla. Thus terminated the so-called battle, or reconnaissance, according to the Turks, of Yeni-Bazar. The Russian account mentioned a loss of 150 men; but the Turkish sabres are said to have done much greater execution; and the withdrawal of their guns, at the leisurely pace of bullocks, into Schumla, seems to prove that they were masters of the ground on this occasion.

The lofty purple-tinged sides of the European branch of the Taurus had gradually become more distinct as the invaders advanced, till all at once more striking scenery burst upon their view. On reaching some swelling ground, almost at the foot of the Balkan, the wooded heights of Strandscha appeared as the fore-ground of the prospect to the right, and those of Tschengel on the left; whilst, apparently as the reward of a toilsome march, the Russians, who did not as yet perceive the intrenchments, were gladdened by the sight of the graceful minarets rising above the pointed red roofs of the houses of Schumla: filling up, as they appeared to do, the space between two abutments of those mountains which still formed the back ground of the view.

CHAPTER IV.

FAILURE OF THE ATTACKS UPON SCHUMLA, AND CONCLUSION OF THE CAMPAIGN OF 1828.

The Russian forces invest Schumla—Fierce attacks of the Turks and Russians—The Emperor Nicholas proceeds to Varna—Progress of the siege—Capture of a Russian redoubt, and its artillery—Repeated encounters before Schumla—The siege becomes a blockade—The Turks assume the offensive—The Grand Vizír fails to succour Varna—Description of that fortress—Progress of the siege—The Russian fleet brings reinforcements—Bombardment by sea and land—Reinforcements brought by the Emperor Nicholas—Sallies and subterranean warfare—Capitulation, and result of the siege—Operations south of Varna—Battle of Kurtepe—Description and siege of Silistria—Retreat of the Russian army into Wallachia—Tête-de-pont of Giurgevo, and operations in that quarter.

The previous state of the defences of Schumla had been known to the Russian Engineers, but they were not aware of the changes recently effected by Hussein Pasha; who had already taken post behind his new intrenchments. These, as in the case of Torres Vedras during the memorable advance of Massena against Lisbon, presented an unexpected barrier to the invaders; who, during the remainder of the present as well as the whole of the succeeding campaign, were destined to find that the Turkish epithet of "Gazi," or triumphant Schumla, was well deserved.

As a first step towards the investment of this position, the Emperor caused a chain of redoubts to be constructed beyond the range of the Seraskier's artillery; and, as part of a second line, the lower portion of the hill of Tschengel was also occupied with a redoubt. But passive defence formed no part of the Seraskier's plan, and he did not long remain inactive. On the 27th of July he made a formidable sortie, and another again on the following day; both of which were attended with severe loss to the besiegers, who held their ground with great difficulty. A Jäger regiment in particular was surrounded by the Turkish cavalry, and was on the point of surrendering at the very moment that it received support.

The details of some of these attacks on the Russian redoubts were related to the author by an individual who took an active part in these proceedings. This was Hemén Pasha, who had brought a force of upwards of 2,000 irregular troops from his government in Konia. These men were animated by the same determined spirit as their chief; whose great anxiety was to serve his sovereign by overcoming the enemies of Turkey. Hemén, in touching upon his own history, mentioned that he was one of the Mamelukes at the time of their destruction by Muhammed Ali; and his Kaïa, or lieutenant, afterwards filled up this outline by informing us that it was Hemén who had leaped his horse over the wall at Cairo: he was, consequently, the solitary individual who escaped that massacre. The expression of Hemén Pasha's dark countenance and rolling eyes, as he related the hope he had conceived during one of the sorties from Schumla, of making the Emperor Nicholas prisoner, are strongly impressed on the memory of the author. "Had this been effected," added he, "we should only have released him on the condition of his restoring the Crimea to the Sultan."

Two days later these attacks were returned by an abortive attempt of the Russians to gain the heights of Strandscha; which was followed by another, made with as little success, on the opposite side of the valley. Nineteen redoubts had been already constructed by the Russians without accomplishing their intended object of cutting off the communications. The space between the road to Silistria and that which leads by Smëadowo and Czalikawak towards Constantinople, was nearly cut off; but the principal communications of the garrison by Rasgrad, Dïoumaia, and Eski Stamboul, were still perfectly open.

Hoping to master the latter post, and cut off these openings, two redoubts were constructed near the hamlet of Matschin. General Rüdiger, with the Hussars and eight battalions of the 19th division, advanced to the village of Chifflik with this view; and, leaving four battalions and four squadrons of cavalry there as a support, he proceeded with the remainder of his force to Eski Stamboul, meaning to push a reconnaissance as far as the village of Kiötej. But a double attack made by the Turks caused a speedy retreat of both corps, on the redoubts which had been constructed for their defence at Matschin.

As these, and other demonstrations elsewhere, did not tempt Hussein Pasha to quit his position, and as no immediate impression was likely to be made against the intrenchments, the Emperor Nicholas, who had but recently joined the army, proceeded towards Varna on the 3rd of August, taking with him twelve guns and some reinforcements. He left Marshal Wittgenstein before Schumla, to continue to observe and blockade that place.

The Emperor's departure caused a fresh disposition to be made of the remaining troops, by which the 5th corps was to occupy the redoubts, while the 7th undertook offensive operations against the rear of the Turks. Accordingly, General Rüdiger, with eight battalions, eight squadrons of cavalry, and some Cossacks, was to renew his attempt to gain possession of Eski Stamboul; securing his communication with the 3rd corps by a part of his own force. On the 7th of August he drove the Turks from Kiötej. They speedily recovered the village, however, and threw up works, both at that place and at Troussi, which were sufficiently strong to defeat General Rüdiger's plans. Other works were also constructed on the slope of the hill between Ibrahim Nazir and Matschin, in order to cover the Constantinople road. From most of these works, particularly from that called Sultan Tabia, zig-zag approaches were carried forward with much ingenuity almost up to the Russian redoubts, with a view to carrying on a subterranean warfare; which, in practice as well as in its early use, is peculiarly a Turkish science.

The activity of the Turks was not confined to the vicinity of their intrenchments, for on the 8th of August they attacked a convoy at Yeni-Bazar, and succeeded in capturing a quantity of cattle. Considering the difficulty in obtaining supplies, this proved a serious loss to the Russians.

With the purpose of closing some of the approaches of the Turkish camp, General Woinov marched against Eski Jumna; whilst Rüdiger renewed his attempt against Eski Stamboul, and Prince Eugene of Wurtemburg advanced at the same time upon Marash. In Rüdiger's attempt, which took place on the 15th of August, 3,000 Turks were driven out of Kiötej, with the loss of one gun and 100 killed; but they repaid this attack with interest, by taking one of their adversary's guns, and driving him back with heavy loss; Lieutenant-General Iwanof being among the slain. Prince Eugene's attempt had no better success, for he was forced to retreat with all speed, in order to defend the redoubts from an attack made on them by the Turks at the same moment. In order to be at hand to support General Rüdiger, the Prince, with eight battalions of the 18th division, took up a position at Marash; from whence he retired on being threatened with a fresh attack. General Rudowitz, however, afterwards intrenched himself at that place to prevent surprise.

These and other affairs which took place in the neighbourhood of Schumla, manifestly to the advantage of the Turks, raised the moral power of the garrison at the expense of the besiegers. The Seraskier, therefore, determined to push his successes by endeavouring to carry by assault two of the principal Russian redoubts ; making at the same time a combined attack upon the position of General Rüdiger at Eski Stamboul, and that of Prince Eugene, who occupied Marash with eight battalions of the 18th division, and six squadrons of Hussars.

Contrary to Turkish custom, the Seraskier commenced these operations by moving against the two redoubts in the middle of the night. The attempts against one of these works failed, but the other was carried sword in hand, with the loss of General Baron Wrede and some hundred Chasseurs of the 15th regiment. Six guns were taken, and the Turks maintained their position, notwithstanding the repeated efforts made by the Russians to regain this post. The Russians attribute the loss of this redoubt to their having been off their guard; but the fact that the Turks brought animals and dragged six battering guns into Schumla, proves that they must have continued masters of the field for some time.

This attempt, however brilliant in itself, was only intended to occupy the enemy, so as to cover the Seraskier's main object of breaking through the Russian line while the attacks on the redoubts were going on. He thus hoped to fall upon the other two positions with a sufficient force to overwhelm them. It proved, however, that General Rüdiger had already retired from Eski Stamboul to a position behind the Kamtchik; having been secretly informed of this intended movement by a Bulgarian.

Issád Pasha, who led the other column during this attack on the night of the 26th, routed the Cossacks; and pursuing them closely, he entered the Russian position at Marash with his cavalry almost at the same instant with them, and was soon followed by his infantry. He found the Russians on the alert, and was received by a volley of musketry and a shower of canister, which drove him back. By this time the day had dawned, and showed two dense columns of regular infantry advancing with a wild hurrah to attack the Russians at the point of the bayonet. These formed the supporting force under the Seraskier, approaching 15,000 men, with which he entered Marash, and threw himself on the right flank of the Russians. Here they encountered a well-directed fire of canister and musketry, under which the Turks deployed with great steadiness and regularity; but a charge of the Wittgenstein Hussars on their right caused some disorder and loss.

The Seraskier now renewed the attempt in another direction; with some battalions of regular infantry, a portion of cavalry, and four light guns, he moved along the valley of the Kamtchik, to attack the left of the Russians, and if possible carry the village, which contained the park and hospital: in the latter were 600 sick. Two battalions of the regiment of Ufa, and another of that of Perin, endeavoured to maintain this post, and showed the most determined spirit. The first battalion of Ufa, which was formed in a square, only saved two officers, and was nearly cut to pieces; when the Turks were attacked in flank by three battalions of infantry and two squadrons of the Orange Hussars, which opportunely debouched from the village for that purpose. They were, therefore, forced to retreat, but carried with them one Russian gun.

Considerable improvement in the knowledge of tactics was manifested by the Turks in these affairs. Not only were the three arms judiciously employed in a combined operation, but they showed a facility of rallying, by re-forming when worsted, very different from their former scattered flight. At least 1,500 men are admitted to have been sacrificed by Count Wittgenstein in these desultory encounters; during which the moral courage of the Russian cavalry soldier had suffered quite as much as his physical condition.

Escort duty in conveying provisions was attended with great labour; and it was still more difficult to procure forage in an exhausted country, with a temperature of from 40° to 60° of Reaumer. The daily loss of 100 to 150 horses soon caused two-thirds of the cavalry to be dismounted, which threw additional duty upon the infantry; who, owing to a scanty supply of food and chalky water, soon filled the hospitals with pitiable cases of scurvy, itch, &c. Added to this, the rear of the invaders was not by any means secure; especially as the heavy Russian horse had been found unequal to cope with the light moving Muslims, who, by sudden and constant attacks on convoys, gave the enemy no rest whatever. In addition to all this, the Russians were now threatened with an attack from the heights of Strandscha; they therefore determined to concentrate the 3rd and 7th corps; holding, however, the six redoubts for a time, as a blind, after the defeat of the 26th; but these were abandoned almost immediately afterwards.

These preparations for concentration enabled the Turks to throw supplies into Schumla, and Hussein Pasha prepared to follow up his former success by attacking the Russians in force on the 10th of September. But the Bulgarians, who favoured the invaders, made this intention known to them during the night of the 9th; Hussein Pasha's spirited attack on the following morning, with 8,000 men against the three redoubts, failed in consequence.

The Turks also made an attack on the left of Prince Eugene of Wurtemberg, while 3,000 cavalry and some infantry marched against the village of Kasaplar. This obliged Rüdiger to attack in his turn, and the Turks were forced to retreat; though without serious annoyance, the Russian cavalry being unable to pursue them with the necessary speed.

These affairs, although not very decisive when taken separately, had considerable influence on the whole; since they obliged Count Wittgenstein to confine his future operations to the mere observation of Schumla from the side of Yeni-Bazar: for which purpose Prince Eugene now abandoned the redoubts hitherto occupied by him near the heights of Tschengel.

Hussein Pasha was not tardy in following up the Russian movements, by sending out his cavalry; one portion of which succeeded in capturing a convoy of provision wagons near Yeni-Bazar, whilst another body of Dellis suddenly fell upon the 3rd Hussars, and made five officers and 200 men prisoners. Nor were these the only successes of the Turkish cavalry, for at this period an officer and a hundred men who were employed in conveying a despatch, fell into the hands of the Dellis; and Halil Pasha, who was sent from Schumla for the purpose, succeeded, by means of an attack on the Russian force near Pravadi, in covering the march of 1,000 men, sent from Silistria to reinforce that place.

The Grand Vizír, contrary to the orders of the Sultan, had continued inactive in Adrianople during these operations. He now at length advanced to Aidos; where he was joined by 14,000 men, detached from Schumla as a reinforcement. But his previous delay and neglect occasioned the loss of Varna; which fortress, next to Schumla, was considered of the greatest importance to the defence of Turkey. The possession of that port and fortress had, therefore, become a paramount object, to which the attention of the Emperor Nicholas was particularly directed; although the means required for this purpose necessarily interfered with his operations against the Danubian fortresses and Schumla.

The defence of Varna was of so remarkable a nature, that the place itself requires a fuller description than that already given, in order that it may be clearly understood. Previously to the siege, the town contained 5,000 houses. and about 25,000 inhabitants. It is situated on the western coast of the Black Sea, towards the northern side of a bay of the same name, which is nearly 3,000 yards deep, and about 4,000 yards wide: *i. e.*, from its northern horn to its southern extremity at Galata Burnu. The houses occupy a kind of spreading valley at the head of Lake Devna, and are chiefly situated on the northern bank of a river of the same name, which conveys the superfluous waters of the lake into the sea. Having the expansive waters of the Euxine on one side of the town, and vineyards, orchards, and the lake just mentioned, on the other, backed by the rounded sides and rounded summits of the Balkan, the appearance of Varna is strikingly picturesque.

The fortifications, which, on the whole, are very respectable, take the shape of a truncated pyramid. A thin loop-holed wall, imperfectly flanked, protects the side towards the sea (or the apex of the figure) and also part of the western side, along the river Devna. A stone bridge crosses the river near the town, and is protected by a *tête de pont* at the commencement of the road leading to Constantinople. The remainder of the *enceinte* is irregularly fortified, having ten flat bastions, with very short flanks and long narrow curtains, and being surrounded by a deep ditch. The scarp and counterscarp are revetted, and (as in Silistria and some other places) the former had, in 1828, a parapet faced with wicker-work hurdles to retain the earth, and a row of strong palisades within, rising a little above its crest. There was also a deep trench, or cunette, in the ditch, which proved to be very important to the defence. Although with only a low relief, the works command the exterior almost to the distance of cannon shot; but, as the necessary consequence of the want of ravelins and covert-way, they might be breached from a distance.

The circumference of the town is nearly three miles; and, before the removal of the guns from the sea face for the defence of Silistria, there were 162 pieces of mounted ordnance of various calibres. Fully one hundred of these, however, still remained in 1828; and, with the exception of one gun on each flank, they were chiefly mounted on the faces of the bastions: the *terre plein* of the curtains being too narrow for the effective use of artillery.

Inside the works, the ground rises to some height, both at the western and eastern quarters of the town. The hills thus form a slope towards the sea; near which stands a Byzantine castle, defended by high square turrets. This work serves as a magazine, as well as a kind of keep or citadel.

In conformity with the Turkish system of defence, three lunettes open at their gorges were constructed at about 500 paces in advance of the western land-front, and another intrenchment, nearly 1,500 paces from the eastern front; which was the expected point of attack.

In addition to these, quite a labyrinth of exterior lodgments was constructed by the Turks, some of which were retained during the siege; and the ground, as will be presently seen, disputed almost to the last moment.

Much time and space would be necessary to detail the various events connected with the siege of Varna; but a succinct sketch will suffice to give the reader an idea of the bravery and constancy displayed by the Turks, up to that trying moment when their noble efforts were paralyzed by the more than doubtful conduct of the Governor.

Count Suchtelen, as already mentioned, appeared before Varna at the head of a weak division on the 14th of July, and on the arrival of General Huchakoff with more troops, the place was invested towards the northern angle on the 15th and 16th. The garrison, which had hitherto been under the command of Yussuf Pasha, had just been strengthened by the arrival of 300 Tofingees (body guard), 800 marines, and about 3,000 Albanians, under the Capudan Pasha; who immediately assumed the offensive, with a force of some 7,000 men. Two days of skirmishing outside the town were followed by a bold *sortie* headed by a dervish; and, as the result of this affair, a cartload of heads was sent as trophies to Constantinople. Later in the war the Turks substituted the salted ears of the Russians, as being more *portable* proofs of their success.

These encounters caused Count Suchtelen to retreat to Kosludsche, leaving General Huchakoff with four battalions and five squadrons to watch the place. The garrison made another *sortie* on the 20th, with every prospect of overwhelming the Russians. Owing, however, to the arrival of a reinforcement which came by way of Devenish, under Count Suchtelen, the besiegers held their ground for a time, and then made good their retreat to the pass of Derbent, where they threw up intrenchments. Some stores and ammunition which had been buried by the Russians, to facilitate their retreat, were found and carried into Varna, and the shops were re-opened, with rejoicings for the safety of the town. During the absence of the besiegers, small detachments of infantry and Topjïs (gunners) with some guns arrived from Constantinople; and a fresh redoubt, called the Islam Tabia, was constructed in front in advance, to the right of the Schumla road.

Towards the end of the month, the Russian fleet anchored within a mile and a half of Varna, bringing three brigades of the 7th division from Anapa; and Prince Menschikoff, now in command, fairly opened the siege on the 3rd of August. According to the Russian accounts, his force only amounted to 9,000 men. Two landing-places were prepared, partly as a means of communication, but chiefly to facilitate the landing of heavy guns from the fleet; the battering-train not having yet arrived. In consequence of a plan of Varna given by a Sclavonian who had deserted from the town, the present attack was commenced at the north-eastern, instead of the south-western side as before.

On the 6th of August a chain of redoubts was commenced at about 2,000 paces from the walls of the town, where the northern face of the latter abuts upon the sea; and a parallel being also completed, the fire of the batteries and a bombardment from the fleet took place simultaneously. The effect of the latter was but partial, however, because the depth of water did not permit ships of the line to approach sufficiently near to do much execution. But a successful boat attack was made from the fleet on the Turkish flotilla, then anchored near the southern extremity of the town, and the greater part of it was captured.

Finding that the progress of the siege was slower than had been expected, and that more troops would be required to reduce the fortress, the Emperor Nicholas left Varna for Odessa, after this partial success; leaving Prince Menschikoff to conduct the operations.

Several partial attacks had already been made on the besiegers by that portion of the garrison which still continued outside, in order to carry on their active though somewhat desultory warfare, under cover of the redoubts and other lodgments. On the 8th, the Arnauts, under cover of the preceding works made a determined *sortie*, through the land gate, which, according to the Russian account, caused a loss of ten officers and 190 men; but the report of the garrison made it much more severe. Instead of returning through the gate, the Arnauts regained the place by leaping into the ditch.

On the 10th, two additional redoubts, the 7th and 8th, were constructed by the besiegers, with the hope of driving in the Turks from the outside, or cutting off their retreat; and a force was detached at the same time to Gebedsche beyond Lake Devna, for the purpose of enclosing the fortress more completely on that side. Both these attempts, however, completely failed. The Turks, as before, maintained their positions outside of the walls, and even succeeded in throwing a reinforcement into the place. About one half of the 14,000 men who had been detached from Schumla, crossed the bridge over the Devna, and quietly entered the town on the 15th and 16th August.

On the former day an additional battery of eleven twenty-four pounders and two mortars opened a fire, in order to dismount the guns of the bastion at the eastern angle of the town. A parallel was constructed on the 18th and 19th within 300 paces of the ditch, and another more to the westward on the 20th, in addition to a sunken battery, which was hastily erected. Next day (the 21st) the Turks sallied out of the town and attacked the Jägers and another regiment, with such determination that it was with extreme difficulty they maintained their ground. The loss on both sides was serious, and Prince Menschikoff being amongst the wounded, the direction of the siege devolved in consequence upon General Pirowsky, chief of the Emperor's staff.

Between the 22nd and 30th another redoubt and several batteries, some armed with field pieces, were erected by the besiegers, to play upon the bastion at their extreme left as well as on the adjoining curtain; and an attempt was also made to storm the Turkish redoubts. The garrison, on the other hand, established an additional counter approach, with the support of which, added to an effective fire of small arms from the ramparts, they made repeated attacks upon the besiegers, and caused them serious loss.

By the Emperor's orders, Count Woronzow took the command before Varna on the 29th of August; which event was signalised by a sortie made in force during the succeeding night, against the right of the Russian trenches. The Arnauts entered the redoubt sword in hand through the embrasures, but were repulsed, after a determined struggle, by the efforts of a regiment called after the Duke of Wellington. The 31st was remarkable for a series of attacks and counter-attacks by the besieged and the besiegers, who alternately attacked the flank of their adversary. Towards the close of the day, the Turks mastered some strong ground near the enemy's right, on which they planted five of their standards ; but during the night General Woinoff regained this position, though with great difficulty. A Turkish lunette was carried at the same moment, but it was retaken next morning by a storming party sent for the purpose from the garrison.

Between the 1st and 8th of September two additional redoubts were constructed by the besiegers, and a second parallel was attempted by flying sap, under cover of fresh batteries. These played directly on the guns of the fortress, instead of the usual and more scientific *ricochet* fire.

At this period the Russians made a movement southward of the Balkan. Two frigates, a cutter, and a sloop, detached for this purpose from the fleet of Admiral Greig, made a successful descent at Neuda, near Bourgas, and carried away twelve guns from the arsenal of the former place.

On the 8th of September, the Emperor Nicholas returned by land, accompanied by reinforcements to hasten the siege, and went on board the *Pallas* line-of-battle-ship for this purpose. The sixteen battalions and sixteen squadrons then brought, in addition to the guards and sappers, gave an effective force of more than 20,000 men before Varna; exclusive of the corps detached to the southern side of the fortress, and of another which occupied Pravadi.

The enterprising spirit of the people of Varna, was elevated rather than daunted by the hosts which now threatened their walls; and perceiving a regiment of Lancers rather in advance, covering a reconnoitering party, 500 Dellis made a sudden dash and drove them back. On this occasion, Lord Bingham, who had accompanied the British ambassador, Sir William A'Court, in the suite of the Emperor, had his horse killed under him.

The operations were, however, pushed with increased vigour; on the morning of the 10th of September the besiegers were within fifty paces of the counterscarp, whilst a force of 5,000 men, who occupied Galata Burnu, and were in communication with the fleet, shut in the garrison on the southern side. But although the greater part of the land front was embraced by the trenches and parallels of the besiegers, the garrison still continued to occupy some of their lodgments outside, and an efficient fire of small arms was maintained against the saps and approaches. These the enemy continued, notwithstanding, to push in advance, with the purpose of mining the body of the place. This operation was, in fact, accomplished on the 15th of September, when a heavily charged mine effected a breach in the bastion at the easternmost angle. Still the Pasha, who was as yet faithful to his trust, indignantly refused to receive a summons to capitulate.

At this juncture, the difficulties attending the transport of heavy guns through Bulgaria had been at length overcome, and the siege train arrived from Brailow to replace the guns landed by the fleet. Additional batteries were therefore opened to render the breach more practicable. A fresh sap was carried at the same time to a part of the counterscarp more to the right, and another towards the tower adjoining the bastion attacked. This tower, although more than half destroyed by the fire of the guns, was still obstinately defended; and the musketry and hand-grenades were so well applied in this part of the works, as almost to silence some of the more advanced guns of the besiegers.

Although a practicable breach existed in the bastion, and another in the adjoining curtain, neither the prospects of the besiegers, nor the state of the campaign elsewhere in Turkey, were by any means encouraging to the invaders. Their attemps to take and afterwards to blockade Schumla, had been total failures; little progress had been made against Silistria and the other fortresses of the Danube; reinforcements, for the purpose of raising the siege of Varna, were actually in sight; and the idea of anticipating this operation by an immediate assault was abandoned, or at least postponed, lest a failure might compromise the safety of the Russian army. It is not, therefore, surprising, that the confidence of the besiegers should have been seriously impaired, notwithstanding the presence of the Emperor; whilst that of the Turks was as naturally increased by the success of their efforts.

Reverting to the siege. Not only did the garrison continue to occupy the ditch, but they there maintained the most singular and bloody warfare that can be imagined. For although the ditch of a fortified place is usually contested, the defence of that of Varna had a peculiar character. Instead of the mere use of shot and shell, as in an ordinary siege, the mining operations and sallies of the Turks were continued without intermission. The inhabitants, like the chivalrous warriors of the middle ages, seemed determined to be buried sword in hand by the mines of the enemy, rather than abandon their perilous position in the ditch, or think of surrendering the town. Unfortunately this noble feeling was not shared by their leader—at least not towards the close of the siege.

Since the successful termination of this siege was made to depend upon subterranean works instead of the powerful effect of breaching batteries, descending galleries were pushed towards the foot of the counterscarp. This operation was materially assisted by taking two of the Turkish lunettes by storm on the 26th, and capturing a gun which till then had actually remained outside of the permanent works. On the 27th, the counterscarp was blown in by the explosion of four globes of compression; but as the cunette was not filled up by the rubbish, as had been expected, the besiegers were more exposed than heretofore to the fire of the curtain, as well as that from the lodgments in the ditch. Since additional guns could scarcely be mounted at this critical period, in the face of an enterprising enemy, another descending gallery was commenced by the besiegers, with the intention of reaching the body of the place by passing beneath the cunette.

After tedious exertions in working through a chalky soil, the Russian sappers perceived by a ray of light that, owing to a miscalculation of the levels, the gallery, if continued, would be exposed to the enemy's fire; luckily for the assailants this discovery was made just in time to close the aperture before it was perceived. The garrison, however, were made aware, by the noise, that mines were advancing, and a fierce attack was made on the covering parties by the Arnauts; who, although completely exposed to the fire of the besiegers, only retired after a bloody contest of upwards of two hours. In order to cover the sappers, blinds were let down into the ditch, but these were burnt by the garrison with firepots and other inflammable materials. Gabions were then resorted to, and after much difficulty, which was only overcome by great perseverance, a lodgment was effected by the besiegers in the bastion on the 28th of September.

Upon this the Turks brought a gun to bear upon the exterior of the gallery, from the adjoining battery; and, an opening being effected, the musketry and grenades took such effect, that the miners were forced to abandon their advanced position and seek shelter in the rear. This retreat was only temporary, for on the following morning they were employed preparing fresh mines in the face of the bastion; whence, however, they were again speedily dislodged.

On the 1st of October, during a thick fog, the Turks and Arnauts stormed the enemy's lodgments in the ditch, and succeeded, by means of this fierce attack, in forcing the miners, as well as the marksmen, to retreat. They then proceeded to burn the materials collected in the ditch, notwithstanding their exposure to the fire of the enemy's lodgments, which completely commanded it. This bloody affair continued nearly three hours; and a small Russian piece called a falconet, and many heads of the enemy, were carried as trophies into Varna.

During the following day the works in the ditch were partially repaired by the besiegers, under cover of a strong body of marksmen; additional mines, as well as opposing countermines, were commenced at the same time by the Turks. A fresh sally took place during the succeeding night, but with less success than on the preceding one; for the Arnauts, of whom it was chiefly composed, retreated after setting fire to the enemy's fascines; the passage of the ditch was in consequence re-established by the besiegers.

On the 3d of October another determined sortie was made by the garrison, with the same purpose of effecting an entrance into the enemy's galleries; but having failed in this attempt, a retreat was effected, after they had been exposed for upwards of half an hour to the fire of the artillery and musketry of the besiegers. These, on the other hand, succeeded in springing a mine in the face of the easternmost bastion; but, although in itself sufficiently practicable, the attempt to form a lodgment failed, owing to an intrenchment constructed by the Turks to defend the interior of the work. The assault was made by 600 Russians, 300 of whom entered the town through a blind alley, and were all killed. A Turkish woman killed one of the Russians herself with a stone, whilst a Kurd of Bagdad made a stand in the street opposite to the breach. The Capudan Pasha at the same time encouraged the men with a stick, calling for horse-bags filled with sand to stop up the breach; working all the while with his own hands. The stand made by the Kurd led to the death of the 300 Russians, and he was made a captain on the spot.

During the two following days, mines were prepared by the besiegers in the second bastion attacked, and in the opposite counterscarp; but the almost insuperable difficulty remained, of conveying the powder across the ditch. For this purpose, a huge mantelet was constructed of thick planks lined with fascines, and provided with loop-holes as well as embrasures for seven guns; it was moved by means of rollers and levers, so that, stage by stage, the transport of the powder might be secured: the latter having the additional protection of boxes covered with skins as a precaution. The Turks immediately opened a powerful fire against this ponderous machine. It was therefore with a heavy loss, and as it were foot by foot, that the besiegers gained ground in the face of their opponents. At length their mines were charged; the breach was rendered more practicable by springing them; and a storming party, followed by some sappers, effected a lodgment in the bastion. The communication being completed across the ditch, the Turks, who had so long and so bravely defended it, were completely cut off, and all on the spot perished sword in hand.

On the 6th of October, in order to recover some of the ground thus lost, the garrison made a determined attack on the bastion; from which the Russians were at length dislodged, with the loss of 80 killed and about 300 wounded. But being reinforced, a fresh attack enabled the besiegers to regain their previous lodgments. The Turks, however, still remained in the gorge of the bastion, and made another attack on the enemy on the 7th, but were repulsed by hand-grenades. Additional mines were also commenced, under cover of field pieces in the Russian trenches, which caused the bastion, as well as the lodgments in the ditch, to be at length finally abandoned. But the Turks only transferred their defence to the houses in rear of the bastion; the adjoining curtain, and the ditch immediately in its front, being still in their possession: and part of the garrison still perseveringly kept possession of some of the lodgments outside of the ditch.

Under cover of the fire of batteries in the trenches, the

besiegers endeavoured to undermine bastion No. 2, and to establish mines against the adjoining curtain; but a shower of hand-grenades interrupted these operations: the besieged being prepared for the assault, and by no means unwilling to come to close quarters with the enemy. But although the destruction of both faces of the eastern-most bastion effectually opened a passage into the town, and the approach of the Grand Vizír with a force destined to raise the siege, was a powerful reason for taking a decided course, the besiegers, either from apprehension about the result, or in the hope of avoiding the alternative by some *other* means, postponed the assault: on which, in fact, the safety of the Russian army in a great measure depended.

A parley was decided upon. It is not often that a council of war leads to a battle, or a parley to the continued defence of a fortress; nor was Varna an exception to the latter case. A communication being opened with the enemy, the Russian General took some pains to convey an impression of the fearful nature of the assault by which they were about to carry the place. The personal negotiations which followed in the Russian camp, terminated by Yussuf Pasha going thither on the night of the 10th of October with nearly 5,000 men, chiefly his followers.

Isad Múhammed, the Capudan Pasha, had strenuously opposed the proceedings of his chief; on whose desertion he immediately retired into the castle, avowing his determination to defend it as long as possible, and when all hope should be gone, to blow it up with all it might contain. But the Russian general, having gained his main object—the possession of the fortress—by the defection of the Pasha, gladly allowed this handful of brave men to quit Varna, with liberty to serve elsewhere.

An English gentleman, the late Mr. Elliot, who served as a medical officer during the siege, related to the author that, at the very moment when Varna was thus shamefully delivered up, there were 8,000 men under arms; who still displayed the same unshaken confidence in their power of defending the place, which had been so strikingly manifested during a siege of eighty-nine days; twenty-seven of which were subsequent to the first practicable breach. The besiegers employed sixty-five guns of heavy and light calibre, and discharged no less than 37,000 shot, 8,600 shells, and 2,500 rounds of case-shot. The labour of 700 sappers and other workmen, who had been employed for eighty-nine days in the trenches, equalled that of 55,000 men for one day.

The heavy loss of 6,000 men incurred by the Russians, both by sickness and by the sword, was no doubt very much owing to the system of their engineers, who carried on the siege without the aid of ricochet batteries. But great as was the destruction of life, it would have been still more serious if the besieged had made greater use of their artillery in the earliest stage of the siege; nor is it going too far to express the belief that, if a little modern science had aided the unskilled bravery of the Turks and Arnauts, the mining operations of the besiegers would have been rendered altogether impracticable. Notwithstanding its unfortunate termination, the siege of Varna claims a high place in the history of modern warfare.

The blot on what had previously been a most brilliant defence, has been attributed, by the partizans of Yussuf Pasha, to the supposed intention of the Sultan to confiscate his property. But a different impression prevailed in Varna at the time; and the subsequent admission of the Russian general who summoned the Pasha of Giurgevo to surrender in 1829, leaves but little doubt that either strong immediate temptation, or apprehension of danger, rather than anticipated injustice, led to such abandonment of duty by the second in command, as to induce him to seek protection for himself and the greater part of the garrison in the Russian camp. It is, however, right to observe that the result of the operations which had been carried on at this time south-ward of the fortress, were calculated to shake the constancy of the garrison, by depriving them of all hope of relief. At best this succour would have been very limited, for an intercepted despatch from the Grand Vizír spoke of being able to spare only 2,000 men for this purpose, provided he were successful.

CHAPTER V.

CONTINUATION OF THE OPERATIONS OF 1828, AND CLOSE OF THE CAMPAIGN.

The Grand Vizír advances upon Aidos and Varna—Imprudent separation of his forces—Omar Vrione repulses General Bistrom and retreats to Kur-tepe—Defeat of Prince Eugene at Kur-tepe—Oversights of the Turkish leaders—Omar Vrione extricates his army from a difficult situation—Continuation of the siege of Silistria—Sallies of the besieged—Progress and termination of the siege—Losses of the Turks and Russians—Retreat of the besieging force—Têtes-de-pont in Wallachia—Defences of Giurgevo strengthened—Defeat of the Pasha of Widdin at Bailisk.

We must now revert to the attempts made towards the close of the siege of Varna to relieve that place, and to the various operations carried on simultaneously elsewhere.

Múhammed Selim Pasha, who was then Grand Vizír, after persisting in continuing to neglect the Sultan's urgent commands to succour that fortress, at length so far forgot his jealousy of Hussein Pacha as to advance from Adrianople to Aidos. He was joined there by some 14,000 men, chiefly Arnauts, from Schumla; and by the middle of September he was in a condition to continue his march towards Varna with nearly 20,000 men.

In addition to a Russian force of 5,000 men, which was placed at Galata Bournu in communication with the fleet, another body of about the same strength, and also destined to cover the seige, had been placed under General Gollowin, in the direct line between Varna and the Grand Vizír. Instead of playing the bold but easy game of falling upon General Gollowin with his whole force, and then continuing his march upon Varna, the Grand Vizír committed the unpardonable mistake of dividing his forces, by taking post himself with 2,000 men, near Dervishkoï on the Kamtchik, and leaving Omar Vrione with the remainder at Hassanlar.

With a view to immediate operations against the principal body of Turks, General Gollowin sent an advance of 1,500 men, under Generals Salutzke and Hartung, on the 26th of September, to reconnoitre the Turkish position. In carrying out these orders, the latter officer incautiously penetrated into the wood, where he found himself most unexpectedly in front of the Turkish position. But instead of retiring, he halted, and opened a cannonade upon the enemy; which was immediately returned by an attack of the Turkish cavalry. Hoping to extricate himself from this dilemma, General Hartung commenced his retreat, under cover of the Jägers; who had, consequently, to support an everpowering attack, attended with very severe loss. General Hartung was wounded, and taken prisoner, and the Russians had ten officers, and 700 men killed.

In consequence of this disaster, a reinforcement was sent to the troops at Galata Bournu; General Bistrom, with about 6,000 men, was thus enabled to take up a position on the flank of General Gollowin, to support his attack; while 5,500 infantry, and 1,400 cavalry, were to advance under Prince Eugene of Wurtemburg, against the opposite or western side of Omar Vrióne's position. General Suchosanet, with 5,000 men, was to operate in rear of the Pasha, from the side of Gebedsche; thus making, in all, a force of nearly 12,000 men, which had been collected by order of the Emperor from the vicinity of Schumla, Varna, and Pravadi.

On the 27th of September, General Suchosanet attacked a part of the Turkish force at Hassanlar, from whence it retired on Kurtepe. On the following day, after making a reconnoisance, he reported to the Emperor that the post was occupied by only 6,000 Turks; and in accordance with the plan of attack which was formed in consequence of this intelligence, General Bistrom proceeded to assault the Turkish intrenchments; but he was repulsed after a spirited contest, with heavy loss. During this engagement, which lasted four hours, the General held his ground against three attacks made by Omar Vrione to overpower him.

The Pasha now placed himself under cover of the intrenchments of Kurtepe, which were rapidly advancing towards their completion; but before they could be rendered effective, the Emperor sent orders to Prince Eugene of Wurtemburg at Hassanlar, to attack the Turkish position. The Prince, who had ascertained from the Bulgarians that Omar Vrione had a considerable force, ventured to represent this fact to the Emperor, and requested reinforcements; but his Imperial Majesty, relying upon the previous estimation of 6,000 men, only repeated his orders.

At 2 P. M., therefore, on the 30th, the troops advanced from Hassanlar in two columns, whilst the forces of Generals Bistrom and Gollowin threatened the intrenchments on the opposite side. Prince Eugene's troops united in a flat saddle of about 2,000 paces in extent, and advanced steadily against the western side of the Pasha's position; notwithstanding the difficulties of the ground, which, being intersected by wooded ravines, was very disadvantageous for infantry, and almost impracticable for cavalry and artillery. The Turks in the mean time did not remain passive, but at once commenced an attack with their irregular cavalry, supported by infantry. This was successfully resisted for a time by the Ukraine regiment, and ten twelve-pounders having been brought up, a cannonade was opened with some effect upon a swarm of Turks. An infantry attack followed against the northern side of the Turkish encampment, during which a battalion of the Body Guards lost about 500 men in their repeated and determined efforts to dislodge the enemy. Two battalions of the Azof regiment advanced next, in the hope that some additional ground might be gained so as to enable them to place another battery of artillery in position; but a charge of the Dellis repulsed this attempt.

At this juncture an encouraging note reached Prince

Eugene from the Emperor, and, incited to fresh exertions by its contents, the Azof regiment renewed the attack in the most resolute style ; but the loss of General Durnowo, and the almost total destruction of the men, were its results. The advance had been supported by five battalions of the Ukraine corps and some Jägers, and succeeded in entering the Turkish intrenchments ; but they were immediately attacked in rear by the Arnauts, and were unable to hold the ground they had thus momentarily gained. The Dragoon Guards and a regiment of Cossacks, under General Nostiz, had attacked the left of the Turkish position at the same time, and with no less perseverance, but had equally failed, and the retreat of the whole force was ordered. This was effected with great difficulty to Hassanlar : indeed, it would scarcely have been practicable if the Turkish horse had not been too slow in perceiving how much might be gained by an immediate pursuit, instead of delaying until the enemy had had time to rally.

The Russians claimed the victory at Kurtesse, but it is difficult to imagine on what grounds, since Omar Vrione maintained his position ; which, although designated a strong intrenchment, could not have been made really formidable during the two days employed in its construction by the Turks, after their retreat thither from Hassanlar. The admitted loss of the attacking force was two general officers and 1,400 men. Prince Eugene himself was amongst the wounded. Immediately after his retreat, the Prince detached six battalions and six squadrons to reinforce General Bistrom, who had remained passive in the intrenchments which had been constructed to cut off the Turkish camp from Varna. This General had already received reinforcements, both from the army besieging the latter place, and also from that acting against Schumla; and with a view to give him more effectual support, Prince Eugene now took post at Osmanjik.

The paramount object of covering the siege of Varna had induced the Emperor to risk the attack on Omar Vrione, at Kurtesse, without calling General Bistrom's force to assist that of Prince Eugene, since he would thus have incurred the possibility of opening the road to Varna.

The Grand Vizír remained so wholly inert on the Kamtchik during these operations, that he did not even detach a few spahis to threaten Prince Eugene's rear. But it is to a total want of military experience rather than to that of good will, that we must attribute his lamentable failure in leaving to Omar Vrione's force the task of relieving Varna; which it would seem the Pasha might still have accomplished, even with the limited means at his command. It is easy to comment on such oversights, but it is scarcely reasonable to expect that an individual quite unaccustomed to military operations, should have avoided those mistakes from which skilful generals are not always free. If, however, Omar Vrione had made a feigned attack on General Bistrom's force on the 27th

September, whilst the real one was directed against the redoubts of General Gollowin which were open to the rear, and thus exposed to the Pasha's troops, an attack on this side would probably have been so far successful as to have enabled him to throw reinforcements into Varna, and possibly to have raised the siege at the same time.

But if the Grand Vizír's oversight may fairly be excused as one of the errors of an inexperienced commander, the same allowance cannot be made for Omar Vrione's neglect of Varna. He remained eleven days at Kurtesse, after defeating Prince Eugene, without making any attempt to succour that fortress, which was about to capitulate under his eyes.

As soon as Varna had passed into the possession of the Russians, Omar Vrione put his force in motion, and succeeded, by a skilful march, in passing the enemy and reaching the Kamtchik. After a warm affair with Prince Eugene, who followed him thither, he retreated to Dervish Jowan, and subsequently to Aidos, leaving some troops to occupy the block-houses which had been erected at the former position. Thus, owing to the want of some strategic skill, or rather to the failure of combined plans, which was at this time the chief defect of the Sultan's army, the invaders made themselves masters of one of the most important fortresses of Turkey.

We must now revert to the operations which had been going on against Silistria. This fortress had, in a great degree, recovered from the calamities inflicted by the siege of Kaminski in 1810. The town, being accessible to small vessels, has all the importance of a second rate port; and it contained in 1828 about 24,000 inhabitants. The short description already given of this place, shows than its defences more nearly resembled field works that those of a permanent fortress, in the ordinary acceptation of the term. An imperfect glacis with a covert way, and a ditch of fifteen and occasionally only ten feet deep, were serious disadvantages, in addition to those of commanding ground at a short distance.

The Turks endeavoured to supply the want of ravelins and other outworks by throwing out some redoubts. Three of these were placed along the south-eastern side of the works; a fourth imperfectly protected the Constantinople gate; and two others were placed outside of the Rustchuk, or western entrance into the town. At this point of the *enceinte* the Bulgarian hills terminate within about 500 paces, and again towards the east within 800 paces of the works; which, not being defiladed from this elevated ground, are subjected in consequence to an injurious command. But the living ramparts counterbalanced these disadvantages to such an extent, that, during the remainder of the campaign of 1828, Silistria triumphed over the best efforts of a powerful besieging army.

Finding it impracticable to effect the passage of the river at Turtokai, opposite to the now celebrated Oltenitza,

General Roth, in order to approach Silistria, was obliged to descend along the Danube, and cross at Hirsova; from whence he moved along the right bank to Kousgoun, and, consentaneously with the movements already described against Schumla and Varna, he continued his march towards Silistria. He arrived before this fortress on the 21st of July, and after an obstinate contest of several hours, he succeeded in carrying the neighbouring heights; he then immediately commenced constructing a chain of redoubts, as a protection against the attacks of the garrison.

The battering train was still on its way from Brailow; but there being a flotilla already on the spot of sixteen gun-boats, each mounting three pieces of heavy ordnance, and twenty others also before the place, with one gun mounted on each boat, there was a sufficiency of artillery to commence the siege.

The defences of Silistria were, without doubt, very inferior to those of Brailow or Varna; but the disadvantages of position were fully compensated by the *personnel*. The armed inhabitants, who numbered at least 6,000 men, had been increased by a part of the garrison of Tuldscha, Matschin, and Hirsova; which gave a respectable force in point of number, and still more formidable from the spirit of determination that animated it. Offensive operations were therefore commenced by the garrison, with the assistance of twelve gun-boats. Sallies were successively made against the besiegers on the 23rd, 24th, and 25th of

July; but without any decided result arising from these spirited attacks. The besiegers continued to work at the redoubts which had been commenced by General Roth, and on the 18th of August completed a chain, that at the eastern side was about 4,000, and at the western about 3,500 paces from the fortress.

But the Turks not only continued to occupy a part of the western heights, but also kept up desultory attacks upon the besiegers till the 28th of the month, when a sortie in force took place. Three thousand men, with five guns, left the place at midnight, and three times succeeded in mastering a portion of the western heights. They were finally retaken, however, by the besiegers, and the Turks retired into the fortress at noon on the 29th, after causing, as well as experiencing, severe loss, during a contest of twelve hours. In the other part of this attack, which was carried on simultaneously against a portion of the hills more to the eastward, the Turks found themselves exposed to the fire of the enemy's artillery when beyond the range of their own guns; they retreated accordingly, followed by the Hulans and part of the Chakow regiment. These two combats cost the Turks 600 men; the Russians admitted a loss of 72 killed, and 312 wounded, including the commanders of two cavalry regiments. The Turkish estimate of the casualties of the enemy was much greater: they also claimed other advantages over the invaders; and the fact that the Turks remained so long outside the walls without any attempt being made to cut off their retreat, gives more than probability to their assertion.

On the 11th of September a combined attack of the garrison, assisted by 5,000 of the inhabitants, was made on the besiegers. It was ultimately repulsed, but not until it had caused them the loss of eight officers and 158 men. Hitherto the Russian works had advanced but slowly, being still some 1,500 paces from the fortress; with the exception of an imperfect parallel, which was occupied by the *tirailleurs* more in advance.

On the 15th of September, the second army corps arrived from Russia under General Tscherbatoff. The battering train was brought up at the same time from the Lower Danube. In consequence of these reinforcements, two divisions of the 6th corps could now be dispensed with from Silistria, and commenced their march to join the army before Schumla. Achmet Pasha, who commanded in Silistria, was not slow in trying the spirit of the newly arrived troops by a fresh sortie, the only result of which was a serious loss of life on both sides.

In consequence of illness, General Tscherbatoff was unable to continue his duties, and the charge of the siege operations devolved upon General Langeron. A period of comparative inactivity followed; for sickness, the usual attendant of fatigue and scarcity of provisions, had almost paralysed the efforts of the besiegers; disease, indeed, became so formidable, that in the early part of October, not less than 500 men perished in the trenches.

The fall of Varna, and the failures against Schumla, had at length placed a larger force at the command of the Russian General, by the concentration of the invading army; which event took place at Aidecha on the 19th and 20th of October though with a loss of 800 men in accomplishing this movement. But although the aggregate force now assembled before Silistria amounted to at least 30,000 men, it was scarcely possible to carry on the siege with any prospect of success at this advanced period of the year, when the rains had commenced, and were already succeeded by snow. As a last resource, therefore, the town was fiercely bombarded for forty-eight hours without intermission, by the flotilla as well as the land batteries. But as this did not intimidate the garrison, it was decided to abandon the intention which had been formed, of a winter blockade; and the retreat was soon afterwards commenced.

The people of Silistria admitted the loss of nearly 3,000 men, during three months of open trenches; that of the enemy, according to their statement, being upwards of 7,000. On breaking up the siege, part of the force was, with some difficulty, transported across the river by the gun-boats; but the bulk of the army had to march, carrying the siege train with them, which now proved a very serious encumbrance. The roads were so soft that two hundred men were sometimes required to drag a single gun; and it is not therefore surprising that a retreat under such circumstances, and before an active enemy, should have become most disastrous. Besides the loss in killed, several guns and many prisoners were taken, before the Russian army recrossed the Danube at Hirsova and took up winter quarters in Wallachia.

As the contending forces had not been inactive in this part of Turkey, during the operations which have been described as taking place elsewhere, it will be necessary, in order to complete the European campaign of 1828, to notice what had taken place on the northern side of the Danube.

When General Roth marched with the principal part of two divisions to reinforce the invading army in Bulgaria, General Geismar remained in Wallachia, with sixteen squadrons of cavalry, two regiments of Cossacks, and twelve battalions of infantry, or about 10,000 men, with a proportion of artillery, to keep in check the Turkish forces on the Upper Danube. The *têtes de pont* of Khalafat, opposite to Widden, and that of Giurgevo, opposite to Rustchuk, were more particularly the objects of his attention; since the Turks, as long as they remained in possession of these *points d'appui*, could at any time make a harassing incursion into Lower Wallachia.

The Pasha of Widden, as Seraskier, had about 10,000 regular and irregular troops in that fortress; while Hamed

Pasha, better known as Kuchuk Hamed, mustered about 8,000 in Rustchuk. He did not, however, remain passively in command of this fortress, but crossed to the left bank of the river, with about 4,000 men, during the early stage of hostilities, and employed all his energies in strengthening the *tête de pont* of Giurgevo. Kuchuk Hamed knew little of the art of fortification, and still less of mathematics, but he had an intuitive perception of the advantages of that position; and he explained to the author, as he rolled from side to side of his divan with restless vivacity, how he had contrived to strengthen his advanced position, by managing a loop-holed flanking defence, as well as a direct fire from the earthen parapets: which he had not only constructed, but successfully defended, up to the signature of the treaty of peace.

Attacks were occasionally made upon the enemy from this position, as well as from Widdin; some of these were combined movements, whilst others were of a desultory character, and chiefly instigated by Kuchuk Hamed: who, according to the Russian account, appeared so often that he allowed them no rest. On the 3rd of June, and again on the 8th of July, the two Pashas crossed the Danube, and made a joint attack upon General Geismar. On the former day continued skirmishing took place without any decisive result, but on the latter the affair was of a much warmer character. Five thousand Turkish cavalry and four thousand infantry had crossed the Danube to attack the Russians, but after an obstinate conflict they were repulsed by General Geismar, and obliged to re-cross the river by way of Khalafat. From the 8th of July up to the approach of autumn, the Russian force held its position in Wallachia, and succeeded in keeping the Turkish troops both at Widdin and Rustchuk in check, by means of a judicious position in the neighborhood of Crajova, almost equidistant from both fortresses. Here it was that General Geismar deservedly obtained so much credit by defeating a superior force of the Turks, under very peculiar circumstances.

The Pasha of Widdin, taking 2,000 Albanians and 1,000 of the Nizam from his garrison, crossed over to the left bank of the Danube, where a force of 10,000 cavalry and infantry was already collected from Giurgevo and the Bulgarian side, thus giving him an effective force of 13,000 men and 20 guns for his meditated attack on the Russians in Wallachia. By means of the Greeks in Widdin, General Geismar was kept perfectly aware not only of all that was passing, but also of all that was intended by the enemy. On the 27th of September he, therefore, concentrated 6,000 men at Czarlow, or rather at Bailisk, according to the Turks. The Pasha arrived the same afternoon, and commenced his attack about four P.M., chiefly with his cavalry, which was received by the Russian infantry in squares. The contest was obstinate, and continued till nightfall, with much loss to the Russians, particularly to the regiment Tomsk.

Night ended a conflict which had been so disadvantageous to the Russians, that the probable result of its expected renewal at day-break was regarded with much apprehension by General Geismar, until the idea occurred to him that he might extricate himself from his critical position by an immediate and daring night attack; for which the Turks are seldom prepared. In the expectation of deceiving the enemy, the Russian commander caused his artillery to double its fire at sunset, as though it were covering his retreat from the field of battle. This ruse had the desired effect; for the Turks, under the belief that the Russians had taken flight, commenced preparing coffee and supper, without any videttes or other precautions. The advance of Geismar's force to the attack in three columns immediately after dark, was, therefore, quite unlooked for; and the surprise was increased by some hay taking fire in the midst of the camp, which speedily extended to the Pasha's tent. Some of the Nizam endeavoured to form, and stood for a time to oppose the enemy; but the general confusion speedily ended in a flight in the direction of Widdin, leaving 300 killed and 7 guns, in addition to 410 Albanian prisoners, in the hand of the enemy. The other fifteen pieces of artillery were, however, carried back to Widdin. General Geismar pursued the Pasha as far as the *tête-de-pont* of Khalafat, which, being undefended by him or his followers, surrendered next day as the fruits of the victory.

In reviewing the various events of the preceding campaign, we find, as the result of its earlier period, a march of 1,100 miles (for a portion of the Russian army), with the capture of Brailow after a resolute defence, in addition to some smaller places in the Dobrudscha. To its latter period belongs the fall of Varna, after a siege by land and sea of eighty-nine days. The other operations were almost entirely in favour of the Turks: such as the combats and attacks near Schumla, the battle of Kurtesse, and the successful defences of Schumla and Silistria; followed, in the latter case, by the retreat of the Russian army across the Danube from before its trenches.

The fall of Varna gave the invaders military possession of the eastern side of Bulgaria; and, as active operations were almost entirely out of the question at that period of the year, the following arrangements were made for winter cantonments. General Roth remained at Varna with the chief part of the 6th and 7th corps; which also occupied Pravadi, Gebedsche, Kosludsche, Devna, and Bazarjik. The Guards moved into Bessarabia. The 2nd and 3rd corps wintered in Moldavia and Wallachia, with head quarters under Count Wittgenstein at Jassy; so that the Russian cantonments extended about 260 miles, from Crajova on the Schyll to the shores of the Euxine at Varna.

This line was, however, cut by that portion of the Danube which was still held by the Turks; and with Silistria, Rustchuk, and Giurgevo inserted like the point of a wedge into Wallachia, added to the firm possession of Widdin at the western extremity, the Turks had a favourable opportunity of continuing their proposed winter campaign.

Between sickness and the sword, these operations in European Turkey are stated to have caused Russia the serious loss of more than 40,000 men; and, according to the accounts received at Bucharest, at least 30,000 horses died. The Russian statements, as might be expected, make it far less; but when the prolonged exposure during the sieges of Brailow, Schumla, Varna, and Silistria, are taken into account, in addition to the ravages of sickness and the defects of the medical and commissariat departments, these circumstances go far to account for so great a loss to an army that was kept more or less complete by reinforcements from time to time. At Bucharest alone the deaths were 19,000: that is, 7,000 of the army, and 12,000 of the inhabitants.

CHAPTER VI.

THE CAMPAIGN OF 1828 IN ASIATIC TURKEY.

Limits of the seat of war—Persian war in 1826—Winter campaign in Northern Persia—Acquisitions of Russia—Preparations for, and commencement of the campaign of 1828—Fall of Anapa—Description and fall of Kars—Storming of Akhalkalaki—Fall of Hertwiz—Mistakes of the Seraskier—Description of Akhaltsikh—Defeat of the Seraskier—Obstinate defence of Akhaltsikh—General Paskevitch burns the town—Severe loss of the Turks and Russians—Capitulation of Atskur and Ardagan—Result of the campaign of 1828 in Asia—Disadvantages of the Turks at its commencement.

THE campaign of 1828 in Asiatic Turkey, which immediately followed the conclusion of peace with Persia, was confined to the territory lying between the Euxine and Caspian Seas.

The tract in question—to which belongs the expedition of the Golden Fleece, together with so many other ancient myths and traditions—extends from the 37° to the 45° of North latitude. The Caucasian chain runs from side to side of this tract at the northern boundary, and from Jebel Judi and the river Tigris to the Araxes at its southern extremity. The eastern limits touch those of Persia, and its western, the mountainous country bordering upon the Black Sea; whilst Ararat and various secondary chains, inhabited by different races, intersect this space, and give rise to a variety of climate and productions.

So long as the Caucasus continued to be a barrier against Russia, Persia and Asiatic Turkey could be defended with comparative ease; but this ceased to be the case in 1801; and, as has been shown already, the gradual progress of that power along the shores of the Caspian, forced Persia to try the fate of arms by invading the Russian provinces in 1826. But the campaign was of short duration, for General Paskevitch, by concentrating a mass of artillery in the centre of his army, gained a decided victory over his adversaries near Elizabethpol, and the Persians retreated into their own territory.

General Paskevitch followed up this success in the spring of 1827 by taking Sardar-abâd and Erivan; and having subsequently penetrated into Azerbaijan, the fall of Taurus or Tabriz, its capital, brought about the preliminaries of peace. But, although signed on the part of the Shah by the Prince Royal of Persia, this monarch, relying on the effective assistance of Turkey as the certain result of the Hatti Scheriff of the 8th of December, 1827, refused to ratify the treaty; in the full expectation that he would have the whole of the succeeding winter left to make preparations. The Emperor Nicholas, however, met this fresh difficulty in a way that was totally unlooked for by the Persians. For, in order to make his Asiatic army quite disposable in the early part of the coming spring, he ordered the campaign to be renewed by entering the northern part of the Shah's dominions, notwithstanding the severity of the season.

Count Paskevitch advanced accordingly, in three columns, through deep snow, as far as the range of the Kaflan-ku. This movement produced the desired effect, almost without firing a shot; for the Shah, seeing no hope of gaining more time, immediately sent Abbas Mirza with full powers to meet the Russian General, and settle the terms of peace. By the treaty signed at Turkman-chai, on the 10th of February, 1829, the Khanats of Erivan and Nak-hitchevan, as well as the fortress of Abbas-abad, were ceded to Russia; in addition to the payment of twenty millions of roubles as an indemnity for the expenses of the war. It was also agreed by the contracting parties, that Russia alone was to maintain vessels of war on the Caspian Sea; which, by this stipulation, became a Russian lake.

The Persian war was thus concluded most opportunely for Russia; since, independently of the preceding advantages, the whole of the Emperor's Asiatic forces could be employed in that part of Turkey, and thus oblige the Sultan to send part of his troops thither, instead of drawing the whole towards his European frontiers.

On the 25th of February, 1828, the Russian troops were put in motion to evacuate Persia; and a few days later, a despatch informed the successful General, that the approaching passage of the Pruth would call for fresh exertions from the army of the Caucasus.

The troops had been put into winter quarters, and the report was spread that no orders had been issued for the commencement of hostilities. As an additional blind, General Paskevitch caused his troops to abstain from everything like a movement; whilst he continued deeply occupied within the Russian limits, in organizing his plans, and preparing those combinations by which he hoped to extend his Emperor's territories at the next treaty of peace. So successful was this ruse, that the Pasha of Kars permitted the people to carry their grain for sale into Georgia as heretofore; and thus he materially facilitated the preparation of supplies for the invading army.

The effective force distined to march into Asiatic Turkey amounted to 23,393 infantry, 6,192 cavalry, and 130 pieces of artillery: 13,860 infantry, 2,391 cavalry, and 42 guns, continued as a reserve in the Russian provinces,* in addition to the fleet and troops acting under Admiral Greig.

The Russian officers believed that, including the Nizam, the Seraskier of Asia would be able to bring into the field some 200,000 men. But if the defensive preparations of the Turks were tardy on the European side, it is certain that they were still more so on the Asiatic; where *everything* had still to be done, even to rouse the people to the consciousness of an approaching invasion.

The first operations took place on the coast. Eight line-

* Tables, pp. 242, 243, La Russie dans l'Asie Mineure, ou Campagnes du Maréchal Paskevitch, par Felix Fonton: Paris, 1840.

of-battle-ships, five frigates, and eleven smaller vessels, proceeded from Sebastopol early in May, under Admiral Greig, who landed about 6,000 men of the 7th corps near Anapa between the 14th and 18th of that month. On the latter day, Colonel Perowski appeared before the place with a reinforcement drawn from the army of the Caucasus, and the siege was commenced under the most promising circumstances ; for, not only had the garrison been driven inside the walls with loss, but two convoys, bringing stores and reinforcements of officers and men, were captured as they approached the harbour. Powerful batteries were immediately opened against the place at less than one hundred yards, assisted by the constant bombardment of the fleet.

On the 8th of June the sorties of the garrison, which had been frequently repeated, were put an end to by a line of contravallation from the sea to the sea ; and on the 23rd of June, the descent of the ditch being effected, and three breaches made practicable, Anapa, with 85 guns and 3,000 men, was taken possession of by the united land and sea forces of the Russians ; which were thus opportunely enabled to take part in the siege of Varna. The fall of Anapa destroyed also the point of union of the Lazian and other tribes hostile to Russia. Now deprived, as it were, of their head, several of these people laid down their arms and submitted to the domination of their enemies.

Either from receiving intelligence of the commencement

of this operation, or some other circumstance, the suspicions of the Seraskier appear to have been at length awakened, and the Governor of Kars was instructed to send a functionary to ascertain the state of affairs at Tiflis, where he was told by General Paskevitch himself that hostilities would be commenced forthwith. In fact, the right wing, comprising six battalions, a regiment of Cossacks, and sixteen light guns, was already in motion towards the Black Sea, under General Hesse; and the left, under General Tchevtchevadze, was proceeding to operate in Armenia, whilst the central and principal line of operations was to proceed against Kars.

By the 25th of May, when the Turkish envoy had scarcely returned with the hostile message, the main force was assembled at Kara Kilisi, near Gumri; and on the 14th of June, 12,000 infantry and four brigades of cavalry crossed the Arpa-Chaï, near the latter place. This movement was supported by 70 pieces of artillery, heavy and light; for which branch of service, more especially with reference to the coming sieges, reserves both of guns and ammunition had been prepared at four principal dépôts, namely, at Tiflis, Redut-Kalá, Baku, and Derbent.*

As the Turkish preparations had as yet scarcely commenced, General Paskevitch advanced almost without opposition to the southern side of Kars; by which rapid and judicious movement, he succeeded in interposing his army

* Ibid, pp. 245, 263-266.

between that fortress and the force which the Seraskier was about to assemble for its support behind the Saganlugh range of mountains.

The city of Kars occupies the semicircular bend which is made by the Kars-chai as it quits a narrow gorge of the Tchildír range. The northern and principal portion of the fortress is protected by a ledge of bold and naturally scarped rocks, rising abruptly from the right bank of the river. The other three sides have a rough stone wall of four or five feet thick and from twelve to twenty-five feet in height, which is flanked by square towers. A bastioned *enceinte* has been thrown up outside of this wall as an additional defence.

At the north-west angle of the town is the citadel of Narin Kalá, which is composed of three separate castellated buildings, whose guns sweep the river both above and below the town; of which this work is the principal defence. The suburbs of Orta Kapu extend eastward from the Kars-chai, along the southern side of the town, and are defended by a simple wall. To these an impracticable marsh succeeds; and again between this and the hills of Karadagh, is the remaining portion of suburbs called Bairam Pasha. Although exposed to the serious disadvantage of houses extending almost to the walls of the fortress, Kars had successfully resisted 90,000 men under Nadır Sháh in 1735, and the Russian forces again in 1807.*

* La Russie dans l'Asie Mineure, &c. &c., par Felix Fonton, p. 279: Paris, 1840.

The Turks had occupied a part of the ground which commands the tower from the left bank of the Kars-chai with an intrenched camp, but having neglected one portion of the hills, General Paskevitch immediately occupied this advantageous position. The garrison instantly made a determined effort to retrieve the error, but failed in the attack, with the loss of eighty men killed; the besiegers were thus enabled to construct four batteries, which not only commanded the intrenched camp and the suburbs of Orta Kapu with much advantage, but also swept the western and southern faces of the fortress itself.

The intrenched camp and the adjoining cemetery were long and bravely contested; particularly the latter, which was defended almost stone by stone, till it was at length carried by the Russians. It was again recovered by a desperate charge of the Turks, but was finally lost.

After another protracted struggle, in which the Turks lost nine of their standards, the besiegers obtained possession of the tower of Temir-Pasha, and the rest of the ground on the left bank of the Kars-chai. Three batteries were now opened from thence, which, owing to their commanding and enfilading position, had a most powerful effect on the works of the tower, and mainly assisted the principal attack, which was directed against the suburbs of Orta-Kapu. Here a breach was speedily effected in the thin walls, and the suburbs were stormed and carried after a severe loss on both sides. The Turkish guns which had been taken, and some fresh batteries which had been erected, now opened a fire upon the walls of the fortress itself; and another bloody assault having put the besiegers in possession of the walls on the 23rd of June, the Pasha consented to surrender the citadel; which alone remained in his possession. Thus, by means of a succession of daring assaults, one of the most important places of Asiatic Turkey fell into the hands of the Russians, together with 129 pieces of cannon, 22 mortars, 33 standards, and a good supply of ammunition and provisions. Thirteen Russian officers and 400 men were put *hors de combat* during the assault of the 23rd; the Turks lost 2,000 men, or nearly one-fifth of the garrison; which, including Dellis and armed inhabitants, was called 11,000 men.*

The surrender of the fortress was barely in time to anticipate its relief. For, although Kiossa Múhammed Pasha, the Seraskier, was without an adequate force to encounter the Russians in the field, he had, with the hope of being able to fulfil his promise of relieving Kars, moved rapidly across the Saganlugh with four pieces of artillery and a part of his force; and his advance was actually in sight when the gates of the citadel were being opened to the enemy.

The appearance of plague amongst the Russian troops at this period, and the necessity of improving the defences of Kars, gave the Seraskier time to collect some 35,000

* Ibid, pp. 290–291.

men, chiefly militia; with which force he took up a position in advance of Ardagan, his left flank being protected by the warlike inhabitants of Akhaltsikh. General Paskevitch, in assuming the offensive, after making the necessary preparations, had the choice of advancing in the direction of Erzerúm, or making a flank movement, either against Akhaltsikh or Akhalkalaki. As both the first and second projects would have increased the distance from his resources, and the former, moreover, would have left an enemy in his rear, the Russian general determined to adopt the third: *i. e.*, that of endeavouring to reduce the fortress of Akhalkalaki.

With this view, a strong demonstration was made on the road to Erzerúm, as far as Tekme, which caused the Seraskier to retreat to the Saganlugh, under the impression that the whole of the Russian army was moving against him; General Paskevitch then hastily retraced his steps to Kars. Six days' march in a northerly direction from thence, with the battering train, through the difficult mountains of Tchildír, enabled him to summon the fortress of Akhalkalaki, but its defenders proudly answered, "that they were not like the people of Eriván or Kars, but warriors of Akhaltsikh, who, having sent their wives and children out of the place, were determined to die on its ramparts."

The town of Akhalkalaki occupies a peninsula at the junction of the Taparawan-chaï, and the Ghendara-su.

The tower has a quadrilateral figure of 300 yards long, by 80 or 100 yards wide, and is difficult of access. Its defences consist of loop-holed walls flanked by towers, and a castellated keep or citadel. It had fourteen guns mounted, and the garrison consisted of 1,000 men. The latter, however, though animated with the best spirit, were but little prepared for the effects of a powerful artillery on such imperfect defences as theirs. Eight heavy guns and eight mortars being opened against the place, its feeble walls were speedily destroyed, and left little or no shelter for its defenders.

As a second summons was rejected with the same unbending spirit, four additional heavy guns and some field-pieces were employed in breaching the body of the place. This was speedily effected, and a column of attack being prepared under Colonel Borodino, another summons was sent; still the Turkish chief and his followers repeated their determination to die on the spot.

By this time the place had become altogether untenable, and the instinct of self-preservation caused some of the garrison to endeavour to let themselves down the walls by means of ropes, in order to escape. But the constancy of the rest of the brave defenders remained unshaken: six hundred of their number perished in the succeeding assault, and three hundred prisoners fell into the hands of the victors, in addition to the mass of ruins of Akhalkalaki.*

* La Russie dans l'Asie Mineure, &c., par Felix Fonton, p. 308. Paris, 1840.

On the fall of this place, Baron Sacken was despatched, with a battering train and upwards of 3,000 cavalry and infantry, against the fortified post of Hertwiz; which, together with thirteen guns and 200 men, surrendered on his approach. The communications with Tsalki and Gumri were thus secured, and reinforcements having arrived from Georgia, General Paskevitch determined to proceed against Akhaltsikh. By undertaking this siege, he would either be enabled to reduce this fortress, or oblige the Seraskier to fight a battle for its relief; and in case of a reverse, there would be the resource of opening a passage to the coast, where the recent fall of Poti had secured another *point d'appui*. General Hesse had moved from Imeritia against the latter place, immediately after the fall of Anassa, and a bombardment of six days caused its surrender on the 15th of July.

The movements against Akhaltsikh are replete with interest, in consequence of the exertions made by the invading army, on the one hand, to master that fortress, and by the Seraskier, on the other, to relieve it; the success of each frequently turning on the energetic employment of only a few hours.

After an exceedingly difficult march of ten days, during which two hundred men were frequently employed to drag a single field-piece, the Russian army succeeded in occupying the hill of Tauchan Pasha, which commands the western front of Akhaltsikh. This was effected just before the Seraskier appeared, at the head of a considerable force, with the intention of relieving the place; and here General Paskevitch intrenched himself in order of battle: with reference to the double object of besieging the fortress, and of either defeating the Seraskier, or keeping him in check during the progress of the siege.

The Turks who, as was the case at Kars, arrived just too late, immediately made a formidable and simultaneous attack on both flanks of the Russians, hoping to capture the battering artillery. In this, however, they failed. After repeated efforts on their part, in which they frequently gained ground for the moment, General Paskevitch remained master of his intrenched position; from which he could at pleasure assume the offensive with advantage, against the Seraskier. After his repulse, the Turkish commander had occupied, with one part of his force, an intrenched camp a little way north of the town; the remainder of his troops being, most injudiciously, posted in three different positions: viz., one to the northward, and the other two southward of the Poskow-chaï; thus, instead of concentrating his force, a weakened line of defence was prolonged to the westward of the town.

The situation of Akhaltsikh is peculiar. It stands within a semicircle formed by the slopes of the Persaat stream to the north, and the rugged banks of the Poskow-chaï on the south, and between the heights of Kaïa-Dagh on the west, and that of Tauchan Pasha on the east. Three ravines, descending from the north, divide this important town into three distinct quarters,—the Jewish, the Mussulman and the Christian. It contains about 5,000 houses, which, being of two stories, and solidly built, are susceptible of a vigorous defence when occupied by Turks; who excel almost all other nations in the internal defence of a town. Akhaltsikh possesses an *enceinte*, consisting of a tower and four bastions, built with sun-dried bricks. A high and strong fir palisade, with a ditch on each side, connects these bastions, on which twenty-two guns were mounted. Some wooden towers, capable of containing a dozen men each, gave additional protection to that part of the town; which, in fact, was only intrenched, and not regularly fortified.

At the southern side of the town is the fortress, an irregular polygon, which abuts to the south upon the elevated and precipitous banks of the Poskow-chaï. The remainder of the defences consist in a double line of walls flanked by irregular stone towers; on these and the castle at the western angle forty guns were mounted.

As the works were commanded on almost every side, the chief strength of the place lay in the bravery of some 10,000 armed inhabitants, and the aid that might be received from the Seraskier's force; which, as has been seen, was separated into four bodies.

General Paskevitch was not slow to take advantage of this fatal mistake; for this purpose he concentrated the whole of his force, and proceeded to make an attack on that part of the Turkish position which covered the northern side of the town. To effect this, a force of 7,000 men and 25 guns, led by Muta-Bei, one of the chiefs of Akhalkalaki, who had been gained by the Russians, made a considerable detour, and under cover of the artillery, attacked the Seraskier's position. The Turks, though partly surprised, displayed great courage; a desperate hand-to-hand struggle was maintained with such obstinacy, that it was only owing to the arrival of the Carabineers of Eriván and the 41st Chasseurs that some little ground was at length gained by the assailants. The Turks, in their turn, took advantage of the explosion of a Russian caisson to charge; but, owing to the steadiness of the troops and the support of the artillery, the Russians held their ground, till the heat of the day gave a temporary respite to the combatants.

The contest was renewed in the afternoon by a feint, which caused the Turks to strengthen the left of their position; the real attack was then made against the right of the camp. Under cover of fourteen horse artillery guns and six field pieces, placed in battery only 160 yards from the palisades, two columns advanced with great intrepidity; but a deadly fire of canister shot, and a sortie of the Turks, yatagan in hand, threw the assailants into disorder: the repulse would have been complete if a fresh attack made by the Russians had not been crowned with success. It was so, however; the intrenchment with its four guns was at length carried, with the severe loss to the Turks of 500 men, or quite one-third of the number exposed. The high ground, which was the key of the Turkish position, having been thus mastered, the other three camps were carried in succession. The Seraskier, who was wounded, made his way into the town, after suffering the loss of ten guns and 1,700 men in killed, wounded, and prisoners. The victors admitted that they had lost 31 officers, and 450 men killed and wounded.*

The remains of the Turkish army took the route of Ardagan, hoping to be able to join the Pasha of Mush; but the intervention of the Russian garrison of Kars, prevented the accomplishment of this purpose.

The capture of the heights northward of Akhaltsikh enabled the besiegers to open a fire on the town from a battery of four mortars, two howitzers, and forty Russian and Turkish guns, at the distance of four hundred yards.

The town was now summoned to surrender, but the people firmly replied "that they were Akhaltsikheans who never had submitted to any enemy, and that they would now, if it were God's will, be buried under the ruins with arms in their hands." Such was the reply of the Muslims; but a different feeling prevailed amongst the other inhabitants. The formidable fire of the artillery shook the fidelity of the Christians, who manifested in

* Ibid, p. 337–340.

consequence a desire to surrender; but as the resolution of the Turks continued unshaken, General Paskevitch was obliged to construct several additional batteries, which soon opened with telling effect on both sides of the Poskow-chaï. On pushing their works more in advance, the besiegers sent another summons into the town, on the 12th of August, with the expectation that a revolt of the Jews and Christians would be the consequence, and that the fortress would be surrendered. But the Seraskier continued firm; and the malcontents having been disarmed, as a matter of precaution, the expectation of a capitulation was at an end. It became necessary, therefore, to press the siege with more vigour, if possible, than before.

On the 13th and 14th, a battery opened a breach in the palisades, which was sufficiently enlarged during the early part of the following day to admit of an attempt being made to carry the town. The besiegers appear to have been made aware that the garrison had been most on the alert every night, in expectation of an attack, and that during the day they were more off their guard. On the 15th of August, at 4 P. M., therefore, under cover of the smoke of a general cannonade from the various besieging batteries, a regiment of Chasseurs and two regiments of cavalry, supported by thirteen pieces of artillery, made a false attack on the left of the town. A second attack was made simultaneously, a little to the right of the former, by two battalions of infantry and two regiments of Cossacks, supported by ten pieces of artillery; whilst a third, and the real attack, was made against the bastion No. 3, by a mass of troops under cover of twenty-seven guns.

The surprise was complete in the first instance; for so little was an assault expected, that the greater number of the garrison were quietly reposing themselves in their houses after the fatigue of the preceding night; and even those who had remained on duty, paid little attention at first to a hostile movement in daytime. Under these circumstances, Colonel Borodino passed through the breach without opposition; and taking possession of the bastion, after bayoneting the gunners and the guard, he proceeded to occupy a position inside the works. This being done, he employed a body of pioneers to improve his communication with the rear, by widening the breach and perfecting the passage of the ditch with gabions and fascines.

In general, the difficulties of a besieging army are nearly at an end when they are firmly established in one of the bastions of a fortress, with a secure communication to the rear; but those of the Russians were only about to begin, since they were now to encounter that fiercely brave but desultory resistance which the Turks almost always display at that particular period of a siege, when more scientific nations usually surrender a fortress as no longer tenable.

The quarter of an hour which enables the besiegers to

master the palisades and bastion, was also sufficient to rouse the sleeping garrison. Five hundred men hastily snatched their arms, and rushed from the Catholic church towards the enemy; but, in so doing, they found that, in addition to the opposition in their front, they were simultaneously attacked by the enemy both in flank and rear. Yet, notwithstanding their most critical situation between three fires, the Turks, supported by the muskets of some of their countrymen from the adjoining houses, maintained the struggle; which became the more fierce and determined as other Turks hastened to the spot to assist their comrades. Advancing step by step, the breach was at length gained by the garrison. The impetuous rush and hurrah of the Turks, yatagan in hand, had almost expelled the enemy from the works, when the timely fire of a mountain gun and howitzer, which had been carried by hand across the ditch, changed the face of affairs.

The breach was recovered, and another battery opened from thence, which drove the Turks out of the bastion. This advantage was followed up by a fresh advance of the besiegers; who, after meeting a most determined resistance, which covered the ground with dead, at length mastered and occupied the Catholic church and the adjoining cemetery. The position they had thus obtained was of great consequence, because it not only secured their right flank, but enabled them to place a howitzer and some cohorns on the roof of the church; from whence a fire was opened, in order to drive the besieged from the tops of the neighbouring houses. But still the Turks continued their attack against the left flank of the besiegers; who were, however, enabled to hold their position—though with great difficulty, and a severe loss both in officers and men, especially of sappers—by opening a passage across the ditch, and bringing more guns and men from the trenches.

About 7 P. M., it was perceived that some of the houses had been set on fire by the howitzers, and general Paskevitch determined to take advantage of this circumstance, by resorting to very unusual means of ending a protracted contest: which for the honour of European warfare will, it is hoped, long continue to be a solitary example of cruelty. A battalion of the regiment of Chirvan and another of the grenadiers of Kherson, provided with hand-grenades, were ordered to advance in the direction of the fortress, whilst the 42nd regiment, under Colonel Reout, similarly provided, entered the suburbs, throwing, in both instances, hand-grenades through the windows and down the chimneys of the houses. The cavalry, at the same time, brought straw and other combustible materials from the villages, to increase the conflagration. Owing to the solidity of the buildings, however, this cruel proceeding was only at first attended with partial success. In some instances, the enraged Turks, poniard in hand, rushed upon the assailants; whilst in others, they continued to defend their burning dwellings: in this manner 400 perished in the flames of one of the mosques. Later in the night, the town presented the fearful spectacle of fugitives passing through burning streets amidst whistling balls, bursting shells, and congreve rockets, to seek an asylum from the spreading flames.

As the fire approached the Russian posts, some fanatics endeavoured to hasten the conflagration, in the expectation that by its extension to a magazine, which had been left in this quarter of the town, their enemies, and, possibly, some of themselves, might be buried in the ruins. This desperate project was, however, thwarted by the opportune arrival of some Russian *tirailleurs;* and the gradual spread of the flames elsewhere, completed the destruction of the remainder of the town by morning. The state of utter misery and suffering thus produced amongst the survivors then put an end to the siege.

The fortress, it is true, was still defensible; but the works had suffered materially: many of the guns were dismounted, the arch of the magazine had been injured by shells, and the means of resistance, especially the *personnel*, were seriously diminished. Ninety-nine of the hundred janissaries, and 370 of the 400 artillerymen who had been engaged, perished in the town, in addition to 1,300 Lazians: including the inhabitants, 4,000 men had fallen, during a fearful and almost unprecedented struggle of thirteen hours duration.

It was therefore time to entertain the fresh overtures made by the besiegers to the Pasha ; and the result was a capitulation, by which the garrison was permitted to quit the fortress with arms and baggage. But the possession of Akhaltsikh, and its sixty-seven pieces of ordnance, had not been gained without heavy loss. According to the official statement, the besiegers had 62 officers, and 557 men, put *hors de combat;* and this was, no doubt, short of the reality.*

The capitulation of this stronghold was followed by the loss of Atskhur and Ardagan. The former place, which is seated in the defiles of Bordjom, and had 24 guns with a garrison of 500 men, capitulated to a force sent against it under Prince Wadbelski. The latter, which had 31 guns and an armed population, occupied the point where the roads to Kars and Erzerúm diverge from the great route towards Akhaltsikh. This place, also, hoisted the white flag, on being cannonaded by a force under Mouravieff operating on one side, and another on the opposite side under Bergmann.

The fall of these places, and the retreat of the Pasha of Mush into his own territory, after being checked by the garrison of Kars ; together with the success of Prince Tchevtzevadze's operations on the side of Armenia, by

* La Russie dans l'Asie Mineure, par Felix Fonton, p. 349-362.

occupying Toprak-Kala and the castle of Bayazid, had made the invaders masters of the country as far as the Saganlugh: thus they were furnished with a base for operations beyond that chain, for the coming campaign.

Anapa, Poti, Kars, Akhalkalaki, and Akhaltsikh, with 313 pieces of cannon, and about 8,000 prisoners, together with the defeat of Kiossa Múhammed Pasha, before the walls of the latter place, were the fruits of a campaign of five months; at the close of which 15,000 Russians, with thirty-four guns, occupied a semicircle, extending from Kars on the right, and by Ardagan to Akhaltsikh on the left.*

The result was no less disappointing to the hopes of the Sultan, than to those of the Muslim people; whose ill-regulated enthusiasm had taught them to believe that they had only to draw their swords and mount their horses, to drive the giaours beyond the Caucasus. It should be borne in mind, however, that Asia Minor was in no way prepared to resist an invasion. Had there even been time to have met the enemy on the frontier with sufficient numbers at the very outset, an untrained people without regular gradations of officers—in fact, without even a military commander—were but ill-suited to oppose a skilful general and experienced soldiers, fresh from a successful war in Persia. The Turks, moroever, were under the extraordinary disadvantage of not having any regular

Ibid, pp. 366, 371, 372.

fortress, the defence of which might have given them additional time; for Kars, and the other places, owing to the defective state of their works and the cover afforded to an enemy in the suburbs, &c., were little more than *points d' appui* for a retreating force.

CHAPTER VII.

FIRST PART OF THE EUROPEAN CAMPAIGN IN 1829.

Number of the invading Russian army—Preparations for taking the field—Strength of the Russian fleets in the Black Sea and Mediterranean—Inadequate preparations in Turkey—Field force of the Sultan, and fleet in the Bosphorus—Sisebolí taken—Attempt to recover it—Movements of the Russian army—First and second attempts of the Grand Vizír to recover Pravadi—Preparations to attack the Grand Vizír—Movements of the contending armies—Defeat of a Russian corps at Markowtscha—The Grand Vizír unexpectedly encounters Diebitsch's army—Position of Kulewtscha—Battle of Kulewtscha—The Grand Vizír's army defeated—His return to Schumla.

The winter of 1828-9 was actively employed by the Russians in preparing an overwhelming force for the opening of the coming campaign. The bravery and persevering resistance of the Turks having not only secured the respect of their enemy, but proved the necessity of increased means of operation, an army was formed consisting of 142,000 cavalry and infantry, supported by 540 pieces of artillery. The cavalry was chiefly armed with the lance, as the most effective weapon against their Turkish adversaries. The guns—of which a large portion was horse artillery, independently of the separate arm attached to the Cossacks—were in the proportion of nearly three for every thousand men; but those divisions and brigades of the army which were more actively employed had four, and sometimes even five pieces, for every thousand men.

Part of the army was to be transported by sea from Sebastopol to Siseboli; and two thousand Turcoman camels were collected to facilitate the march of the remainder of the force. Two months' provisions were prepared on the Danube for the troops destined to besiege Silistria, in addition to three months' provisions for 50,000 men, which were placed in dépôt at Varna.

At the end of March, and the beginning of April, the invading army commenced its march towards the Danube under a new commander, General Diebitsch. He had, in addition, the effective assistance of a fleet of eleven sail of the line, eight frigates, and twelve corvettes, destined to threaten Constantinople from the Euxine; whilst eight sail of the line, seven frigates, and twenty smaller vessels, were employed under Admiral Hamlin, who menaced the capital by blockading the Dardanelles.

The Turkish authorities had also been preparing, in some measure, for the coming struggle; but the predestinarian feeling, that bane of the Muslim's exertions, operated on the inclinations of the people, particularly in the European side of the empire. The contingents of the Servians and Arnauts were unusually small; while the Bosnians, who had always displayed the greatest bravery, kept back theirs entirely. To the difficulty of raising a sufficient army was added neglect of putting the fortresses in a defensible state.

By way of illustration, it may be mentioned that in 1829, when the sieges of Schumla and Silistria were resumed, the trenches, parallels, batteries, and forts, were found just as they had been left by the besiegers in 1828.

Reschid Múhammed Pasha, the new Grand Vizír, who had been employed in Greece, arrived at Schumla on the 21st of March; where he found 10,000 men as the nucleus of his intended army. Taking the highest estimate, that of the Russians, the total Turkish force eventually collected for the campaign, might be about 150,000 men; of which nearly 100,000 were irregulars, distributed in Rustchuk under Hussein Pasha, and in the other fortresses. A part of the remainder, or Nizam, was employed in Asia; and 12,000 men were in the lines thrown up at Ramid Tchifflick to cover the capital; thus there remained about 36,000 infantry and 10,000 cavalry, with nearly 100 guns drawn by bullocks, to oppose the enemy in the field. But if such a number of men actually joined the Sultan's standard, which is not impossible, it could only be made out by taking into account the levies which arrived at successive periods; for there is no reason to believe that anything like 150,000 men were under arms at the same time. The effective force may, however, have equalled that of 1828. The fleet consisted of eight sail of the line, two frigates, and thirteen smaller vessels.

Marshal Diebitsch, who had been adjutant-general, was selected for the chief command of the Russian forces, and left Jassy on the 14th of April to accompany the army. Acting more systematically than his predecessor, Count Wittgenstein, and wishing to take advantage of his command of the Black Sea, he arranged that his operations should be preceded by a movement of part of the Russian fleet against Siseboli; for which the Turks were quite unprepared. This place had been entrusted to a thousand Albanians; but the greater part of this force had been required elsewhere, and only a small detachment remained as the garrison of this important post. It was, therefore, taken by Admiral Kumani, after very little resistance; its works were then strengthened, and it was strongly garrisoned by the Russians.

Hussein Pasha, the Seraskier, was immediately ordered to advance from Aidos to retake Siseboli. But although usually so energetic in his movements, he, on this occasion, allowed no less than seven weeks to be consumed in making his preparations, before he appeared with a force of 4,000 infantry and 1,500 cavalry before this place. During this interval, the Russian intrenchments were completed, and General Wachten was placed in command with a garrison of 3,000 men and two field pieces.

The Seraskier, advancing at the head of his force, made a formidable and well sustained attack on Siseboli, with the full expectation of recovering this fort, which was the more important on account of its proximity to the capital. The Turks entered the works sword in hand, and had almost succeeded in their enterprise; but, owing to the want of the usual supporting force in such cases to maintain the attack, they were eventually compelled to retire. Being also disappointed in the expected co-operation of the fleet from Constantinople, they retreated to Bourgas. The Sultan had despatched his whole fleet to engage that of the Russians, and to endeavour to regain the supremacy in the Black Sea. His ships, numbering twenty-three sail of various sizes, encountered four Russian frigates and a brig, and having captured one of the former, they returned with their prize to Constantinople, without attempting anything at Siseboli.

As the capture of this place had secured to the Russians the important object of a position south of the Balkan, as well as the means of supplying provisions to the invading army from the fleet, the former immediately advanced, and reached the Danube on the 8th of May, at two points: viz., the bridge of Hirsova, and that of Kalaratsch, immediately below Silistria.

General Roth, who had wintered in Roumelia, with a part of the 6th and 7th corps, commenced the campaign by placing himself in front of the Grand Vizír, whose camp covered Schumla. The position thus taken up by the invading army was protected on the left flank by Lake Devna and Varna.

After the passage of the Danube, which was simultaneously effected between the 8th and 9th of May, the Russian light troops and some Cossacks were pushed forward to various points in advance; Silistria being one of the most important objects. But before detailing the progress of the siege of that place, the operations in connection with it, and which preceded its termination, require some notice.

The Cossacks, and other troops already mentioned, were so posted in rear of General Roth, as to keep up the communications in a direct line from Turtokaï on the Danube to Jenibazar and Pravadi; whence a second chain of defensible posts swept in a curved line from the environs of Schumla to the vicinity of Rustchuk. The camp of General Diebitsch was so placed, at the centre of the chain, that support could be given to any point of the line which might be menaced; whilst, at the same time, it covered the operations of the siege from any attempt that might be made from the side of Rustchuk, by the force of Hussein Pasha. Under these circumstances, the Grand Vizír had only the choice of either continuing at the foot of the Balkan, watching the course of events, or of assuming the offensive. In the latter case, his intrenched position would have served as a *point d'appui*, and be the means of covering his retreat.

Reschid Pasha, who had lately come from Greece to assume the Grand Vizírate, was not long in deciding upon active operations. His plan was to endeavour to overwhelm General Roth, and retake Pravadi; in the hope that, after the fall of that place and of some of the other forts, he might possibly recover Varna, and finally relieve Silistria.

In accordance with this brilliant plan, the success of which might have terminated the campaign, the Grand Vizír made a demonstration against Pravadi on the 17th May; but not finding the expected support from Hussein Pasha, who was to have co-operated with him from Rustchuk, he retired to Schumla, carrying with him four guns and some prisoners. It proved that Reschid Pasha's letter, giving the details of his plan and requiring the co-operation of Hussein Pasha, had fallen into the hands of the Cossacks; thus he found his own movement anticipated and his combinations defeated, and he was unable to make any impression on Pravadi. The place had been most carefully fortified by the enemy: an inundation, covered by a battery, protected the northern side of the town; a hornwork had been constructed on the commanding ground to the west; and the town itself, being surrounded with a wall flanked with tenailles, was perfectly defensible notwithstanding its position in a deep valley.

The check thus experienced showed the importance of Pravadi, and the serious oversight committed by neglecting to recover it from the enemy during the preceding winter. The Grand Vizír, therefore, determined to repair his error if possible, and an ample force was forthwith put in motion for this purpose; with little expectation that one mistake would lead to another followed by more serious consequences.

Confident of success, the Grand Vizír again advanced against Pravadi, at the head of the whole garrison of Schumla: with the exception of four battalions, which he left behind under Ibrahim Pasha. Taking post on the heights south-west of the town, he commenced an irregular siege, by opening from thence the desultory fire of a battery against the crown work, and making attacks, chiefly with cavalry, against the garrison; which, according to some of the officers who took part in the defence, numbered at least 8,000 men. And thus he continued in thoughtless security before the place, without making any impression whatever; whilst General Diebitsch planned and executed, with infinite skill and success, those manœuvres by which he managed to interpose his army between Schumla and Pravadi.

The deep and narrow valley of Pravadi, which runs nearly north and south, forms the base of a triangle, the second side of which is the valley of Kalugre, or Newtscha, and the third that of Markowtscha, the apex being at Matara, a little beyond Kulewtscha. These valleys, more particularly those of Pravadi and Markowtscha, are enclosed on each side by mountains, rising to about 2,000 feet.

The activity and bravery of the Turkish garrison had caused the siege of Silistria to languish; and, the month of June arriving without any material progress having been made, it became necessary to attempt something more, either there or elsewhere. General Diebitsch, being quite aware of the actual position and negligence of the Grand Vizír, left the three corps under General Krassowski before Silistria, and commenced a rapid march with the purpose of throwing himself on the enemy's line of communication; thus occupying the only road leading from Pravadi to Schumla, so as to force on a general engagement under the most unfavourable circumstances for the Grand Vizír. The corps of Roth and Rüdiger, assisted by the garrison of Pravadi, were ordered to co-operate by occupying the defiles in rear of that place; thus preventing the retreat of the Turks, until the Russian army should have time to accomplish the intended detour.

Count Pahlen, with the advance of the army, reached Kuchuk Kaïnardji on the 5th of June, and on the 8th a communication was opened by General Matadoff with General Roth at Molatch. General Kreutz, whose advance was at Kizil Childir, in front of the valley of Newtscha, found the main body near Koargou, an elevated and strongly intrenched position. Continuing to advance, the main body was joined on the 8th at Alexfat, by parts of the 6th and 7th corps, bringing the intelligence that the Grand Vizír still continued on the plateau of Rowno, with Roth opposite to him at Eski Arnautlar. Favoured by a dense fog, and by the ignorance of the Turks, the Russian army reached Tauchan Kosluche during the night of the 9th, and the advance under Count Pahlen was pushed onward at the same time to Yeni-bazar, where his Cossacks encountered some Turkish cavalry. These proved to be the advance of a force under Veli Pasha, which had quitted Schumla, by order of the Grand Vizír, to threaten the rear of Roth and Rüdiger. Count Pahlen, having driven the Pasha back almost into that fortress, turned to the left, and established himself at Madara, on the direct road between Pravadi and Schumla.

On the following day another important movement took place, when General Roth, leaving two regiments to watch the Grand Vizír, effected his junction with General Deibitsch by a daring flank march. This was the more hazardous, since it was parallel to the line by which the Grand Vizír might have been returning to Schumla at that very moment, and he could, in this case, have crossed the hill to overwhelm him.

Towards the evening of the same day, the 10th, the capture of two Tartars informed the Russian General that the Grand Vizír's army was in motion. Uncertainty as to the direction of his march caused some alarm in the camp; since from a position near Markowtscha, which is midway between Schumla and and Pravadi, the concentrated force of the enemy might overwhelm any part of the exposed line of the Russians, extending as it did from Boulanik, by Madara, Yeni-bazar, and Tauchan Kosluche, to Pravadi, a distance of twenty-five miles. There was, however, but little occasion for uneasiness ; for the various posts which had been occupied with reference to the siege of Silistria, had so completely cut off the Grand Vizír's communications with that fortress, that he was still entirely ignorant of General Diebitsch's march.

Under the impression that the demonstration against Veli Pasha was the precursor of an attack upon Schumla, Ibrahim Pasha, who was in that place, had summoned the Grand Vizír to his aid. He marched accordingly in that direction, with the full expectation of being able to overpower the forces of Roth and Rüdiger ; which, as he supposed, threatened his rear. Instead, therefore, of proceeding southward by Marash, or more northwardly by way of Eski Arnautlar and Tauchan Kosluche, he chose the direct central line. The first part of his march was parallel to that of the Russians, from whom the Turks were separated by a mountain chain, whence their movement was watched by Russian videttes.

On reaching Markowtscha early on the morning of the 11th, the Grand Vizír found a strong body of cavalry posted in his front, with six guns, and supported by infantry in the rear. This force had been rapidly brought from Pravadi by General Kuprianoff, in the full expectation that his very strong position would enable him to prevent the passage of the Turkish army, which now suddenly appeared in his front.

Kara Djehennem,* the general of the Ottoman artillery, immediately planned the following attack upon the supposed corps of Roth and Rüdiger. The cavalry advanced, masking five field pieces which eventually opened upon the enemy at a suitable distance; and the charge which took place under cover of their fire was completely successful, for the Russian cavalry was routed, with the loss of five guns, and 400 killed. The infantry, however, was more fortunate; for, by rapidly changing front, they gained the protection of a neighbouring wood.

Having thus opened a road across the mountain, the Turks continued to advance, till, on reaching the other side, they discovered the advance of the Russian army; which, under General Ostrochenko, had in the interim occupied the defiles between Tschirkowna and Kulewtscha; while behind the latter place other divisions of the enemy's army had been successfully forming.

The position of General Diebitsch was particularly strong, comprising as it did a succession of wooded hills separated by deep ravines. The principal of these ravines is about 1,600 yards long, with a breadth varying from between 100 to 200 yards. The narrowest part is that touching the mountain near the village of Tschirkowna, and this necessarily became the first position of the Turks;

* Kara Djehennem (meaning Black Hell) was the name, or more properly the *nom du guerre* of this artillery officer, who was so instrumental in routing the Janissaries at the Etmeïdan. He died some three years ago, after attaining the rank of Ferik or Brigadier-General: his name being Ibrahim, he was called Kara Djehennem Ibrahim Pasha.

who had, consequently, very little room for either their cavalry or infantry. The Russian position was much more favourable, for at the other extremity of the defile, the hills are rather lower, and terminate at the village of Kulewtscha, in an open plateau.

On this advantageous ground, five battalions were posted in chequered squares, supported by two pieces of artillery, with orders to maintain their position *at all risks*, until the expected support, which was in full march, could arrive from the direction of Kalugri and Madara. On the other side of this position, there is a succession of gentle hills crossing the Schumla road, in the shape of a crescent, which at once encloses, and most advantageously commands, the valley of Pravadi.

The Turkish army is said to have numbered 33,000 men, and, including the siege artillery, they had fifty-six guns. The Russians, including the force with the baggage, had about the same number; but their 146 guns gave them a decided superiority, independently of the fact that the greater part of the Turkish force was composed of militia.

By changing front and making a rapid flank movement by way of Marash, the Grand Vizír might still have reached Schumla without a battle; but, nothing daunted by finding the whole instead of a part of the Russian army in his front, he determined to attack General Diebitsch forthwith. With this object, a battery opened its fire from the commanding ground against the plateau occupied by the enemy, and at 8 A. M., the loud hurrahs of the Turks were heard as they advanced through the smoke of the artillery.

Notwithstanding the extreme difficulty caused by broken ground, a mixed body of cavalry and infantry charged the Russians with such impetuosity, that, according to the account given to the author on the spot by a Russian* officer, two of the squares were broken, and one of them, 1,600 in number, of Múrom's regiment, was entirely cut to pieces as the men stood in their ranks. Six guns were also taken; the villages of Kulewtscha and Tschirkowna were carried; the plateau was nearly cleared, and the remainder of the Russians were actually giving way, and about to be exposed to the sabres of the victorious Turks, when the Hussars under Count Pahlen arrived most opportunely to save them from their impending fate. Had the Grand Vizír followed up his victory by bringing up his reserve to attack the enemy's right wing, the day must have been completely his; but he contented himself with driving the Hussars back, and then resumed his former position: which gave the enemy time to bring up more troops, and attack in his turn.

General Arnoldi, with the Hulan division and a twelve-gun horse battery, came up from Matara, and assisted by Count Pahlen with fourteen battalions and thirty-five guns, made an attack on the left of the Turks, which was led by General Budberg. Although the Turks suffered

* Lt. Schaufuss, who shared in the battle of Kulewtscha.

severely from the fire of the enemy's guns—which their artillery, consisting chiefly of battering guns slowly drawn by buffaloes and oxen, could not adequately return—they yet succeeded in repulsing this attack.

During the progress of these two affairs, the main body of the Russian army continued to arrive, and formed on the crescent-shaped hills already mentioned, which outflanked the Schumla road, as well as the Turkish position on both sides. Towards noon, Reschid Pasha, with the view of throwing back the Russian right wing on the main body and thus opening a road to Schumla, made a grand attack with his infantry, which advanced by the valley, from the left of their position. In carrying out this movement, they got beyond the plateau; and the latter would have been turned and the passage to Schumla opened, had it not been for some Russian troops and guns, strongly posted to defend that road: the corps of Roth and Rüdiger, which had just advanced from Matara, were among the number.

General Diebitsch, having now his whole force in hand, prepared a decisive attack upon the Grand Vizír; who had resumed his original position, at the edge of the wood behind Tschirkowna. For this purpose, the Jägers were formed under General Ostrochenko near this village, and five divisions under Count Pahlen still farther to the right. Two of Roth's divisions were posted, under General Zoll the chief of the staff, so as to outflank the left of the

Turks; having in reserve twenty-four battalions, and some hussars. The second division, under Kuletza, was detached to Marash, to operate against the rear of the Grand Vizír.

These arrangements being made, General Arnoldi, with four battalions and a twelve-gun horse battery, supported by two battalions with another twelve-gun horse battery and some hussars, led the attack. The ground narrowed as they advanced; but, as the Turks remained firm, it became necessary to resort to a cannonade on both sides. This was of course greatly to the disadvantage of the Ottomans, owing to the limited space occupied by them; and the battery of General Arnoldi did fearful execution with case shot.

Notwithstanding this, the contest was maintained without losing ground, up to four P. M.; when the fire of the Russian battery caused the explosion of two caissons in the very centre of the Turkish army. A similar mischance occurred to two other tumbrils, which had a disheartening effect. According to Lieut. Schaufuss, the officer already mentioned as having been present, this gave the turn to the battle; confusion ensued, and was succeeded by flight. The Grand Vizír endeavoured to rally the fugitives; and, for this purpose, posted the fourteen regiments of the Nizam most advantageously in strong ground, that might have been defended, without difficulty, sufficiently long to effect this object. But these troops abandoned their post without resistance, and the flight of the Turkish army became general: it fled through the wood of Markowtscha, leaving the six Russian guns which had been taken, together with the rest of the artillery and baggage, in the hands of the enemy. The fugitives being met near the village of Markowtscha by the garrison of Pravadi, turned to the right and crossed the wooded mountains towards the Kamtschik; thus, by a considerable detour, they succeeded in reaching Schumla.

It has been already mentioned, that the Grand Vizír, on breaking up his camp near Pravadi, had despatched orders to the garrison of Schumla to make a diversion in his favour by attacking the rear of the Russians. This was accordingly attempted, and with some success; but it was not sufficiently followed up. On meeting a slight check, Veli Pasha retired within the lines of Schumla; and in so doing he committed the second mistake, by abandoning entirely some of those exterior redoubts which had been such serious impediments to the enemy in 1828. If, therefore, General Diebitsch had instantly pursued the retreating garrison, he might, and probably would, have carried the important intrenchments of Schumla, on the evening of the 11th, or even on the morning of the 12th of June; for on the former day the Russian army was only a few miles from the place, and under the most favourable circumstances, it having already accomplished the double object of cutting off and defeating the Turkish army.

But the Russian General lost the opportunity of putting the finishing stroke to his brilliant march and well-combined manœuvres; and he contented himself with despatching on the 12th a force under General Roth to Marash, with the object of intercepting the retreating enemy. General Matadow, who commanded half the right wing of this force, was attacked between Tschengel and Kasanlai by 1,000 or 1,500 Turkish cavalry, who were supported by three redoubts, constructed in 1828. They maintained the contest until the arrival of the Russian artillery decided the affair: the redoubts were carried, and the greater part of their defenders put to the sword. The grand object of this march, however, failed; for the Grand Vizír, with the cavalry, made his way through the enemy, and reached Schumla by a circuitous route on the morning of the 13th. He was followed by his infantry; who continued to make their way through the woods in small detachments; and at the expiration of ten days there were, including a recent reinforcement of about 3,000 Albanians, some 30,000 men re-assembled under the Grand Vizír.

The Turks had lost upwards of 3,000 men, and the Russians, according to their own admission, not less than 63 officers and 2,500 men, at the battle of Kulewtscha. The former had about 33,000 men and 56 pieces of artillery, and the latter 31,000 in action, and 2,000 with the baggage. But the Russians, taking into account their 146 guns, had a decided superiority in the field, independently of the mixed composition of the Turkish force.

When it is remembered that the Nizam, though nominally regular troops, were then but imperfectly organized, and that the remainder of the Turkish army simply consisted of untrained armed men, it must be admitted that this battle, although lost, did honour to the valour and perseverance of the Osmanli. Their zeal and irregular courage enabled them for many hours to oppose a regular army, commanded by an experienced general; and this successfully, until the shock of a fearful explosion in the midst of their forces, threw them into confusion, and gave victory to the Russians. The battle of Kulewtscha proved to be the fatal turning point of the two campaigns, and in the sequel, placed Turkey, for a moment, at the feet of her invaders.

CHAPTER VIII.

FALL OF SILISTRIA AND CONCLUSION OF THE CAMPAIGN OF 1829.

Continued demonstrations againt Schumla—Force employed against Silistria—Progress of the siege—Mining operations—Fall of the fortress—General Diebitsch marches into the passes of the Balkan—Retrograde movement—Fall of Adrianople—Signature of the treaty of peace—Intended renewal of the war—March of General Diebitsch across the Balkan.

THE day after the battle of Kulewtscha, General Diebitsch endeavoured to open a negotiation with the Turks; but he was referred by the Grand Vizír to the Sultan on this point; and Silistria being still successfully defended, he determined to employ his army in threatening Schumla. As in the preceding campaign, he adopted for this purpose a series of demonstrations, rather than a regular attack with a view of storming the place: which, considering the nature of the defences and the bravery of the garrison, scarcely promised success.

The attempts made by the Russians on certain parts of the intrenchments could have little interest for the reader, beyond showing the spirit displayed by the besieged; who did not fail to repay their adversaries with interest on almost every occasion. Amongst the number, however, may be noticed the serious affair under Colonel Howe on the Kamtschik, on the 1st of July, which lasted for some time without any marked result on either side; and again another on the 11th close to Marash. On this occasion the Turkish cavalry, whilst foraging, encountered and drove back a body of Cossacks, until the support of a force in skirmishing order under General Rüdiger gave the latter the advantage. The Turks were in their turn reinforced, with the additional support of eight guns, and a formidable affair of out-posts ensued; the Grand Vizír himself was present, encouraging his men, who eventually drove the Russians back.

After Schumla had been menaced in this way for four weeks, during which time Silistria had fallen, the third corps joined the army on the 13th of July, with a view to more active operations. But before noticing these it will be proper to revert to the siege of Silistria.

The Russian forces consisted of 21,000 men and 88 pieces of cannon, with a covering or reserve army under General Diebitsch of 65,000 men with 240 guns. The attack commenced with the flotilla of Admiral Paniotto, who forced the Turkish gun-boats to retire under the guns of the fortress. Against this the besiegers had marched simultaneously in three divisions. The centre, under General Laskievitch, met but little resistance; but it was quite otherwise with those of the left, under General Krassowski, and of the right under General Pahlen. The former especially encountered the most formidable opposition.

As an acknowledgment of the brilliant defence of Silistria in 1828, the garrison had recently been replaced by 8,000 Albanians; these, together with some of the Nizam, gave an effective of about 10,000, instead of 12,000 men as before. The Pasha met the enemy on the heights near the town, and after a sharp action which lasted about six hours, the Turks retreated into the fortress, after losing 800 men; leaving the Russians masters of two redoubts, in addition to the trenches and batteries of the former year, which the Pasha had most unaccountably neglected to destroy. The siege was therefore renewed, as regarded the besieging army, precisely where it had terminated when the Russian army retreated from before the town in 1828; and the batteries being forthwith animated, a fire was opened against the fortress in the course of an hour's time.

It has already been mentioned that the trenches were re-opened against Silistria on the 18th and 19th of May, but not with that advantage which usually attends a powerful besieging force. The besiegers had been informed by some deserters, that Seret Pasha, a man of seventy, and a portion of the inhabitants, were ready to give up the fortress rather than endure the hardships of a second siege. Under these circumstances, it was naturally expected that a bombardment would have caused its surrender; and this might, in fact, have been the case, had it not been for the determination evinced by Múhammed Pasha, the second in command, and his followers from Asia, who were resolved to defend the place to the very last.

On the morning of the 19th of May, a sally was made in force by the besieged. The Russian *tirailleurs* were driven back and suffered severely, before reinforcements came to their support; and even then they succeeded with difficulty in repulsing the Turks. Other sallies were made, with the same kind of spirit, on the night of the 21st, and again on that of the 28th of May. The latter took place against the left of the Russian trenches; and, as it happened, most inopportunely for the Turks, at the moment when the relief was taking place; thus an additional hostile force becoming available, they were eventually driven back.

A still more formidable sally took place on the night of the 5th of June; but, secret intelligence having put the besiegers on their guard, the sally ended by the retreat of the Turks into the garrison, after a fierce struggle, which caused the besiegers the loss of five officers and 113 men. By means of hooks and cords, the Turks carried, or rather dragged their wounded into the town. The movement against the Grand Vizír, which took place almost immediately after this event, reduced the force of the besiegers to some 12,000 men.

Fresh embrasures were now opened in the works,

counter-mines prepared, and even some counter-approaches established by the Turks to cover their sorties. On the 13th of June, the besiegers made known to the garrison the defeat of their countrymen at Kulewstscha; which occasioned, as it was intended it should, some disunion in the fortress. The courage of Múhammed Pasha, however, continued unshaken. With the view of ascertaining the real state of the case, he sent two pigeons to the Grand Vizír, one white, the other black, with a request that the former might be sent back if the intelligence were false, the latter if it were true; and the ominous black-coloured bird accordingly made its way back to Silistria. The defence, however, was still maintained, notwithstanding this discouraging news, and the still greater trial of the continued bombardment of rockets and other missiles. These were poured into the fortress almost incessantly, until the guns of the besiegers in the third parallel had nearly silenced those of the besieged, and reduced the defence almost entirely to musketry.

At length the fourth parallel was established, and between the 17th and 20th of June the glacis was crowned, and the explosion of four mines partially blew in the counterscarp. At this juncture, the Turks, hoping to destroy these works, made a determined sally; but other mines were exploded by the besiegers, who descended by galleries, and on the 21st succeeded in occupying an unflanked cunette in the ditch. On the 22nd, a sally was made by a part of the garrison, who were assisted by the stones launched by their comrades from the parapets, in addition *to burning combustibles.* The latter were of a very novel but effective description. They consisted of earthen pots, having gunpowder at the bottom, with pitch above it; these being thrown down, after igniting the pitch, the pots soon exploded with such formidable effect, that the enemy was driven out of the cunette.

Following up this advantage, the Turks effected an opening into the besiegers' galleries, and carried the contest as far as the glacis; but the garrison being driven back, and more mines prepared, an animated and chiefly subterranean contest succeeded at the counterscarp; and it was afterwards continued in the cunette, particularly during the interval from the 23rd to the 26th. The Turks, on perceiving that both of the bastions of the front attacked were being mined, prepared a counter-mine, which, by some accident, exploded almost simultaneously with that of the enemy; the whole front of No. 4 bastion was thus completely opened, and the bastion itself occupied by the besiegers in consequence. The garrison, after making an ineffectual attempt to recover the bastion, continued to defend themselves with grenades, stones, mines under the cunette, and fire-pots. An intrenchment was at the same time constructed, extending along the whole of the side attacked, and on which thirteen guns were mounted. But as there were two practical breaches, and three other openings in the body of the place (which still existed when the author visited Silistria in 1829), the Pasha, whose ammunition was now almost expended, agreed to capitulate instead of risking an assault: which was, in fact, all that was wanting to complete the brilliant defence of Silistria.

About 9,000 men laid down their arms, and the Russians got possession of 238 garrison guns, in addition to 31 others belonging to the flotilla. The loss of the garrison, between the 17th of May and the 1st of July, was between 3,000 and 4,000 men; that of Russia was admitted to be 115 officers, and 2,566 men killed and wounded.

Agreeably to the original plan of the campaign, the siege of Rustchuk was to have followed that of Silistria, and the line of the Danube was to have been maintained till the spring. But the battle of Kulewtscha caused a change, by preparing the way for more decided operations.

The Russian general was aware of the moral effect produced on the Turks by the loss of this battle; he also knew that much dissatisfaction prevailed at Constantinople on account of the Sultan's reforms, and more particularly in consequence of the organization of regular troops instead of the Janissaries. Encouraged by these and other circumstances, General Diebitsch determined on the daring step of passing the Balkan, in preference to the alternative of undertaking another siege to secure more effectually his lines of communication. His plan being formed accordingly, he proceeded, on the approach of the troops hitherto employed in reducing Silistria, to make a more formidable demonstration against Schumla. So closely was this place invested, that the Grand Vizír, in expectation of an immediate assault, recalled a portion of his troops from the mountain passes, to aid in the defence of a position on which, in his opinion, everything depended. The defenders of the Balkan being thus seriously di minished, it only remained to attempt the passage before the Grand Vizír had time to discover and remedy his fatal error. In order to complete the deception, 10,000 men under General Krassowski were to press Schumla closely, whilst the main force, with an effective of about 30,000 men, feigned a retreat towards Silistria.

On reaching Yeni Bazar, a distance of about six leagues, General Diebitsch suddenly, and to the Turks most unexpectedly, turned to the right. General Roth, with thirty-two guns, ten battalions of infantry, sixteen squadrons of cavalry, and two regiments of Cossacks, moved on Devna; General Rüdiger, with another force, reached Kupriquoi, whilst General Pahlen, with seventeen battalions, eight squadrons of cavalry, and thirty guns, occupied Yeni-Bazar; to which the head-quarters were removed on the 18th of July. General Roth had, in the mean time, ascertained that only 3,000 Turks, with twelve guns, were encamped at Pod-Bashi, on the Kamtschik. The advance commenced forthwith. Each soldier was provided with four days' provisions, and ten more were carried in the wagons attached to each regiment. General Roth found the Kamtschik almost undefended, and advancing to Dalgurado, carried the works on the height at that place ; while Rüdiger easily turned and drove 1,000 Turks from Oxymale, where he took four guns and some of their baggage. A bridge was then thrown over the Kamtschik, and on the 19th, head-quarters were established at Dervish-Jowan.

General Krassowski had orders to assault and carry Schumla, in case the Grand Vizír should pursue the Russians, with nearly the whole of his force ; but the moment that Reschid Pasha became aware of the real object of General Diebitsch, he detached 10,000 men to intercept him at the pass of the Kamtschik, which he hoped was still maintained. But the handful of men who occupied that post, only 120 in all, could not offer any real resistance ; the Russians therefore had already passed the bridge in question, as well as the most difficult part of the country in advance, and were far on the road towards Eski Bashli before the Grand Vizír's move was made. Head-quarters, in fact, reached this place in nine days from Schumla.

In the mean time, General Roth advanced along the coast of the Black Sea to Misivri, which capitulated on his approach ; and he was thus enabled to push on to Bourgas, and open a communication with the fleet. The figurative comparison of the number of Diebitsch's army to the leaves of the forest, which had been spread by the reports of the Bulgarians, acted like magic ; Aidos, with all its stores, was abandoned, in consequence, by the retreating Turks. They were taken so completely by surprise, that they had not even offered any substantial resistance to the *coup-de-main* march by which the principal passes of the formidable barrier of the Hœmus had been already scaled.

At this juncture, the posts occupied by General Diebitsch covered about 800 miles of country, viz., from Bourgas to the vicinity of Selimnia, and again from Tschenga to Omar Faki; with the additional serious disadvantage of a long line of communication with the Danube, which might be cut off. In fact, the latter consideration, together with the reported junction of Hussein Pasha and the Grand Vizír, caused such uneasiness, that General Diebitsch concentrated nearly the whole of his force, and made a retrograde movement on Selimnia with 25,000 men, and ninety-six pieces of artillery. But, instead of encountering the expected army, he only found a small force of cavalry posted near the town, which gave way, after a smart affair, and the place was occupied. General Diebitsch now left a force to secure his communications, and resuming his advance forthwith, he encamped before Adrianople on the 19th of August in three divisions, with the right of the army leaning on the river Tschenga. Although the city was not fortified, and is, moreover, a good deal exposed to the fire from the Derbent heights and other commanding ground, the town might have afforded a strong *point d'appui* for defence; since those quarters which are separated from one another by the rivers Toncha, the Maritza, and Adra, could have successively offered serious resistance to the entrance of an enemy. But no preparations whatever had been made for this purpose, and a hasty capitulation enabled the Russians to enter Adrianople on the following morning.

The *coup-de-main* thus successfully accomplished, and the retreat of some 20,000 Turks on Constantinople, had given the undisputed possession of the ancient capital of European Turkey to the enemy; but great and unexpected advantages were not unattended by causes for deep and serious consideration.

By opening a communication beyond his left flank with the fleet at Bourgas, General Diebitsch would have obtained the supplies requisite for a forward movement; which, if successful, might have enabled him to complete his brilliant march by occupying the long-coveted shores of the Bosphorus and the seat of the Constantines; and in case of a reverse, he could either have retraced his steps by endeavouring to recross the Balkan, or have made a flank movement for the purpose of reaching one of the fleets. The Euxine fleet was on one side of his line of march, and on the other, that which had so long menaced the Sultan's territories by blockading the Dardanelles.

General Diebitsch felt that there was no middle course between bringing about peace and the destruction of his army; and his critical situation caused such anxiety at St.

Petersburgh, that the Emperor Nicholas not only ordered a fresh levy of 90,000 men, but also made arrangements to obtain a loan of forty-two millions of florins in Holland, to prosecute the war in case the mission of Baron Muffling to Constantinople should fail to bring about peace.

Like Cortes, under somewhat similar circumstances, the Russian commander determined to risk everything by taking a bold course; and, as in the case of the Spanish adventurer, circumstances favoured his demonstration, projected with a view to second the efforts of the Russian envoy in the capital by intimidating the Divan.

It was under these particular circumstances, and with an effective force of about 21,000 men, that a demonstrative advance was commenced on three points The extreme left, with the support of the fleet, captured different places on the shores of the Black Sea as far as Midiah; which place, only sixty miles from the entrance of the Bosphorus, was occupied on the 7th of September. The right wing, under General Siewers, had been pushed on at the same time by Demotika to Enos; by the fall of which a communication was opened on the 8th of September with the Russian fleet in the Mediterranean. On the same day, the central column of advance, under General Roth, took post at Eski Baba, while the Cossacks extended as far as Loule Bourgas. The line thus occupied reached from the fleet anchored in the Euxine at Midiah, to that in the Mediterranean at Enos, a distance of about 140 miles

But as the greater part of the invading force had been employed in these demonstrations, the means nowhere existed of supporting any one of them in attacking the formidable positions in their front.

If the 20,000 Turks who reached the capital between the 26th and 28th of August, had simply shown a bold front at Adrianople and elsewhere, as they retired, the march of the Russian army would have been delayed sufficiently long, not only for their reduced numbers to have been ascertained, but also to have enabled the Grand Vizír and Hussein Pasha to act in rear of the invaders; and thus might have been prevented a humiliating treaty, which was entered into by the Divan, under the firm belief that hosts which had been compared to the leaves of a forest, numbered at least 60,000 men.

To put an end to such an alarming invasion, and save Constantinople, was a paramount object with the British Ambassador, Sir Robert Gordon; more particularly as considerable anxiety was felt lest there should be an outbreak in the capital for the restoration of the Janissaries. A treaty of peace was signed, in consequence, at Adrianople on the 28th of August, 1829.

It is said that Sultan Mahmoud's usual firmness deserted him on this occasion, and that he shed bitter tears on affixing his signature to what he so justly considered a disadvantageous and even humiliating treaty. It is pretty certain that he would have continued the war at all hazards, had he been aware that at that moment the Russian commander, now Marshal Diebitsch Zabalkanski, had not more than from 15,000 to 17,000 bayonets. A defective commissariat, and a still worse medical department, caused disease to commence its work as soon as the invaders reached Adrianople; at a grand review which took place on the 8th of November, 1829, and at which the author was present, there were scarcely 13,000 men of all arms in the field.

An unexpected difficulty arose at this period. Whilst the treaty of peace was on its way to St. Petersburgh for ratification, the Pasha of Scodra, who had been very dilatory in taking the field, and who was not inclined to do anything when he was there, took the extraordinary course of objecting to the terms of peace, and declared his intention of renewing the war. He marched at once to Philippopoli, with a force which appeared to the author to number fully 25,000 irregular troops. Such a movement, coupled with a message that he would be in Adrianople within eight days, naturally caused Marshal Diebitsch the greatest uneasiness. He ordered the troops to hasten with all speed from Wallachia to join the army, and desired General Kisselef to come from the neighborhood of Schumla for the same purpose.

Accordingly General Geismar, at the head of the former, crossed the Danube at Rachova with about 12,000 men; and, being conducted by a Greek who was well acquainted with the mountain passes, he turned and afterwards forced the pass of Anatza, which was but feebly defended by the Pasha. By continuing a rapid march, General Geismar placed himself in the rear of the Albanian force near Sophia; whilst General Kisselef, the second in command, reached Gabrova with thirty guns at nearly the same time, by another route. Both halted, however, on finding that the peace had not been interrupted, and that the Sultan's orders had at length been obeyed by the Pasha of Scodra.

Had the Pasha really desired to be serviceable to the cause of his master, he might have turned the scale in favour of the Sultan, even after the Balkan had been crossed. For, by forming a junction with the Grand Vizír, either at Jamboli or Selimnia, there would have been, after leaving an adequate garrison in Schumla, at least 50,000 men to act in rear of the invading army. It appears that he remained almost inactive near Widdin during the winter of 1828 and the spring of 1829, expecting that the necessities of the Sultan would give him the necessary weight to bring about the re-establishment of the Janissaries. This, in fact, was the real object of his march towards Adrianople, or Constantinople, as he himself gave out. Nor was he the only individual of high standing in the empire who hoped to see the Sultan forced by the exigencies of the war to return to the former state of things, and submit once more to the thraldom of the Janissaries: the Prætorian guards of Turkey.

During the more active part of the campaign, which continued from the 8th of May to the 28th of August, or nearly four months, about two-thirds of the Russian army were employed in besieging Silistria, and one-third in the field. The proportions were afterwards reversed, for the larger number was in the field after the surrender of that fortress. This siege, a battle, and a march of about 1,400 miles, constituted the principal events of the campaign in European Turkey. Soon after the signature of the treaty at Adrianople, an officer of rank was despatched to make the conclusion of peace known to the Seraskier in Asia. The Turkish army, owing probably to habits of greater cleanliness, was comparatively free from disease, and its losses were, therefore, confined to those of the sword. About 16,000 men are said to have perished on their side; the loss of the Russians from sickness and the sword probably exceeded 50,000 men and 20,000 horses.

CHAPTER IX.

ASIATIC CAMPAIGN OF 1829.

Projected recovery of Akhaltsikh—Ahmed Bei assaults Akhaltsikh—Siege of the citadel—Failure of the Turks—General Paskevitch moves against the Turkish position—Defeat of Osman Pasha—Capture of the intrenched camp—Advance to Erzerúm—Bayazid taken and retaken—Defeat of the Russians at Khart—Fresh attempts of the Turks—Recapture of Khart by the Russians—General Sacken's perilous retreat from the Ajar country—The Russians prepare to enter winter quarters—Hostilities renewed by the Seraskier—Intelligence of the signature of a treaty of peace in Europe—Loss of the Russian army—Result of the campaigns in European and Asiatic Turkey—Relative situation of Turkey and Russia when the war commenced.

Having now brought the campaign in European Turkey to a close, we will revert to the operations which were being carried on in Asia, consentaneously with those which have just been described; and which were brought to a close by the arrival on the scene of action of the messenger who carried to the belligerents the intelligence of the treaty of Adrianople.

Operations had commenced in Asiatic Turkey at an unusual period of the year: or rather, they had never been suspended by the Turks; for on the attempt of the Russians to retire into cantonments for the winter of 1828, they continued their defensive measures, with a view to recover the ground which they had lost during the summer. The Sultan ordered fresh levies. Hajji Salegh, the

Pasha of Maïdan, replaced the former Seraskier; and Hagkhi, the Pasha of Sivas, as his Kaïa or second in command, succeeded Kiossa Múhammed Pasha. About 10,000 men, the remains of the former army, continued behind the Saganlugh, as the nucleus of a force which was expected to number 80,000 men and 66 guns in the spring.

The Seraskier's plan was to assume the offensive by a demonstration against Kars; making the recovery of Akhaltsikh, however, the main object; it being one of the bulwarks of Islamism. This service was confided to Ahmed Beï, Prince of the Adjares, who, in the depth of winter, marched at the head of 15,000 Lazians, hoping to master that fortress; of which, by way of encouragement, the firman of the Sultan had nominated him Pasha. The Seraskier was to second this operation by threatening Kars, whilst Osman Pasha of Trebizonde should make a similar demonstration against the Ghuriel. But, as the Russian General was aware of the real object of the Turkish movements, he not only reinforced Akhaltsikh in good time, but also caused the neighbouring defiles to be occupied by another body of troops, to cover the fortress.

On the 18th and 19th of February, Ahmed Beï had concentrated his followers in the vicinity of Akhaltsikh, and having successfully stormed the outer walls he advanced through the suburbs to attack the fortress. In spite of a shower of balls, the assailants placed their ladders against the walls and endeavoured to mount them, notwithstanding the loss caused by the bursting of hand grenades and the deadly effects of canister shot. The gaps made by these missiles were filled up as quickly as they occurred, and the assailants continued to pass over the bodies of their companions, hoping by renewed attacks to overcome the determined spirit of the garrison. But the heavy loss, caused by more than half an hour's exposure at the foot of the walls, showed that an open assault was impracticable in the face of a numerous garrison. The escalade was, therefore, abandoned, and the besiegers took possession of the adjoining houses; from which a musketry fire was opened against the ramparts.

Ahmed Beï, whose scientific knowledge was not great, continued for a time to press the siege in this desultory manner; but, on perceiving that the garrison, by closing the embrasures and raising the parapets with sand-bags, were protected from the fire of the houses, he resorted to a battery; which was, however, so badly constructed, that the guns were speedily silenced by those of the fortress. Ahmed Beï now endeavoured to cut off the supply of water from the besieged, but the Ajars posted for this purpose were dislodged by a sortie of the garrison. A solid intrenchment was next constructed, close to the gates of the town, for the same purpose. This was so far successful that water could not be obtained in day-time, and, a force being employed under Avdi Beï the brother of Ahmed to defend the neighbouring passage of the river Kura, it was hoped that the garrison would be thus completely cut off. But a skilful manœuvre of the Russians under Burtsoff, followed by an attack in flank, drove Avdi Beï to a distance, and enabled them to continue their march to relieve the place. The sudden appearance of a force coming up in the rear, produced a decided effect upon the unorganized followers of Ahmed Beï, and a sortie of the garrison at this opportune moment put the greater part to flight. That portion of Ahmed Beï's followers which was posted in the tower, being cut off by the retreat of the others, endeavoured to defend itself in the houses; but the enraged Russians set fire to the buildings, and put some of the Lazians to the sword, while the remainder perished in the flames.

The loss of the Russians on this occasion is said to have been only 100 men, while that of the Turks exceeded 3,000. 8583 cannon and 72,882 musket shots, in addition to 1,354 hand grenades, were discharged from the fortress in repelling the brave but desultory attacks of Ahmed Beï and his followers, and the suburbs were reduced to a heap of ruins by the preceding struggle of twelve days and nights.

At this period the Turks* also experienced a check on the shores of the Black Sea. Kiaja Aglou, the Pasha of

* La Russie dans l'Asie Mineure, &c., par Felix Fonton, p. 388-398.

Trebizonde, occupied the intrenched position in advance of that city, with 8,000 men. Here he was attacked in force by the Russians, under cover of a formidable battery of artillery; and at the same time by another force of 1,200 men and some field guns under General Hesse, who turned his right flank. The Pasha made an obstinate defence of four hours, but was forced to abandon his position with the loss of 163 killed, and a great many wounded.

Changes in the Turkish functionaries at this period, and the failure of the attempt to recover Akhaltsikh, had an unfavourable effect on the defence of Asiatic Turkey, which was greatly increased by the defection of the Pasha of Mush. He was decoyed over to the Russian service by the two former Pashas of Kars, who were then Russian prisoners, and who were instigated to this step by their new masters. The loss of the services of the Pasha of Mush deprived the Turks of 12,000 Kurdish cavalry; which was an immense disadvantage to them. The Seraskier, also, had only been partially successful in assembling troops for the approaching campaign; although it was understood that he had about 50,000 men at Hassan Kale, behind the Saganlugh, and that it was his intention to march against Kars with about 30,000 men, whilst his Kaïa, or lieutenant, endeavoured to retake Akhaltsikh with the remainder of the force. The Russian general, who had been strengthened by 20,000 men, determined to anticipate these movements; and as the position of General

Pankratief under the walls of Kars secured this fortress against the right of the Turks, Ardagan, which had been carefully strengthened of late, became the pivot of a combined movement against their left wing, which was chiefly composed of Adjars, under Ahmed Beï. This portion of the Turkish force was advancing rapidly at this juncture from Schaumchett towards Akhaltsikh.

Accordingly, a force under General Muravieff, with fourteen guns, manœuvred on its left flank, while General Burtsoff formed the advance of the intended attack on the Kaïa's force in front. The cavalry of the latter, numbering about 3,000, had already arrived at the village of Dighur, scarcely eight miles from Akhaltsikh, when a part of the Russian force under Hoffman was perceived by the Turks, who immediately attacked it both in front and flank; but as he was advantageously posted, his squares resisted the repeated charges of the enemy, and he maintained his ground until three in the afternoon, when General Burtsoff came to his assistance from one direction, and Muravieff from another: the Kaïa, thus threatened on both sides, retreated precipitately at nightfall into his camp near the village of Tchaborié.

The combinations of the Russian general had thus placed nearly 7,000 men and twenty-two pieces of artillery in an advantageous position. At daylight, on the 2nd of June, Burtsoff commenced the attack on the right, while General Serghéïeff, with cavalry and infantry supported by eight field pieces, was to attack the left flank and rear of the Turks. Burtsoff advanced with great intrepidity, but found himself attacked in turn by the enemy's cavalry, and with difficulty maintained his ground by forming squares. Subsequently, however, he reasumed the offensive, and, supported by a battalion of Count Paskevitch's regiment, at length forced the Turkish right by a successful charge. Notwithstanding this severe check, the Kaïa, under cover of two guns, brought up reinforcements, and renewed the attack, sending a strong body of troops at the same time to outflank the right wing of the Russians, and occupy the village of Dighur. But the timely occupation of a defile by a part of the Kherson regiment, prevented its execution. An obstinate contest now took place, and was maintained between the villages of Tchaborié till the charge of two Russian battalions at length decided the affair; and the Turks retreated, after having lost 1,200 men, and some provisions, in addition to a gun, a mortar, and a number of camels and horses.

The retreat of the Kaïa's force having completely disengaged the right wing of the Russians, General Paskevitch was enabled in consequence to concentrate a force of 12,-340 infantry, 5,770 cavalry, and 70 pieces of artillery on the 9th of June; with which he decided to advance from Kotanly, ten miles from Kars, and cross the wooded Saganlugh in two columns.

On the other hand, Salegh Pasha, the Seraskier, with

about 30,000 men, prepared to cover Erzerúm, by occupying the route thither at Zevinn; whilst his Kaïa, Haghki Pasha, was strongly intrenched at Medjingherte, in the gorges of the Milli-Duz, with some 20,000 chiefly irregular troops and 16 field pieces, so posted, that he could take in flank and rear an enemy moving towards Zevinn.

Having ascertained that Zevinn was only about to be occupied, General Paskevitch determined to endeavour to anticipate the Seraskier's plans by a daring manœuvre. For this purpose he formed the invading force into two columns, one of which so completely occupied Haghki Pasha by a series of demonstrative and false attacks, that the other, without being perceived, gained the crest of the Saganlugh by a rapid night march; and whilst the Seraskier was on the point of executing his manœuvre, the space between the two divisions of the Turkish army was occupied on the 14th of June, and the communications between them almost entirely cut off.

With the hope of remedying this state of things, 1,200 infantry and 400 cavalry were despatched on the 17th of June from the camp at Milli-Duz, under Osman Pasha; who, by means of a detour, succeeded in interposing his force between the Russian column and Zevinn, and immediately commenced intrenching his position, with the hope of being able to maintain his ground till the Seraskier could come up. General Paskevitch was not slow to perceive that the fruits of his late brilliant manœuvre must be lost, if time were given to Osman Pasha; and he attacked him forthwith in his isolated position. The struggle that ensued was of a very determined character, and sustained for some time—the combatants occasionally fighting hand to hand with alternate success, until numbers prevailed, and the Russians at length mastered the Turkish position. The road onward was thus opened just in time; for some troops, on being pushed forward, found the Seraskier's advance near Zevinn, and in full march to support Osman Pasha. But the success was not as yet complete, for the two Turkish armies, then forty miles apart, were actually endeavouring to unite by means of a concentric movement on Zaghinn. As the least delay might have been fatal under these circumstances, one Russian column continued as before to threaten Haghki Pasha, whilst the other, by a flank movement, occupied the intended point of junction of the Turks at Kaïnly.

Still hoping to gain his object, the Seraskier caused his cavalry to advance on the 19th of June, endeavouring with one portion of this arm to outflank the right of the enemy, whilst the Dellis attacked the left. Their onset was so impetuous that the Russians only maintained their ground by the great steadiness of the squares and the supporting fire of a powerful artillery. The engagement soon became general, and was at first favourable to the Seraskier: but he having weakened his centre too much by the withdrawal of troops, General Paskevitch brought a mass of artillery to bear on this point, and assumed the offensive by an oblique attack, which was followed by several charges of cavalry with much advantage. The Turks opposed a vigorous resistance, and endeavoured to carry the guns; but their concentrated fire, and the timely charge of Colonel Simonitch, with two battalions, four squadrons of cavalry, and eight guns, enabled the Russians to maintain their ground; although in some instances the artillerymen had been sabred at their guns.

The Seraskier now retired to a strong position in the rear, where, with one flank on the Kaïnlychaï and the other resting on some commanding ground, he purposed remaining till the expected reinforcements should enable him to renew the engagement. But the Russian General having ascertained the Seraskier's intentions from a deserter, determined upon an immediate attack, and forthwith advanced for this purpose in three columns. Muravieff, with one portion of the army, was to turn the enemy's left; another under Pankratieff was to threaten the right, and cut off the communication with the other camp at Milli-Duz; whilst the main force, with the cavalry and artillery, was directed against the centre. As the Russian army appeared to be throwing up intrenchments in the evening, the Turks were totally unprepared for their attack; and the sweeping fire of a powerful artillery advantageously placed, put an end to anything like resistance. Twelve guns, with their caissons and ammunition, together with the baggage, and about 500 prisoners, were the fruits of this victory. It was, however, on the very point of proving fatal to the Russian commander himself; for General Paskevitch had only just quitted the Castle of Zevinn, when a mine exploded, which had been carefully prepared for his destruction by some of the Seraskier's followers.

By the dispersion of the Seraskier's army on the night of the 19th, the intrenchments at Milli-Duz were completely turned: they could be taken in reverse by marching along the southern side of the plateau, which was done accordingly. The protection of the park and provisions, &c., being entrusted to a corps under Burtsoff, 12,000 cavalry and infantry advanced to the attack, covered by 36 guns; and the intelligence of the defeat of the Seraskier, received at this moment, acted like magic upon the undisciplined followers of Haghki Pasha. The camp, therefore, fell into the enemy's hands after a short resistance, together with 3,000 prisoners, 19 pieces of cannon, and 19 standards, in addition to the tents, baggage, and provisions.

As the Asiatic forces were chiefly composed of militia, the double defeat had so diminished the followers of the Seraskier, that he had no resource but that of leaving some cavalry at Hassan Kalá, and of endeavouring to concentrate the Lazian militia and the followers of the Pasha of Mush, as well as the Kurds, at Erzerúm.

Pursuing his advantages, General Paskevitch continued

his advance in three columns, and having ascertained from the people of the country that the force left by the Pasha at Hassan Kalá had almost dispersed, he pushed on at the head of some cavalry, and on the 23rd of June obtained possession of the provisions, stores, and twenty-nine guns belonging to the castellated building at that place. This, although it had not been defended, was, in fact, the key of the valley of Erzerúm.

Information which General Paskevitch here obtained from the Christians was turned by him to still better account. Relying upon the state of disaffection that was known to prevail in the capital of Asiatic Turkey, he hastened his march thither. The inhabitants of Erzerúm were almost exclusively Armenians, and on the appearance of the Russians before the city, they (aided by the timely demonstration of some batteries from the heights against the town) caused the Seraskier to surrender the place on the 27th of June, with its arsenal, which contained 150 pieces of artillery. Although not a regular fortress, Erzerúm would have been capable of a respectable defence, had it been occupied by a sufficient body of Turks.

The operations elsewhere had been of a mixed character, although, on the whole, favourable to the Turks. The extreme left of the Russian army had been weakened by the grand operation against the capital, and the Pasha of Vann prepared to take advantage of this circumstance. Proposing to strike a blow, he moved at the head of a considerable force, and appeared before the town and castle of Bayazid, on the 19th and 20th of June; he carried the former by assault, with the loss to the Russians of 300 men and four guns. The castle, or citadel, however, was still maintained, and the opportune arrival of a reinforcement enabled the besieged troops to renew the engagement.

A fierce struggle, which lasted two days, ensued; but the town was finally recovered by the Russians, notwithstanding the most determined efforts of the Pasha and his followers to maintain it; and on receiving intelligence of the fall of Erzerúm, he retreated, in order to protect his own pashalik. The total loss of the Russians at Bayazid amounted to twenty-four officers and 400 of the garrison.

The capture of Kniss, twenty-three miles south-east of Erzerúm, had followed that of the capital; and General Paskevitch, on learning that the inhabitants of Baïburt were ready to submit to his arms, detached a force of cavalry, infantry, and artillery in that direction, under General Burtsoff. Five hundred men, posted in the mines of Miss-Maydani, two hours short of that place, made some show of resistance; but the miners, who were Greeks, joined the Russians, and the spahis then retired to Baïburt; which place, with four guns, and two petards, fell into the hands of the invaders, without resistance, on the 7th of July.

Encouraged by this success, General Burtsoff determined to attack the neighbouring village of Khart, which had been intrenched, and was occupied by some of the Lazians. He put his force in motion accordingly, in two columns, which were to meet so as to make a joint attack on that post on the 19th of July. But as some accident had retarded one of the columns, Burtsoff, on arriving with the other, commenced the assault without waiting for it. He was successful in the first instance, and the Lazians were driven out of the cemetery into the adjoining part of the town. The contest that followed in the narrow winding streets, was most obstinate and protracted, for the Lazians poured volleys of musketry on their assailants as they defended the town, house by house. Seeing that little or no progress could be made, Burtsoff, as a last resource, ordered the other column, which had just appeared, to take the Lazians in flank from the western commanding ground; but whilst he renewed the attack in front consentaneously, he was brought down by a pistol-ball. The assailants, after continuing their efforts for a time, retreated out of the town, and reached Baïburt on the 20th, after the loss of eighteen officers and 300 men.

This serious defeat encouraged the inhabitants of Erzerúm and Bayazid to make fresh exertions, which the Pasha of Vann was preparing to support by a renewed movement in the direction of the latter place; and even the Pasha of Mush was ready to break through the net of intrigues which had, for a time, shaken his fidelity to the Sultan.

Under these circumstances, the Russian general decided

on taking the bold step of marching against Khart, with the double object of avenging the death of Burtsoff, and of restoring the moral tone and confidence of his army.

Having, as a precautionary measure, placed a strong force under General Pankratieff in Erzerúm, General Paskevitch advanced, and on the 25th of July he reached Baïburt; from whence, by making a rapid detour, he succeeded in turning the village of Khart, and anticipated the force coming to its relief. Two intrenchments which had been constructed as an additional protection, were carried in the first instance, and the greater part of the Lazians put to the sword; the four faces of Khart itself were stormed simultaneously on the following morning, and carried after a loss to the garrison of about 300 men.

Osman Pasha, who had just arrived from Trebizonde, on finding that he was too late to succour the intrepid Lazians, immediately retraced his steps; thus giving a practical proof of the mischievous effects of entrusting military commands to civil functionaries. Osman Pasha was quite aware of the importance of hastening to Khart in good time; nor did he fail to perceive that something might still be done to remedy his previous tardiness. It was, in fact, his anxious wish to prevent the onward march of the invaders; but, owing to his want of military experience, he did not take advantage of the strong ground as he retired. Instead of occupying the Tchifflik in force, by which he might readily have stopped the enemy's advance, he merely left a few spahis as he retreated; thus a brief skirmish put the Russians in possession of this important position, from whence they could, at pleasure, either move against Sivas, or continue the march upon Trebizonde.

After due consideration, the latter course was adopted by General Paskevitch, on account of opening a communication, through the Euxine, between the Russian ports and the army. The main body advanced, accordingly, along the route of Kara Hissar, and Sivas, as far as Temlia; whilst a strong column diverged to the right, under Simonitch, and reached the well-known mines of Ghumish Khana, on the 14th of August. But, although scarcely forty-six miles from the important port of Trebizonde, difficulties presented themselves which proved to be insuperable. Instead of experiencing, as at Erzerúm and other places, the support of the Armenian people, the Russians found, as they advanced through a country almost impracticable for artillery, that their communications were seriously threatened by the Adjars, and other Muslims carrying on an irregular warfare. These circumstances, added to the recent success of the Kurds, in retaking Khniss, caused the Russian commander to abandon his previous purpose of opening a passage to the sea, in order, with the assistance of the fleet, to secure the whole line of this part of the coast. During the retreat, which was determined upon in consequence, Baïburt was evacuated and the works blown up, previous to the concentration of the Russian forces at Erzerúm, which took place on the 27th of August.

Operations did not, however, cease altogether in other places. General Hesse attacked the intrenchments of Mukha-Estatt, opposite Fort St. Nicholas, on the Black Sea, and carried them by storm on the 8th of August, under cover of a powerful artillery, with the loss of sixty-eight guns, and 500 men, to the Turks. Ghuriel submitted in consequence.

The attempts made at this period by the Russians, to subject the Adjars, had a very different result. With the purpose of putting an end to the constant and seriously annoying incursions of the Adjars, General Sacken marched from Akhaltsikh with four battalions, two regiments of Cossacks, and four mountain guns. With this force he boldly entered the territory of Ahmed Beï, burned several villages as he proceeded, and took possession of Khuli, the seat of government, on the 16th of August; receiving, after the retreat of the Beï, the keys of the town from his wife.

General Sacken continued the pursuit of Ahmed Beï; but finding that he occupied an inaccessible fastness in the mountains, and being disappointed in receiving the expected co-operation from General Hesse, the scarcity of provisions made it necessary to think of a retreat. But as this was found to be impossible, owing to the passes in his rear being occupied by the Adjars, he decided on making a flank march to the frontiers of Ghuriel: fully expecting to meet the force under General Hesse in that direction. Accordingly, dismounting his guns, and carrying them piece-meal by manual labour, he found himself entangled in a difficult country, presenting narrow pathways and precipitous defiles. The Adjars, who of course knew their own country thoroughly, alternately opposed his march in front or attacked him in flank and rear; by which, during his perilous progress on the 19th, seven officers and 142 men were put *hors de combat.*

On the following day, he entered a more favourable country; and, therefore, only lost 12 men; and on the 21st, General Sacken reached the Sarnomli range, on the borders of Ghuriel. Here he expected to obtain supplies; but disappointment awaited him in this respect, as well as in that of receiving such a reinforcement from General Hesse as would enable him to assume the offensive; he was, therefore, forced to continue his retreat through the Sandjak of Kooblian, to Akhaltsikh. On reaching that place, he found that his letter, containing the project of a combined operation against the Adjars, had not reached General Hesse in time to divert him from another operation which he was about to commence.

In consequence of the heavy rains which, in the beginning of September, indicated the approach of an early and severe winter, the Russian general ordered the troops into cantonments; and part of the army was already on its march towards Georgia for this purpose, when it became necessary to take the field once more, to oppose Osman Pasha; who, with the intention of doing something to distinguish himself in his recent appointment as Seraskier, had invited his countrymen, the Lazians, and others, to join his standard.

In consequence of his urgent appeal to the Muslim people, about 10,000 men had assembled about the beginning of September, at Baïburt, the capital of Lazistan, and 6,000 more at Tchifflick. These, with the addition of a corps at Ghumish Khana, to keep up the necessary communications, formed the left wing of Osman Pasha's army; 4,000 Dellis, Spahis, &c., composed the right, and were posted at Terdjan and Pun, under the Pasha of Vann. The latter commenced operations by moving against Miklacheoski, who was posted on the road between Ach-Kala and Pekeridge; but the arrival of Muravieff enabled him to drive back the Turks, and to pursue them as far as Pun, capturing a gun and some provisions.

General Paskevitch now prepared to strike a blow against the Seraskier: who, as has just been mentioned, occupied both Baïburt and Tchifflick with his reserve at Ghumish-Khana. Leaving an adequate force both at Erzerúm and Ach-Kalá, with the purpose of concealing his plans, he formed the remainder of his troops into two columns; which, after making demonstrations against the former places, effected a junction at Miss-Maydan on the

26th of September. Since his real purpose must now have become apparent, General Paskevitch resorted to a rapid night march, by which he threw himself between the Seraskier and Baïburt; after a brisk affair with the Turks, he succeeded in occupying some commanding ground, which completely cut off all reinforcements from the place. Instead of making the best of their position by defending the place, the Turks committed the serious mistake of making a sortie with 4,000 infantry and 2,000 cavalry. Paskevitch did not fail to take advantage of this fortunate circumstance. He hoped to be able to enter the town with the fugitives, and therefore caused Muravieff to make an attack, which was well supported; and the Turks, after most determined efforts, were driven back. Seizing the critical moment when their retreat masked the guns of the place, the cavalry was ordered to charge, and succeeded in cutting off the greater part of the fugitives from the town. Some of the Lazians renewed the fight by occupying strong ground at the entrance of the village of Daduzar, and others in the town continued a desultory resistance for some time, which was terminated at length with the loss of six guns, 700 killed, and 1,236 prisoners. The Seraskier, who now appeared at the head of a considerable force when it was too late, retreated to Balakhor, where he received intelligence of the termination of hostilities in Europe, in consequence of the treaty of Adrianople.

The loss of the Russian army during the preceding campaign of four months, is said to have been only 3,900 men although four fortresses and 262 pieces of cannon had been captured.*

A retrospective glance at the invasion of Turkey will give us a march of about 1,150 miles, the capture of two fortresses, Brailow and Varna, after lengthened sieges, the drawn battle of Marash, and a retreat from before Schumla as well as Silistria as the results of the campaign in European Turkey of 1828. In Asia Minor three fortresses were reduced, and a battle gained before one of them, viz : Akhaltsikh.

The results of the succeeding campaign in European Turkey were the same lengthened march for a portion of the army, followed by one important battle, that of Kulewtscha, the reduction of Silistria, and a *coup de main* march across the Balkan. In Asia Minor the chain of the Saganlugh was forced in face of the Turkish army, and the subsequent defeat of the Seraskier led to the fall of Erzerúm and of some smaller places. The well-earned distinction of a Field Marshal's bâton awaited Count Paskevitch as the reward of his skilful and successful operations. Count Diebitsch, the leader of the European forces, received, in addition to a similar distinction, the title of Zabalkanski (the crosser of the Balkan), conferred as an acknowledgment of his successful march across that

* La Russie dans l'Asie Mineure, &c., par Felix Fonton, p. 399-532.

hitherto impassable barrier, as well as of his having subsequently opened a communication with the Russian fleet in the Mediterranean.

The two empires presented the most striking contrast at the commencement of hostilities, when the height of power and prosperity belonged to one of the contending powers, whilst the state of the other was almost the very reverse.

The well-equipped army of about 120,000 men, which took the field in May, 1828, does not give a fair estimate of the force employed by Russia on that occasion against Turkey; for, as in the case of the British troops in the Peninsula, its numbers and efficiency were kept up in spite of the serious drain of human life, consequent on the reverses in Bulgaria and the adjoining territory. Moreover, this force had the advantage of operating in a tract of country which was already known by previous campaigns, as well as in consequence of more recent topographical examinations.

On the other hand, Turkey was worse than unprepared to resist the sudden invasion of Russia. An exhausting struggle of six years' duration in Greece had just been terminated at Navarino; and, in addition to the loss of the command of the Euxine by the destruction of her fleet in that unequal contest, the internal state of the country was far from being favourable to its defence. Several projects of reform and improvement occupied the attention of Sultan

Mahmoud at that moment; among which the most prominent was the organization of the army. This serious undertaking had already been commenced with a bold hand on an enlarged scale. Consequently, the empire was in a transition state, from the iron rule of the Janissaries to the more manageable and milder substitute of an organized force. In commencing this task, the Sultan caused mere lads to be selected for the ranks, as being freer from prejudices and more amenable to discipline than grown men. To borrow the words of a celebrated Russian diplomatist, when speaking of the war undertaken by the Emperor, "If the Sultan had been allowed sufficient time to give his organization solidity, he would have made that barrier impenetrable which we found so much difficulty in surmounting, although art had hitherto done so little to assist the efforts of the nation."*

Considering that the experienced soldiers of Russia encountered half-drilled recruits, and a levy *en masse* hastily assembled, whose numbers were very limited when compared with the time of the Janissaries, the surprise must be that so much was done by the Turks during the campaigns of 1828 and 1829 to resist an invasion, for which the most ample preparations had been made for some time previously.

By the hasty treaty of Adrianople, the Sultan engaged

* Extract of a very secret despatch from Count Pozzo di Borgo: Paris, Nov. 28, 1828, p. 349 of the Portfolio.

to pay a large sum into the Russian treasury, as an indemnity for the war which Russia herself had caused. Additional territory was also gained by her in Asia, viz.. the fortress and Pashalik of Akhaltsikh, with a portion of the coast of the Black Sea, in addition to Brailow (in Europe), and a tract of country lower down; which, to a certain extent, enables her to control the entrance of the Danube. And, what is still more serious than all these acquisitions, Russia acquired the right of interference in the concerns of the Turkish provinces of Moldavia and Wallachia; which has already, for the second time, produced most baneful effects.

CHAPTER X.

CAUSES OF THE PRESENT WAR BETWEEN TURKEY AND RUSSIA.

Exactions of Russia in consequence of the treaty of Adrianople—Secret article in the treaty of Hunkiar Skellessi—Occupation of the Principalities by Russia from 1848 to 1850—Mission of Prince Menschikoff to Constantinople—Ultimatum of Russia—Dignified conduct of the Porte—Cessation of diplomatic intercourse—Circular of Count Nesselrode—Russia invades the Principalities—The Porte protests against this aggression—France and England also remonstrate—The four western powers propose terms—Modifications suggested by the Porte—Russia rejects the proposals—The Grand Council of Turkey decides on a contingent declaration of war against Russia—Disadvantages suffered by Turkey from delaying this step.

If the author has been in any degree successful up to this point, the preceding chapters will have given the reader some idea of the resistance that was offered by the Turks to the Russian invasions of 1828 and 1829, and will also have enabled him to form some estimate of what may be expected from the Ottomans, if left to continue the present contest single-handed.

But before touching upon the relative means of Russia to accomplish a march to the banks of the Bosphorus, and those of the Sultan to defend the peculiar description of country which intervenes, let us briefly pass in review the *ostensible* causes of the present war.

These would seem to go back at least to the treaty of

Adrianople. Russia at that time violated the engagement made on the 6th of July, 1827, "not to seek any increase of territory, or exclusive advantage in commerce;" and violated also her own declaration of war (26th of April, 1828), disclaiming all intention of territorial aggrandizement, "since," as she stated, "sufficient people and countries already acknowledged her sway." Notwithstanding these express declarations, she obtained possession of the fortress and Pashalik of Akhaltsikh, with a portion of the sea coast of Asia, in addition to the left bank and islands of the Lower Danube, as well as the Sulina mouth of that river. This last was claimed on the ground of establishing a quarantine for the general good.

Further, the Porte agreed to pay, on account of the war which Russia had commenced, 10,000,000 ducats of Holland, and 1,500,000 ducats besides, as an indemnity to Russian merchants for losses which they *might have sustained* in the course of this, *or any preceding war.* The larger sum was to be paid by instalments, and a portion of territory was evacuated as each succeeding payment was made: first, Adrianople was relinquished, next the Balkan, then the Danube, and finally, the Principalities. A portion of this contribution was, however, remitted by Russia when Ahmed Pasha repaired as Ambassador to St. Petersburgh after the peace. Not, as might be supposed, from motives of generosity, but in consideration of the concession by Turkey of the fortress of Poti and the adjoining territory in Asia to Russia; which were more than equivalent to the 5,000,000 ducats which were remitted.

The Porte retained the suzerainty in the Principalities, and a small revenue, but surrendered the fortresses and everything else to Russia, including even the soil itself; in which no Mohammedan subject of the Porte was to hold any possession beyond the period of eighteen months, which was the time allowed for the sale of their property. Nor was this all: the treaty of Adrianople secured to Russia the right of interference in the internal concerns of the Principalities, and the power of sending troops thither under certain circumstances.

Thus were realized the words which are understood to have been used by the Russian Ambassadors, when writing from London to St. Petersburgh, in 1829:—"It is in the midst of our camp that peace must be signed. Europe must learn its conditions only when it is concluded. Remonstrances will then be too late, and it will patiently suffer what it can no longer prevent."* And so it proved; for France and England remained quiescent, whilst Russia pursued the advantages she had gained by the destruction of the Ottoman fleet. Nor does it appear that more was done by either of these two powers, than to remind their former ally that a desperate war, and the terms secured by the treaty of Adrianople, were in direct violation of the

* Despatch from Prince Lieven and Count Matuszewich, addressed to Count Nesselrode. London, June 1, 1829, Portfolio, vol. 1, p. 171.

engagements made on the 6th of July, 1827. It is right to observe that the Sultan had become a party to this treaty a short time before the signature of that of Adrianople.

The arrangements connected with this treaty had not been long completed when the internal difficulties of the country produced fresh complications. The refusal of England to give assistance to the Sultan after the battle of Konia, caused him to apply for aid to Russia, and a Russian fleet and army promptly appeared in the Bosphorus, to protect Constantinople against the Egyptian army.

As the price of this assistance, and before the return of the Russian forces to their own country, Russia exacted from Turkey the offensive and defensive alliance of 1833. By the treaty of Hunkiar Skellessi, both powers were reciprocally bound to furnish succour in case either were attacked; while, by a secret article appended thereto, Turkey was bound to close the Dardanelles against any power with whom Russia might be at war.

These clauses were calculated to involve momentous considerations; but the separate act of the treaty of Adrianople more immediately concerned the peace of Turkey.

Had this memorable and unjustifiable settlement of an unprovoked war been limited to tho loss of treasure and territory by Turkey, it might have been bearable; but it went much further: for by it the seeds were sown of still greater future mischief.

The people of the Principalities were not free from the

revolutionary contagion of 1848, and a movement in that direction commenced in Moldavia, whence it extended to Wallachia; there it was carried still further, and the entire abrogation of the *réglement organique* was loudly demanded.

The Porte, on being applied to by the people, took the prudent course of deputing a commissioner, Suleiman Pasha, to examine their requests. He proceeded to Wallachia, and finding the people ready to submit to his authority, he did not hesitate to proclaim an amnesty.

But as this peaceful settlement of affairs was not quite agreeable to Russia, she made a pretext of a reported conspiracy, and, under the supposed sanction of the 4th article of the treaty of Balta Liman, the military division of Podolia passed the Pruth, and occupied Moldavia. The Porte was invited at the same time to send troops to Jassy. This it declined doing, and a Russian force of between 40,000 and 50,000 men continued to occupy the Principalities. It was only after lengthened negotiations with Great Britain, and the advance of about 10,000 Turkish troops, that this force was withdrawn in 1850.

The treaty of the 1st of May, 1849, at Balta Liman, only provided that both powers should enter the Principalities together, and this under peculiar circumstances, with an equal force; therefore, Russia had no right whatever to enter the territory alone, and still less excuse for making the people responsible, as she did, for the expense of this occupation.

Thus were the Principalities freed for a time, and their grain, instead of being prohibited from exportation in order that it might be consumed by the troops of the Czar, again competed with that of Russia in the markets of Europe. Before the end of the year 1,400,000 quarters of wheat were sent to England from the port of Galatz alone.

But the trade and consequent prosperity of these border provinces was not of long duration; for the settlement of a trivial dispute between the Greek and Latin Churches has been made the pretext for covering a deep design for attempting one of the long cherished objects of the Czars.

Prince Menschikoff, who had for a time commanded the Russian army before Varna in 1828, proceeded to Constantinople in the appropriately named *Foudroyant*, and landed on the 28th of February, 1853, accompanied by a train of admirals, generals, and other officers of all grades in the naval and military services.

On the 2nd of March the Prince paid his official visit to the Porte, in the very unusal attire, on such an occasion, of plain clothes. He also offered the further slight of not visiting the foreign minister as usual, and Fuad Effendi resigned his portfolio in consequence.

As the question of the privileges of the holy places had been already set at rest by a Hatti-Scheriff, Prince Menschikoff made known the real object of his mission on the 22nd of March, by demanding on the part of the Czar the so-called Sened, or convention, for a protectorate over the Greek Christians of Turkey. This demand was repeated on the 29th of April, and again on the 5th of May, with the addition, that the Prince required an answer to be sent within five days, and that longer delay would impose upon him the *most painful obligations.**

In the mean time, England and France had not been inattentive to what was passing at Constantinople. Our own ambassador, Lord Stratford de Redcliffe, arrived there the very day that this demand was made, and Monsieur de la Cour, on the part of France, on the following morning; and the fleets of both nations anchored close to the Dardanelles a few days later.

Although the peremptory and almost insulting demand which had been again sent to the Porte, indicated but too clearly what was to be expected from the extensive warlike preparations in Bessarabia and Sebastopol, a temperate but decided refusal was returned by the Reis Effendi on the specified day, the 10th of May, to the unjustifiable demands of Russia. On this occasion it was stated that the Sultan had at all times considered it to be a sacred and imperative duty to maintain the religious privileges of his Christian subjects, but that he could not enter into a treaty which would annul his sovereign rights over a large portion of his people.†

On the following morning, Prince Menschikoff replied

* Appendix I. † Appendix II.

briefly to the Reis Effendi's letter, and repeated his demand still more peremptorily than before, giving three additional days to allow the decision of the Porte to be sent in.*

In the hope of producing a more amicable tone, three of the Turkish ministers proposed a meeting to the Prince at the Yali, or summer residence of the Grand Vizír, on the Bosphorus, on the 13th, to which the Russian ambassador agreed. But instead of going to the meeting, he proceeded at the appointed hour straight to the palace of the Tchengan, and insisted on seeing the Sultan. It was in vain that he was told it was Friday, and that, except to attend the mosque as usual, the Sultan was keeping his apartment, on account of the death of his mother the Sultana Validí, which had taken place on the 1st instant. Notwithstanding this, Prince Menschikoff remained three hours at the palace; after which the Sultan agreed to give him a brief audience. During this interview the Sultan explained that his ministers were acquainted with his intentions, which would be made known to the Prince. He was about to reply, when the curtain suddenly dropped in front of the Sultan, and left the ambassador and his dragoman by themselves in the apartment. A few seconds afterwards the Sultan's chamberlain came to request the ambassador to await the arrival of the Grand Vizír and the Reis Effendi.

* Appendix III.

They did not appear, however; for, owing to the slight they had already experienced, and the disgust felt in consequence of the offensive proceedings at the palace, both ministers immediately requested the Sultan to accept their resignation.*

On the 15th of May, their successors addressed a note to the Prince, in which, with reference to the necessity of considering so important a question *de novo,* they expressed their desire to reply in the course of five days, or sooner if possible.† But, instead of consenting to this reasonable delay, the ambassador gave his reasons on the 18th for considering his mission terminated.

A further attempt at conciliation was made by the Porte on the 19th, calling the Prince's attention to the firmán just issued to the Patriarch of the Greek Church; which ought for ever to have put an end to all anxiety respecting the exercise of the rites of the religion of his Majesty the Emperor.‡

This, however, was so far from being at all satisfactory to the Russian ambassador, that when quitting Constantinople with his imposing suit of attachés on the 21st, he replied by a kind of protest, in which he stated that if the firmán should be found to invalidate any of the other privileges or immunities of the orthodox religion, it would be regarded as an act of hostility to Russia and her religion.§

* Question d'Orient devant l'Europe, par M. A. Ubicini: Paris, E. Denton, 1854, p. 59.

† Appendix IV. ‡ Appendix VI. § Appendix V.

Under these circumstances, Reschid Pasha submitted to the ambassadors of the four Western Powers the draft of the treaty which Prince Menschikoff had sent to the Divan. Their reply, "that they did not consider themselves authorised to give any advice on the subject,"* coupled with the position of the French and English fleets in Besika Bay, seemed scarcely to evince a more friendly feeling towards the cause of the Turks than towards that of the Russians.

Five days after the receipt of this communication, an official note was forwarded to the ministers of the four powers who had been parties to the treaty of 1841. In this, it was expressly stated that the Porte was determined to maintain all the religious privileges and immunities voluntarily granted to the Christians by former Sultans: but it added, as had been explained to the Russian minister, that concessions thus accorded are entirely different from a Sened or treaty taking the form of a convention; which would, in fact, be contrary to the rights and independence of the government itself. The note went on to state, that since the departure of Prince Menschikoff, no assurance had reached the Porte that war would not be the result of those extensive preparations then making by Russia on the confines of the Ottoman territories, both by sea and land. Whilst, therefore, the Porte repudiated, in the face of the allied powers, any and

* Appendix XII.

every aggression and hostile intention on its part, it had found itself under the painful necessity of taking (purely as a matter of precaution) certain measures of self-defence: these comprised the movements of troops, and some attention to the state of the imperial fortresses on the other side of the Balkan, on the banks of the Danube, and other important points, which required to be put in a proper state of defence.

A communication to the same effect was published in the Constantinople papers, with the view of explaining the situation of the Porte more fully to Europe at large. The interests of all classes had been already secured by a Hatti-Scheriff previously addressed to the Greeks, the Armenians, the Catholic Armenians, and the Jews, by which all the religious immunities conceded to them *ab antiquo*, were confirmed.*

The next communication in this singular correspondence was in the form of a letter from Count Nesselrode, at St. Petersburgh, dated the 31st of May. In this he announced to Reschid Pasha, that in the course of a few weeks the Russian troops would receive orders to cross the frontier; "not to make war upon a sovereign who had always been considered as a faithful ally, but in order to secure a material guarantee until the Ottoman government should give those proofs of equity which had hitherto been sought for in vain." Count Nesselrode continued, almost in the

* Appendix VI.

tone of a mandate, to press that the Pasha should obtain the Sultan's signature to the ultimatum, without any alteration.* This demand seems in reality to have been made with the object of furnishing an *ex post facto* excuse for the long meditated occupation of the Danubian provinces.

Reschid Pasha's reply, on the 16th of June, was still eminently pacific. He explained, in the most conciliatory terms, the reasons which prevented the Porte from acceding to the terms of the cabinet of St. Petersburgh. His tone, however, was firm at the same time; especially when reminding the Count of the threatened march of troops into the Principalities, as being completely at variance with the *peaceable assurances* which his letter appeared otherwise to contain.†

A few days subsequently to the despatch of the preceding letter, Count Nesselrode's circular of the 11th of June, addressed to the ministers and agents of Russia at foreign Courts, reached Constantinople. In this they were told that there "is no pretension on the part of the Emperor to any religious protectorate, which would have a tendency to exceed that which we exercise in point of fact, and traditionally in Turkey, by virtue of former treaties." That "His Majesty does not aim at the ruin and destruction of the Ottoman empire; which he himself, on two occasions, has saved from dissolution. On the contrary, he has always regarded the existing *statu quo* as

* Appendix VII. † Appendix VIII.

the best possible combination to interpose between European interests ; which would necessarily clash in the East, if a void were actually declared; and that, as far as regards the Russo-Greek religion in Turkey, we have no necessity, in order to secure its interests, of any other rights than those which are already secured to us by our treaties, our position, and the religious sympathy which exists between 50,000,000 Russians of the Greek persuasion and the great majority of the Christian subjects of the Sultan."

Expressly passing over the fact that the Eastern Church, as it exists under its own patriarchs and synods in the dominions of the Porte, is very different from the Russian branch of the church, whose head is the Czar ; the Sultan was required, in the following terms, to subscribe to a Sened or convention by which the whole of the Eastern Church would have become subject to the Emperor of Russia, and the sovereign authority over Christians in Turkey would have been as completely set aside, as if the Roman Catholics of Great Britain were to look to the Emperor of Austria instead of Queen Victoria for their future immunities and privileges :—

"After three months of laborious negotiations, and after having exhausted even the last possible concessions, the Emperor is now compelled peremptorily to insist on the unconditional (pur et simple) acceptation of the draft of the note. But still influenced by those considerations of patience and forbearance which have hitherto guided him, he has granted the Porte a fresh reprieve of eight days, in which it has to take its decision. That period passed, and, painful though it may be to his conciliating disposition, he will be compelled to think of the means of obtaining, by a more decisive attitude, the satisfaction which he has in vain sought by peaceable means."

The most striking fallacies contained in this document were ably answered by the French Minister of Foreign Affairs; and, in doing so, M. Drouyn de l'Huys clearly showed that neither the treaty of Kuchuk-Kaïnardji, nor any other, could serve as a basis for the pretensions of the cabinet of St. Petersburgh.*

A second circular from the pen of Count Nesselrode appeared on the 2d of July, in which it was again stated that if the Porte should refuse the demand of Russia, it would be necessary to resort to more decided steps. Count Nesselrode went on to say:—"En posant cet ultimatum à la Porte, nous avions plus particulièrement informé les grands cabinets de nos intentions. Nous avions engagé nommément la France et la Grande Bretagne à ne pas prendre trop tôt des mesures, qui d'un côté, auraient pour effet d'encourager l'opposition de la Porte, de l'autre, engageraient plus avant qu'ils ne l'étaient déjà dans la question, l'honneur et la dignité de l'Empereur. J'ai le regret de vous annoncer aujourd'hui, que cet double tentative a

* Appendix XI.

malheureusement été vaine. La Porte, comme vous le verrez par la lettre ci-jointe de Reschid Pasha, vient de faire à celle que je lui avais addressée, une réponse négative, ou au moins évasive.

" D'autre part, les deux puissances maritimes, n'ont pas cru devoir déférer aux considerations que nous avions recommendées à leur serieuse attention. Prenant *avant nous* l'initiative, elles ont jugé indispensable de dévancer immédiatement, par une mésure effective, celles que nous ne leur avions annoncées que comme purement eventuelles. . . . . Elles ont sur-le-champ envoyé leurs flottes dans les passages de Constantinople. Elles occupent déjà les eaux et ports de la domination Ottomane à portée des Dardanelles. Par cette attitude avancée, les deux puissances nous ont placé sous les poids d'une démonstration comminatoire, qui, comme nous le leur avions fait préssentir, devait ajouter à la crise de nouvelles complications.

" En présence du refus de la Sublime Porte, appuyé par la France et l'Angleterre, il nous devient impossible plus que jamais de modifier les résolutions qu'en avait fait dépendre l'Empereur.

" En conséquence sa Majesté Imperiale vient d'envoyer au corps de nos troupes, stationné en ce moment en Bessarabie, l'ordre de passer les frontières pour occuper les principautés.

" Elles y entrent, non pour faire à la Porte une guerre

offensive que nous éviterons au contraire de tout notre pouvoir aussi longtemps qu'elle ne nous y forcera point, mais parceque la Sublime Porte, en persistant à nous refuser la garantie morale que nous avions droit d'attendre, nous oblige à y substituer provisoirement une garantie matériélle ; parceque la position qu'ont prise les deux puissances dans les ports et eaux de son empire, en vue même de sa capitale, ne pouvant être envisagée par nous dans les circonstances actuelles que comme une occupation maritime, nous donne en outre une raison de rétablir l'equilibre des situations réciproques, moyenant une prise de possession militaire."*

The Porte postponed answering this statement of Count Nesselrode's till after the passage of the Pruth, which the Western Powers still hoped might be averted. But all doubts were set at rest by the *St. Petersburgh Gazette* of the 9th of July, containing the manifesto of the Emperor Nicholas, and appealing to the religious feelings of the Russian people, who were told by their Emperor that the solemn oath of the Sultan had been perfidiously broken.†

In accordance with the circular of Count Nesselrode, of the 2nd of July, and of a proclamation addressed to the inhabitants of Wallachia and Moldavia by Prince Gortschakoff, the second, fourth, and fifth corps passed the Pruth

* The reasons adduced by Count Nesselrode in this despatch for the conduct of Russia are so peculiar, that the author has felt unwilling to weaken them in any degree by a translation.

† Appendix IX.

on the 3rd of July, and advanced by Leova and Sculeni to fulfil the orders of the Emperor.

The excitement occasioned at Constantinople by this news was very great, and the call for immediate hostilities caused much uneasiness in the Divan. As, however, they were told that a favourable result might still be expected to follow the efforts of the allied powers, the Porte, instead of taking the natural course of declaring war, was content to await the issue of events; using its best endeavours in the mean time to calm the feelings of the people.

On this occasion Turkey presented a striking contrast to the state of things in 1828. At that time, opposition to the Sultan's reforms caused, to say the least of it, lukewarmness on the subject of the Russian invasion. But in 1853, the movement was, as it were, that of one man, who was prepared to sacrifice his life, and expend his all in opposing the enemy. In Constantinople the people brought their money or jewels to increase the public funds, and the rich gave their horses to the artillery, in addition to other contributions. Troops and ships were hastened from Egypt, and men from Arabia, from Syria, from Barbary, and from Albania; with, in many cases, funds provided for their support. One private individual at Aleppo is said to have raised 5,000 men to serve the State. Nor was the Government negligent on its part. Mules were purchased, and brought from Spain for the artillery service, and the greatest exertions were made to arm the fortresses and equip the fleets, so as to be well prepared for the expected struggle.

In this state of preparation a mild but firm protest was issued by the Sultan on the 14th of July,* in which the aggression on his territory, and the consequent sufferings of the peaceable inhabitants of the Principalities, were strongly contrasted with the reiterated peaceable *declarations* of the cabinet of St. Petersburgh. The questions at issue were then discussed with an equal degree of calmness and candour; and after stating what had been done by a firmán and by other means, to remove difficulties and satisfy complaints, the document concluded by repeating the desire of the Sultan to do away with every reasonable cause of dissatisfaction.

On the 15th of July, just one day later than this Turkish manifesto, Count Nesselrode's second circular was answered in Paris by M. Drouyn de l'Huys,† and on the following day Lord Clarendon's reply to Sir Hamilton Seymour‡ was despatched from London. In both these documents the fallacy is shown of Count Nesselrode's statement that the invasion of the Principalities was the consequence of the movement of the combined fleets to Besika Bay. Indeed it is clearly pointed out that the orders for the fleets to move from Salamis and Malta to Besika Bay, could not have reached St. Petersburgh before the 17th of June, whereas the circular issued by the Emperor Nicholas an

* Appendix X. † Appendix XI. ‡ Appendix XII.

nouncing his intention of invading the Principalities, bore date the 11th of June.

It might also have been added that the proclamation of Prince Gortschakoff to the inhabitants of the Danubian provinces, was issued on the borders of Moldavia on the very same day—the 2nd of July—as Count Nesselrode's circular in St. Petersburgh; and as the fleets only reached Besika Bay seventeen days previously, it was absolutely impossible that this movement could have been known at St. Petersburgh, when instructions were given to Prince Gortschakoff for his proclamation, and orders to march were issued.

On the 24th of July a grand council of the Ottoman Empire was held, at which the Grand Vizír presided; when it was resolved to send the draft of a fresh note to St. Petersburgh, proposing, in the most conciliatory terms, to guarantee to the Greek Church all the privileges that were compatible with the sovereign rights of the Porte, and offering to send an ambassador to St. Petersburgh to enter into negotiations for this purpose.

But on the following morning, before this note could be despatched, a courier from the Prince of Moldavia brought copies of the orders issued to him by the Russian government.* In one of these Count Nesselrode thus addresses that Hospodar:—"There remains, however, still one point on which we must acquaint the two Hospodars with our opinion for their guidance.

* Appendix XIII.

"We refer to their relations with Constantinople and the Ottoman ministry. These relations must cease on the day that our troops take military possession of the Principalities; on which, consequently, all influence and all measures of the sovereign power must remain temporarily suspended."*

It is worthy of remark that this letter was addressed to the Russian Consul General, at Bucharest, for his guidance on the 15th of June, and thus expressly violated the public declaration subsequently made to the inhabitants of Wallachia and Moldavia, by Prince Gortschakoff, "that there was no intention of modifying the political position guaranteed to them by solemn treaties."

It was also proclaimed on this occasion, in the name of his Imperial Majesty, that the presence of his troops would not impose any charge or contribution on the people of the Principalities, who were to be paid for all provisions furnished to the army, agreeably to a scale to be settled by the Russian and Wallachian authorities.† The Porte, however, learned from the Hospodar, that while appearing to fulfil this part of their engagement, the Russians subjected the people of both provinces to the most refined oppression.

The price of flour, &c. was fixed by them at the low rate of an abundant harvest, and no increase of price allowed when food became scarce and dear. In addition to this indirect exaction, the unfortunate inhabitants were

* Appendix XIII., enclosure 2.

† Appendix XIII, enclosure 1.

exposed to another, by being called upon to pay the interest on the expenses of the previous occupation of their country by the Russian army from 1848 to 1850.

The supposed ill-will of the Wallachians and Moldavians towards the Turks, was made the ground of interference by Russia; but the rising of some of the people to oppose their invaders, and the flight of others to escape from them, are, perhaps, a sufficiently conclusive answer to this statement. Had any doubts still existed as to the real nature of the Russian occupation of these provinces, they were put an end to a little later, on the 30th of October, by Prince Gortschakoff's taking possession of the public funds, and nominating General Budberg governor of the Principalities.

The intelligence received from the Hospodars of Moldavia led to a letter being prepared by Reschid Pasha, on the 25th of July, ordering them to quit that territory. This, however, was not sent; but an explanatory manifesto was issued on the 27th, addressed to the Turkish people, and signed by the Grand Vizír, the Sheikh-ul-Islam, and sixty other dignitaries of the empire. In this document, the whole question was ably, and, it may be added, conclusively discussed.

Commencing with the warlike preparations of Russia by land and sea, it passed in review the various demands of that power; more particularly the question of making the spiritual privileges of the Greek Church, and those of its monks, the subjects of a special treaty between the two powers. It stated, in reply to this, that the present Sultan had recently confirmed the various privileges granted by his predecessors, and that he was ready to give assurances to *the whole world*, that this spontaneous act should neither be restricted nor withdrawn. But, it added, His Majesty never would consent to the exercise by a foreign power of the right of interference with the religious privileges granted to millions of his subjects. Yet, it continued, Russia had violated existing treaties, by seizing the Principalities as a material guarantee until this demand should be complied with.

The document then went on to say, that as the Sultan never could agree to sacrifice his sovereign and independent rights, "he had determined, while waiting to see what phase the question would take, and with a view to provide for his own safety by precautionary measures, to assume an armed attitude on the Danube and on the Asiatic frontiers; without, however, in any way discontinuing to follow up the course of negotiation."*

While Russia had thus been pursuing her object of establishing an indirect authority over the subjects of the Sultan, both by diplomacy and by extensive armaments, the hope entertained by others of averting the calamities of war, which had never been quite abandoned, seemed now on the point of being realized.

* Appendix XIV.

On the 10th of August, a fortnight after the publication of the Sultan's manifesto, an extraordinary courier reached Constantinople, bringing the Vienna project for settling the differences between Russia and the Porte. This note emanated from the Austrian ambassador; and being so worded as to secure indirectly the objects of Russia, it was readily accepted by that power. The Sultan's acceptance was now, therefore, all that was necessary to terminate the long-pending negotiations.

Experience of the past had taught the Porte to give this document, as well as the autograph letter of the Emperor of Austria which accompanied it, most careful consideration.* The Divan perceived that it would give Russia undue authority in Turkey, which would be detrimental to the sovereign rights of the Sultan, and at once declined to accept the proposition, unless with one or two modifications; the reasonableness of which will be seen by comparing the proposed changes with the original note.

Paragraph 3, of the Vienna note: " Si, à toute époque, les souverains de Russie ont témoigné leur active sollicitude pour le maintien des immunités et privilèges de l'Eglise orthodoxe grecque dans l'empire Ottoman, les Sultans ne se sont jamais refusés à les consacrer de nouveau par des actes solennels qui attestaient de leur ancienne et constante bienveillance à l'égard de leurs sujets chré-

* Appendix XV.

tiens. . . . . . . Le soussigné a reçu d'ordre, en conséquence, de déclarer par la présente que sa Majesté le Sultan restera fidèle à la lettre et à l'esprit des stipulations du traité de Kainardji et d'Adrianople, relativement à la protection du culte chrétien, et que sa Majesté regarde comme étant de son honneur de faire observer à tout jamais et de préserver de toute atteinte, soit presentément, soit dans l'avenir, la jouissance des privilèges spirituels qui ont été accordés par les augustes aïeux de sa Majesté à l'Eglise orthodoxe d'Orient, et qui sont maintenus et confirmés par Elle, et, en outre, à faire participer, dans un esprit de haute équité, le rit grec aux avantages concédés aux autres rits chrétiens par conventions ou dispositions particulières."

The corresponding passages in the amended note ran thus:—"Si à toute époque les souverains de Russie ont témoigné de leur active sollicitude pour le culte de l'Eglise orthodoxe grecque, les Sultans n'ont jamais cessé de veiller au maintien des immunités et privilèges de ce culte et de cette Eglise dans l'empire ottoman et de les consacrer de nouveau par des actes solennels, qui attestent," etc., etc. . . . . . and . . . "que sa Majesté le Sultan restera fidèle aux stipulations du traité de Kaïnardji confirmé par celui d'Adrianople, relatives à la protection du culte chrétien, et de faire connaître que sa Majesté regard comme étant de son honneur," etc., etc. . . . . and again, "à faire participer dans un esprit de haute équité, le rit grec aux avantages accordés ou qui seraient accordés aux autres communautés sujettes ottomanes."

The cabinet of St. Petersburgh, as might have been expected, rejected the modifications of the Porte, and the explanations offered by Count Nesselrode for so doing, showed that the object of Russia for the last six months had been to establish a religious and political protectorate over about twelve millions of the Sultan's subjects.

Before the publication of this note the conduct of the Porte in making difficulties had been loudly blamed, and although there was a change in this respect after the Russian explanation appeared, the ambassadors at Constantinople still pressed the Porte to accept the note "pur et simple."

It was under these circumstances that the grand council of the Turkish nation was assembled, and that after deliberating for two days, it was determined to persist in the modifications proposed by the Porte. This, however, was not its only resolution. It had become absolutely necessary to take some steps to calm the excited feelings of the people, who had come forward as one man with their persons and their means to oppose the aggressions of Russia; and who were beginning to apprehend that their Government, as well as its allies, were about to sacrifice their honour and their interests for the sake of peace with Russia.

At the close of this remarkable meeting, therefore, the

Sheikh-ul-Islam issued a fetva (sacred ordinance), legalizing its decision as sacred and irrevocable: this decision declared war against Russia. But in resolving upon this necessary step, it was determined, in the faint hope of still preserving peace, to make hostilities conditional. The General-in-Chief, Omar Pasha, was commanded to make known to Prince Gortschakoff that the Turkish army would commence hostilities in the course of fifteen days, unless the Principalities were evacuated in the mean time. To this letter the Prince returned an evasive answer, and the Pasha, perceiving the inevitable result of the truce, immediately began to collect boats, so as to be able to cross the Danube on the day of its expiration.

War is an evil so much to be dreaded, that the statesmen of Europe are entitled to the greatest respect, and even gratitude, for their continued efforts to avert this calamity; which must fall the heavier on Europe in consequence of the prosperity which has been the result of thirty-six years of peace.

These considerations deserved every possible weight. But they should not have been carried to the extent of overlooking the past aggressions and well-known policy of Russia with regard to Turkey; nor the fact that her extensive armaments must have had a more important object than the adjustment of a monkish dispute. It may, therefore, be asked whether a serious mistake has not been made by appearing to put faith in the peace protestations of Russia, and allowing her to pass the Pruth without considering this as an act of war. Had negotiation, as she asserted, been her only object, it could have been carried on quite as well from the northern as from the southern side of that river.

Had Turkey determined, or rather, had she been allowed by her allies to take her stand alone, it is obvious that on the promulgation of Count Nesselrode's letter of the 31st of May, her troops would have hastened to meet the invaders on or near the banks of the Pruth. If forced to retire from this position, and even if obliged ultimately to abandon the defence of the Principalities, the Sultan's forces would, in *the worst case,* have been able to prevent the enemy from taking advantage of their resources, and gaining, as he has been allowed to do, the left bank of the Danube without firing a shot.

But this would not have been the case. Judging from what Turkey was able to do during the campaigns we have described, when unanimity of purpose and military organization were wanting, we can scarcely doubt what would have been the result now, had she been allowed to meet her invaders on the Pruth, with her fine army, her well-appointed artillery, and, above all, with the unanimous and ardent spirit of her people.

The advantage arising from the uncontested possession of the Principalities, was not the only advantage gained by Russia by the postponement of hostilities. In addition to the inactivity which had been recommended to the Ottoman fleet, the revenue and finances of Turkey suffered to an alarming extent by this delay; which could also scarcely fail to damp the almost unparalleled enthusiasm of the Turkish people.

The natural impatience of those who had come from the most distant parts of the empire to repel an unjust aggression on their country, obliged the Porte at length to take the initiative, in order to appease the growing, and even alarming discontent which prevailed among them.

CHAPTER XI.

ON THE PRESENT RESISTANCE OF TURKEY TO RUSSIA, AND THE MEANS OF DEFENDING THE EMPIRE.

Turkish and Russian forces at the commencement of hostilities—Affair of the Russian flotilla—Omar Pasha crosses the Danube—Battle of Oltenitza—Avowed peaceable intentions of the Emperor Nicholas—Destruction of the Turkish flotilla at Sinope—Predicted fall of Turkey—Commerce of Turkey—Her importance to Europe—Possible invasion of India—Disadvantage caused to Turkey by delaying hostilities—Commerce of Odessa—Attacks of fortresses by fleets—Supposed movement against Sebastopol—State of Turkey in 1828—Russian fleet and army—Turkish fleet and army—Kurds and other irregulars—Supposed coup-de-main march towards Constantinople—Proposals for defending Turkey—Supposed marches of the invaders, and their probable Results.

When the well-known patience of the Turkish people had been so completely exhausted that the Porte was constrained to declare war against Russia, the most advanced troops belonging to each of these powers were separated from each other by the river Danube.

The Turkish force in the field at this period, which occupied various posts in Bulgaria, under the Seraskier Omar Pasha, was called 100,000 men, but in reality scarcely exceeded 70,000 Prince Gortschakoff's troops, which amounted to about 79,800 men, before sickness thinned their ranks, were stationed at different places in Moldavia and Wallachia.

On the 23rd of October hostilities were commenced, by two Russian steamers with eight gun-boats attempting to force the passage of the Danube. On this occasion, the Russians had a lieutenant-colonel and twelve sailors killed, and fifty-nine men wounded, by the fire of the fort of Isaktchi.

A glance at the map will show that Omar Pasha's position in Bulgaria partly out-flanked that of the enemy, by the bend of the Danube above Widden, and again still more completely by its northerly sweep at the Dobrudscha. The Turkish commander, therefore, might either have broken through the Russian line by a central movement towards Bucharest; or, by crossing the Danube at one or other of the preceding points, he could have turned either of Prince Gortschakoff's flanks, and thus have obliged him to change front, and concentrate with all speed to meet an attack.

The centre and left appear to have been the choice of the Pasha, and he effected the passage of the river at three points—in the vicinity of Giurgevo, at Khalafat, and again at Turtukai. Several attacks made by the first corps, failed against the strong *tête-de-pont* of Giurgevo, but Khalafat and Turtukai were occupied by the Turks on the 2nd, 3rd, and 4th of November.

This most brilliant operation will be best described in the modest language of Omar Pasha's bulletin; which has been confirmed from several sources, including even the Russian: all agreeing substantially with this account of their defeat.

"The possession of the island situate in front of Turtukai having been considered indispensable, I had effected the passage of troops, and in the space of the night of the 1st managed to raise tolerably strong fortifications. On the following day, the 2nd, two battalions of infantry, three pieces of cannon, and a hundred of the mounted police, were conveyed in large boats to the locality, with ammunition, provisions and great coats.

"They had scarcely landed, when from the batteries of Turtukai we opened a fire on the lazaretto situate on the left bank. After the first discharge, the Russians quitted this position, and the imperial troops took possession of the building, which is of solid construction, with vaulted chambers. Without loss of time 400 workmen, under the direction of staff officers, commenced raising fortifications, for which purpose 2,000 gabions had been already prepared. On the 3rd, again, other troops were sent to fortify the *tête de pont.*

"As soon as the imperial troops had landed on the left bank of the river, the Russians, quartered in a large village at about an hour's distance, turned round, and began to retreat. A body of cavalry was despatched to reconnoitre, and, having encountered at Oltenitza an outpost of Cossack cavalry, they killed five, and rejoined our lines with a loss of three men. We found at Touzla, on the left bank, a great number of boats, which were sent to Turtukai.

"The number of boats at our disposal having facilitated the construction of the bridge, we were enabled without delay to place in the fortifications twelve large guns, which were brought from Schumla.

"On the 3rd, at 4 P. M., three battalions of Russian infantry, with eight cannons, a regiment of cavalry, and a party of Cossacks, entered the village of Oltenitza. Our troops, posted within the works constructed on the left bank, awaited them with firmness. This same night I caused a bridge to be constructed at the conflux of the Argisch and Danube, and flanked it with redoubts.

"Yesterday, Nov. 4, at 6 A. M., we began to perceive the movement of the Russian forces. As soon as their march was well defined, I caused a reinforcement of one battalion to be embarked and conveyed to the lazaretto. The evening before I had placed on even ground a battery of guns calculated to check any attack which might be made. The Russian forces amounted to twenty battalions, three regiments of cavalry, one of Cossacks, sixteen mounted batteries, and sixteen on foot. They formed in order of battle, with fourteen pieces of cannon in the rear of twelve battalions, and the regiment of Cossacks in lines beyond the reach of our guns, and fronting the centre of our works. They advanced, supported by the fire of their artillery, and at the same time two battalions, with two cannons, came on, threatening our left flank. Having commenced the assault, another stronger division—consisting of six battalions, with four cannons, and having in the rear three regiments of cavalry supporting and outstripping their left flank—took its position and formed in two lines, with artillery, horse, and foot, in *echelon*, attacking our right flank. After an exchange of some cannon shots, the centre gave the assault, whereon they charged both our wings. The centre attacked three different times, and each with a fresh battalion,—twice on the left, and once on the right.

"A well-directed fire from our fortress at Turtukai soon dispersed their right column, and the centre gradually fell back, after having suffered severely, and half its numbers being disabled. The battery of the island, also mounted with powerful guns, and commanded by Khalid Pasha, did admirable execution on the enemy's right wing. The Russians advanced with coolness and resolution almost to the brink of the trench, and on this account their loss was considerable, amounting to a thousand men killed and double the number wounded.

"The engagement lasted four hours, from noon till 4 P. M. During this interval the wagons never ceased carrying off their dead, and twenty were observed heavily laden even after the conflict. With a view of facilitating this duty, as long as it lasted, we abstained from molesting the enemy and from firing a single shot, but found, nevertheless, 800 bodies on the field. A private carriage, moreover, was remarked; and, from the pains taken in the search, we conjecture it must have been destined to receive the body of a general officer.

"At 5 P. M., a total confusion ensued in the Russian ranks; their lines were completely broken and their retreat was precipitate. An hour later some few rallied in the neighbouring villages, but the remainder fled in disorder. Some of our men pushed forward in pursuit of them beyond the lines, but were summoned back by trumpet to their own quarters.

"Our loss amounted to 106 men. We found on the field of battle 500 muskets, *sacs*, cartridge boxes, equipments, &c.

"OMAR."

The bravery of the Turks was very conspicuous on this occasion, and the Minié rifle, used with the coolness and steady aim of the Muslims, did great execution.

Omar Pasha continued to occupy Oltenitza, notwithstanding the increased Russian force in his front, until the continued rains, &c. so flooded the country as to oblige him to quit the low tract occupied by his troops. He recrossed the river, therefore, without any kind of molestation, leaving about 15,000 men in the *tête-de-pont* of Khalafat; to which strong intrenchments have been recently added, armed with guns of heavy calibre, for the more effectual protection of this passage into Lower Wallachia.

In commencing hostilities for the recovery of the Turkish territory, the Porte has shown no desire to interfere with commercial transactions. Fifteen days were allowed for Russian vessels to quit the ports of Turkey; and when asked what should be done with those vessels which did not comply with this requisition, the following was its dignified and considerate reply:—

"The Sublime Porte knows too well how the Russian authorities in Moldavia and Wallachia have molested and vexed the Ottoman merchants and ships by ordering them to quit the Principalities in forty-eight hours; nevertheless, the Imperial Government, reflecting that the present war is carried on only between the two Governments, and that commerce ought not to suffer from it, will never depart from the system of moderation which it has adopted; and it will be always disposed to accord to Russian vessels all possible facilities which do not occasion prejudice to the rights and interests of its own subjects. In conformity with those principles, and in virtue of an Imperial decree, the Ottoman authorities have been ordered, not only to afford to Russian merchant ships which from good cause may prolong their stay in a Turkish port all the time that may be necessary for them, but also, in case when Russian ships, passing from an Ottoman port to the Black Sea, or the Mediterranean, may be constrained, not by commercial causes, but by contrary winds, to take shelter in any other Turkish port, to receive them amicably until the weather changes; and also to afford them every assistance of which they may be in need. As relates to the commerce with Europe, the Imperial Government will never permit any impediment to be offered to it, considering that, in consequence of the scarcity of corn, now so severely felt, every facility should be afforded to it. Considering, moreover, that Russian ships about to carry grain to the Black Sea, or to the Mediterranean, are at this moment either laden or not yet so, and on account of the short distance they have yet to go, a very long term is not necessary to them, they shall have granted to them a further term of forty-five days, during which they shall be enable to effect, without any obstacle, the entry of the Bosphorus on coming into the Black Sea, and going out of the Dardanelles.

"Lastly, as regards Russian merchant ships which are on the coast of Europe or of Africa, or on the ocean with cargoes belonging to merchants of friendly countries, we believe that a term of three months will be sufficient for them to return by the Dardanelles into the Black Sea; and instructions to this effect have been sent to the officers commanding the two Straits. Orders have in like manner been given to the officers in command of ships of war not by any means to molest during that period the merchant ships under other flags.

"The Sublime Porte does not doubt that the foregoing is conformable to the desire expressed by your Excellency, as also to the interest of those above mentioned.—

"I have the honour, &c.,

"REDSCHID."

The Emperor Nicholas, although invading the territories of the Sultan, declared that he was not at war with Turkey. Therefore, so far as words go, he appeared equally anxious with the other powers to avoid unnecessary hostilities. We learn from the recent statement of M. Drouyn de L'Huys that it was announced to the Emperor of the French, through his Ambassador, General Castelbajac, that the Court of St. Petersburg had intimated its intention "*to abstain from taking the offensive anywhere* in the contest so unhappily begun in Turkey."* Most unfortunately, this assurance—or rather what, under such circumstances, was a positive engagement—was unscrupulously set at nought both on sea and land.

If the commencement of hostilities by the Russian flotilla on the 23rd of October be passed over as a trifling affair; and supposing it to be admitted that the subsequent passage of the Danube by Omar Pasha might excuse the repeated attacks made on his position at Oltenitza, instead of the Russians remaining on the defensive as had been the professed intention of the Emperor Nicholas;—admitting all this, what redeeming point can be found in

* Appendix XVI.

justification of that Navarino of the Euxine, the carefully planned and gratuitous attack on the Turkish ships in the harbour of Sinope?

A powerful Turkish fleet of line-of-battle ships had recently returned to the Bosphorus, in order, as it would seem, to avoid any collision that might mar the hope of peace: a squadron only, consisting of seven frigates, three corvettes, and two steamers, being left at Sinope. Some accounts state that part of this flotilla had been employed in conveying stores, &c., to the Circassians, consequently, in a service hostile to Russia. Whether this were so or not is but of little importance, since it is clear that the ships were quietly anchored at Sinope, where they had been for some little time.

Admiral Nachimoff, who was cruising off that port with three line-of-battle ships and six frigates, despatched a steamer to Sebastopol for reinforcements. On the arrival of three additional line-of-battle ships, on the 27th of November, the Russian fleet, consisting of six line-of-battle ships, two frigates, and four steam-frigates, entered the harbour of Sinope on the 30th, under cover of the fog and rain, and anchored within 500 yards of the Turkish frigates, which were lying promiscuously, close to the shore, quite unprepared for hostilities.

The action was commenced by the Turks; and their fire, designated by Admiral Nachimoff as "terrible," began about 10 A. M. But the Paixhans, or shell guns, of the three-deckers caused fearful destruction among the

Turkish squadron. At 2 P.M., the relentless massacre of an unequal contest had pretty well terminated; for it appears that, after that hour, the guns of the Russian fleet were turned upon the unhappy town, the principal part of which they reduced to ashes.

The Turks fought with the utmost bravery; and in some instances, set fire to their own vessels in order that they might be blown up rather than fall into the enemy's hands. The result was that two frigates blew up during the battle, five were burnt by the enemy the next day, one steamer escaped, and another was driven ashore. One frigate was taken out of the harbour, but she went down before reaching Sebastopol.

Admiral Nachimoff, in his letter to the Austrian Consul, deplores the necessity he was under of firing shells into the town and harbour. He "*sympathizes* with the sad fate of the town and of the inoffensive inhabitants," and concludes this extraordinary explanation by saying, "that the imperial squadron had no hostile intentions either against the town or port of Sinope."

Prince Menschikoff hastened to inform his imperial master that his orders had been "brilliantly executed by the fleet of the Black Sea," and the *victory* of Sinope was celebrated at St. Petersburg by a Te Deum, and every possible demonstration of joy.

In the days of chivalry, the wholesale destruction of a squadron of frigates by a fleet of line-of-battle ships would *not* have been considered a victory, even at St. Petersburgh : and if the utilitarian spirit of the present age had been less preponderating than it is, the Ottoman Empire would not have been so long left to struggle alone, as she was in 1828, and as she has been also in 1853.

For nearly two centuries the fall of Turkey has been constantly predicted; and, in addition to numerous schemes for partitioning the country, a good deal has been done of late to effect the fulfilment of this prophecy, by separating Servia, Greece, the Principalities, and, to a certain extent, Egypt also, from the Ottoman Empire. Yet she still exists ; and we have been told by a statesman who is no mean authority in this case, that "Turkey has made greater progress and improvement during the last thirty years than any other country."*

Such a spirit of advancement as that here alluded to deserves to be fostered. But hitherto, time has never been granted to Turkey to perfect any of her reforms. The various improvements introduced by Sultan Mahmoud, in the departments of justice, of finance, and in the organization of the army, were checked in their very commencement by the Russian invasions in 1828 and 1829. And scarcely has the country rallied from the exhausting effects of those campaigns, than a fresh attack from Russia puts a stop to the Tanzimat and all that Abdel-

* Speech of Lord Palmerston in the House of Commons, 16th August, 1853.

Meschid was doing to consolidate and carry out the wishes of his father.

The integrity of Turkey, however, claims support on other and yet stronger grounds than those of her advancement, which deeply interest almost every civilized nation.

The fall of Turkey would not only cause a disruption of the balance of power, but would also be attended with the fatal consequence of putting an end to the ordinary European commerce in that part of the world. The possession of Constantinople by Russia, would, as a matter of course, be followed by that of both shores of the Euxine, together with the eastern portion of the Mediterranean, including Greece. In fact, both European and Asiatic Turkey, with the adjoining territories of Syria, Mesopotamia, and Egypt, as well as the commerce by land of those countries, must of necessity belong to the masters of Constantinople.

Therefore, if under these circumstances a consolidated peace, such as we have just supposed, were at length to succeed an aggressive war which might cause the Ottoman territories, as such, to disappear from the map of the world, the mercantile advantages at present enjoyed under the most favourable terms by European nations, would be almost entirely lost.

Some of our travellers have misled us a good deal by representing Turkey to be in a state of hopeless decay, whilst others from a neighboring nation, taking nearly the same view, have made a similar mistake. One French traveller complacently tells us that the Ottoman Empire is nothing but a "cadavre;" and another delights in saying, that the Turks are only "campés en Europe." Their encampment, however, has been a tolerably lengthened one; and let us hope, for the sake of Europe in general, that it may continue permanent, and that time and opportunity may thus be given for the increase of those benefits which Turkey, in her steadily advancing course, is conferring upon Europe.

The trade of Turkey, exclusive of Prussia, which has been overlooked, shows:

	Value of Imports in Turkish Piastres.	Value of Exports in Turkish Piastres.
Great Britain, Malta, and the Ionian Islands,	252,300,000	130,500,000
Transit to Persia,	217,500,000	217,500,000
France,	108,702,150	229,971,450
Austria,	113,765,550	185,310,000
Russia,	97,266,000	74,263,200
Holland,	26,434,950	9,017,550
Belgium,	4,650,150	2,079,300
Sardinia,	3,658,350	10,426,950
Greece,	1,740,000	18,705,000
Persia (direct trade),	108,750,000	6,525,000
Switzerland, U. States, &c.,	91,832,850	59,651,550
Egypt and Servia,	99,445,350	61,826,550
Moldavia and Wallachia,	56,761,500	37,845,000
Total in Turkish* Piastres,	1,182,330,000	1,064,445,000

Total in sterling money:—imports, 11,823,300*l.*; ex-

* The Ottoman Empire and its Resources, &c., by Edward U. Michelson, Phil. D., pp. 191, 192: Simpkin, Marshall & Co., London.

ports, 10,644,450*l.* Another author* makes the proceeds rather less, stating them at 11,390,833*l.* imports, and 9,402,500*l.* exports. But neither of these statements appears to include the indirect trade with Turkey; such as that from the three presidencies of India to the Persian and Arabian Gulfs, and also through the fairs of Leipsic, and other places in Germany. From some data in his possession, the author feels justified in estimating this additional trade at quite Two Millions each way, thus giving about 26,467,750*l.* for the trade of Turkey.

This being the case, it is evident that Europe at large is deeply interested in maintaining existing relations; and it may be asked whether any power that might or could replace Turkey, would give the same commercial advantages to all countries as she has hitherto done.

But passing from general to individual considerations, we shall find that the integrity of the Ottoman Empire is of the last importance to the three great powers, Austria, France, and Great Britain.

Were Bosnia, Wallachia, and Bulgaria to be severed from the Sultan's territories, the independence of Austria would necessarily be compromised; since the main outlet of the Danube would then be completely under the control of another power, by whom she would be outflanked, and *might be* cut off politically as well as commercially

* Letters sur la Turquie, &c., par M. A. Ubicini, première partie, les Ottomans, pp. 400, 401: Paris, 1853.

from her exterior relations: which, with Turkey alone, give her commercial transactions of 2,990,955*l.* sterling.

The exports of France, in cotton goods, woollens, sugar, paper, glass-ware, and fancy goods, with the imports in raw silk, linseed, sesamum, wool, goat's-hair, oil, tobacco, and gallnuts, amount to 3,386,736*l.* This would all be lost, if her vessels were to be excluded from the Black Sea and the commerce of the Levant in general; which must be the case if Constantinople were to become Muscovite. Alexandria, Syria, Asia Minor, and Greece, would naturally follow, and even Africa would suffer from such a change.

In the case of Great Britain, taking a lower estimate than that of Ubicini—

The direct exports to Turkey, according to the *Bankers' Circular*, were, in 1850, ...	£3,113,679
From Bengal to the Persian and Arabian gulfs, . . .	178,582*
From Madras do do . . .	117,407*
From Bombay do do . . .	525,705*
From England to Syria, ...	72,616
Indirect English trade through Leipsic and the rest of Germany, ...	700,000
Total, independently of Egypt and Barbary, ...	£4,707,989

Whereas, it appears from the *Bankers' Circular*, that the exports to Russia in 1850 were only £1,454,771.

But, beyond the value of this amount of trade, Turkey is the keystone of one great branch of our commercial prosperity. Her maintenance as a nation and an inde-

* From official returns given in the Expedition to the Euphrates and Tigris by the author, vol. ii. pp. 677, 683.

pendent power, is, on political as well as on commercial grounds, of momentous importance to Great Britain.

Since the Ottoman Empire in its fall would carry with it its Syrian and Egyptian dependencies, England, in case of such an event, must be content with an inferior place among nations. The overland communications with India, which only the other day were but an occasional luxury, must be sacrificed at a moment when they have become an ordinary part of the wants of almost every family. And, in addition to the chance of seeing another formidable maritime power in the waters of the Mediterranean, probably preparing to dispute the empire of the seas elsewhere also, the possibility of an invasion of India must cause uneasiness with regard to the safety of our Eastern possessions, independently of the expense which must be the consequence of such a threat.

It is not necessary to dwell upon the three lines by which British India may be approached—that through Arabia, through central Asia, and by way of Persia. In a former work the author had occasion to notice these lines of march, in connection with the projects of Napoleon for the invasion of India.* In each case, however, very serious difficulties would have to be overcome. But on the other hand, it should be remembered, that the fascinating prospect of the spoils of Indian wealth would be sufficiently attractive to smooth even still greater difficulties than

* Expedition to the Euphrates and Tigris, vol. ii. pp. 536, 537.

those in question; and would also secure the invader enthusiastic support and assistance throughout his lengthened march. It is only sixteen years since a Persian army, provided with an ample battering-train, marched a distance of about 1,260 miles from Tabriz to Herat; and during the seige of the latter place, which continued from the 22nd of November, 1837, to the 9th of September, 1838, bread continued to be as cheap as in the market of the city they had left.*

The author conceives there can be but little doubt entertained of the possibility of invading India; and it is his belief that, in the event of a general war, the attempt will be made. In such a case he ventures to affirm, that it is on the bravery of our troops, rather than on the difficulties of the march to India, that we must rely for the security of our possessions.

The central position of Turkey as a non-aggressive power, serves England, therefore, as a barrier towards India, protects the interests of France in the Black Sea as well as in the Mediterranean, and is necessary to the very existence of Austria.

But these considerations, even when coupled with the commercial advantages depending on Turkey, should weigh as nothing in comparison with the great principles of justice. These apply as closely to nations as to individuals, and a departure from them seldom fails to bring

* Ibid, vol. i. p. 165.

its retribution. Since, then, it is almost universally admitted that an unprovoked and unjustifiable aggression has been committed by Russia against Turkey, is it not incumbent on the four great western powers heartily to espouse the cause of their suffering ally? If the voice of Europe were to be thus raised on the broad grounds of right and justice, a consolidated peace, with security to Turkey for the future, must be the consequence of this determination; and it is to be hoped that indemnification for the late heavy expenditure, to which her exchequer and her people have been so unjustly subjected during the last twelve months, would form a part of all stipulations for her future welfare.

The same result for Turkey may be looked for, although probably not without a serious struggle, should France and England alone take the initiative without the conjunction of the other two allied powers. This, in fact, has now become doubly a duty on their part. For if it be true, as it is stated, that England and France prevented Turkey from declaring war against Russia at the time the Czar announced his intention of invading the Principalities, the most favourable moment for Turkey was thereby lost. Indeed, judging by the progress of the contest, both in Europe and Asia, notwithstanding the disadvantageous circumstances under which it has been commenced by the Turks, we are surely warranted in assuming that still greater success would have attended the Sultan's arms, had operations been commenced on the Pruth in the month of June, instead of on the southern bank of the Danube on the 28th of October. It is now well known that at the former period the Russian army was only beginning to prepare for the intended invasion, but even had it been otherwise, Turkey would have been spared a heavy expense, as well as the general derangement of the agricultural and commercial relations of the empire; in addition to the acknowledged difficulty of keeping irregular troops for a lengthened period in the field.

But it is to the existing state of things, rather than to the past, that our attention should now be directed. Let it not, however, be forgotten by France or England that the present must not be regarded in the light of an isolated attack upon Turkey; it is another step in advancing that hereditary and encroaching policy of Russia, which has been the cause of all her aggressions against the Ottoman Empire since the time of Peter the Great. In this case, the fruits of Russian intrigue have been visible in the court of Persia; and, if the author be not mistaken, in the efforts also to close the Sound against the combined fleets: all showing that preparations have long been making for the present position of the Russian troops in Turkey.

The English and French fleets have at length entered the Euxine, to give, as it is understood, material support to the Sultan. If, therefore, hostilities should commence, the combined fleets, or even only one of them, will be quite sufficient to clear the waters of the Black Sea of every Russian vessel that floats; causing her ships to remain inactive in the ports of Taganrog, Sebastopol, and Odessa.

Some idea of the injury which would thus be occasioned to Russian commerce may be formed by a statement of the trade of one of these ports.

The total amount of the foreign trade of Odessa last year was 34,605,076 silver roubles: viz., exports, 24,777,-717 silver roubles; imports, 9,827,359 silver roubles. The principal production of the country is corn, and wheat was exported to the amount of 14,066,031 roubles; rye, 1,884,179 roubles; barley, 212,059 roubles; maize, 1,594,-324 roubles; flour and meal, 150,808 roubles. Among the other items are,—linseed, 1,644,302 roubles; wool, 4,268,-144 roubles; tallow, 439,732 roubles; cordage, 126,002 roubles.

A simple blockade would have the effect of placing the trade of this and other Russian ports in abeyance, without resorting to any hostile attack on Sebastopol, or elsewhere.

It is the author's belief that Sebastopol would be safe against the action of the combined fleets. No doubt the hitherto unequalled efficiency of a steam fleet, with its present armament, would effect all that can be accomplished by skill and bravery; but the result of attacking a well defended fortress with a fleet, remains, as yet, a problem for the future.

It is true that three remarkable instances have occurred in modern times, which may seem to favour the superiority of ships over stone walls. These are Copenhagen, Algiers, and Acre. In the first case, it is understood that Nelson was only relieved from a critical position by sending a letter on shore, which caused the batteries of Copenhagen to cease firing against the fleet.

In the second instance, the attack on Algiers was made during a state of peace. We know that after our fleet had entered the harbour, not in line of battle, but almost ship by ship—and consequently, greatly exposed to the fire of the garrison—the *Queen Charlotte*, by the advice of an engineer officer, Sir William Reid, K.C.B., now the distinguished Governor of Malta, was placed with her broadside on the flank of the grand or mole battery. The rest of the fleet had also taken up advantageous positions without a shot being fired by the garrison, until Lord Exmouth waved his hat, as the signal for the fleet to open its fire simultaneously.

In the third case, that of Acre, the fleet was also allowed to take up positions which had been previously arranged, without any opposition. Buoys had even been placed beforehand, and what had been a state of peace up to that moment, was only broken by the opening of a terrific fire of shells and shot, when everything was ready: at least on our side.

It is not, however, to be expected, that the defenders of

Sebastopol would be equally tardy in opening a fire of shells and hot shot on their assailants, and testing, with these terrific missiles, the relative strength of stone against "wooden walls." But we are here treading on difficult ground. Therefore, while expressing a hope that the attack of Sebastopol, if it should take place, will be with an adequate force by land, rather than by a *coup-de-main* attack by sea, let us give due weight to the remarkable words of the late Duke of Wellington, when speaking of our success against Acre. His Grace, after expressing his cordial approbation of the services performed by the navy in the Mediterranean, and of those who were engaged in this glorious expedition, goes on to say:—"He had a little experience in services of this nature, *and he thought it his duty to warn their lordships, on this occasion, that they must not always expect that ships, however well commanded, or gallant their seamen might be, were capable of commonly engaging successfully with stone walls.* He had no recollection, in all his experience, except the recent instance on the coast of Syria, of any fort being taken by ships; excepting two or three years ago, when the Fort of St. Juan D'Ulloa was captured by the French fleet."

* * * * * *

"He would repeat, that this was a singular instance, in the achievement of which great skill was undoubtedly manifested; but which was also connected with peculiar circumstances, which they could not hope always to occur.

It must not, therefore, be expected as a matter of course, that all such attempts in future must necessarily succeed.*

The recent chequered success of the desultory warfare of the Turks in Asia, leads to the inference that but little is required to turn the scale in their favour. A comparatively small European force landed in the Crimea would produce a rising of the people of that country in favour of their ancient masters, the Turks; and trifling assistance to the Caucasians, especially in arms and military stores, would suffice to expel the Russians, who, as it is, can scarcely hold their trans-Caucasian provinces.

The difficulty would scarcely be greater of giving support to Turkey by a force operating on the western side of the Euxine. The principal passages of the Danube are of themselves sufficiently difficult, and could be easily protected by a steam flotilla and gun-boats; while a comparatively small force acting in the rear of the enemy, under the protection of the fleet, must (considering the difficulty attending supplies and transport) render the advance of an invading army utterly impracticable. For the passage of a large body of troops, with artillery and provisions, across the Balkan, would be no easy task of itself, if no opposition whatever were to be offered to their march. Nor would the facility of defending the passes be much changed by the addition of the Austrian forces to

* Hansard's Debates, House of Lords, 4th Feb., 1841, vol. lvi. p. 254.

those of Russia; for it is still as true now as it was in 1739, with regard to a campaign in Turkey, "that a large army would be starved, and a small one destroyed."

Such circumstances have told powerfully in former wars in favour of the Turks, and it is believed that they would be sufficient now to enable them to maintain a defensive warfare successfully.

The following observations on the means which Turkey possesses, in case of the necessity of sustaining a contest with Russia single-handed, are based upon the difficulties she has experienced during her past campaigns, which were carried on under most adverse circumstances. And to show that this was the case, it is only necessary to remind the reader that to the disadvantage of an imperfect organization, which only comprised as yet thirty infantry regiments, was added that worst of all calamities, a divided country. Mahmoud's intended reforms had diminished the confidence, if not completely alienated the affections, of a large portion of the Muslim people. He had become an object of suspicion to one large section, and of latent hostility to another, which was prepared for the horrors of civil war. To this it is believed the Christians had been taught to look as the probable means of removing their infant seat of government from Athens to Constantinople. The encouragement given to the discontented by foreign emissaries, had prepared the way for what might have been a fearful crisis, had less firmness been shown at this trying period. But if the Sultan's presence, and several timely executions, saved the capital from an insurrection, it was effected at the expense, in some degree, of the more energetic defence of the frontiers.

The Nizam had been retained in Constantinople during the early part of the campaign of 1828, with a view to preserve order in the capital. And when a portion was at length sent under Hussein Pasha, the Sultan's purpose of speedily following with the remainder (see p. 73) was frustrated, by the necessity of still keeping some regular troops in the city in order to keep down the malcontents.

If, under such circumstances, Turkey resisted the well-appointed and numerous army of a first-rate power and its successive reinforcements, up to the close of a second protracted campaign in Europe, and caused immense loss to her invaders—whilst a very creditable defence was maintained against Marshal Paskevitch by other levies hastily assembled in Asia—it is surely not too much to expect that, under the greatly improved circumstances which have enabled Turkey to take a respectable army and an enthusiastic people into the field, she will be able to offer a still more successful resistance to the fresh attempt now being made to conquer the country.

Without entering at much length into the question of throwing a force by sea into the Golden Horn, it may be safely assumed that the defences of the Bosphorus are too formidable to be forced by a fleet; and that Constantinople is not liable to be taken in this way by a *coup-de-main*—at least not in war time, at any rate.

The Russian fleet in the Black Sea consists of thirteen ships of the line, in addition to eight frigates, six corvettes, and twelve smaller vessels. These would not afford the means of transporting 30,000 men to the Bosphorus; and even if she had sufficient ships, and if her fleet were to succeed either in passing the batteries of the Bosphorus, or in landing the army near the entrance of the Straits in preference, such a force would be insufficient to take Constantinople, much less to hold it against an excited people.

In endeavouring to accomplish the invasion of Turkey, the Russians must therefore advance from the Principalities, and avail themselves of their command of the Black Sea as a means of lessening their difficulties, by transporting part of the provisions and stores by the fleet.

Russia possesses the most numerous, and, as regards the means of recruiting and equipment, the least expensive army in Europe. It consists of eleven corps: *i. e.*, one of the guards, one of grenadiers, six of the line, two of cavalry, and one of dragoons. These comprise 368 battalions, 460 squadrons of cavalry, 14 squadrons of Hulans, amounting in all to 480,000 men ready for the field, and 996 guns. In time of war this force may be increased by a levy of 213,000 men, and 472 guns. In addition to this, the local reserve would give 385,000 men, 93,000 Cossack cavalry, and 33,000 Cossack infantry, with 224 guns; making a total of 1,214,000 men, and 1,692 guns. Of this prodigious force, however, only 290,000 men, and 800 guns, can be marched to a distance, and kept effective.

Although the bravery and passive endurance of the Russian soldier cannot be surpassed, the army of that nation cannot claim a first-rate place amongst European powers; although the talents of the generals and that of the staff are by no means inferior. Whatever may be the efficacy of a *corps d'armée*, and however perfect it may be with regard to the relative proportions and arrangement of the three arms on taking the field, there exist two defects in the Russian service, which seldom fail ere long to thin the ranks and diminish the effective force with which a campaign may have commenced. These are the medical and commissariat departments; on the efficiency of which so much depends. These two branches are, or rather were, inferior to other parts of the Russian service. Supplies frequently failed in consequence during the last campaigns; and as regards medical care, the writer may state, that in going from the Turkish to the Russian stations in 1829, he found the former free from plague, while the latter were suffering from that calamity.

The high name acquired by the Cossacks elsewhere in Europe, was not, nor is it likely to be, maintained in Turkey, where they were speedily overmatched by the Dellis; and the heavy, massive dragoons, shared the same fate. If the author were to venture to compare the Turks and Russians—and an opinion on this subject is offered with some hesitation—he would give a preference to the Russian infantry, as the principal part of an organized force, over that of the Turks; whilst the cavalry of the latter had, and will probably continue to have, the advantage in the field.

The resistance of Turkey to so large a disposable force as that of Russia, with the additional advantage of being kept complete by drafts from her reserves, would, at the first view, seem to be out of the question; if the nature of the country did not, in a great measure, counterbalance the inferiority of numbers, as well as the want of combined military skill which at present exists in the Turkish forces. A Russian army invading Turkey is necessarily at a great distance from its base of operations, as well as from its supplies and its resources generally. Stores, reinforcements, battering trains, the whole warlike materiel in short, must be brought from the very heart of Russia; and the depôts and magazines thus formed could only be renewed and kept up, at or near the seat of war, by means of unceasing labour, and at a vast expense.

Under such circumstances, difficulties of no ordinary kind must be connected with the invasion of either European or Asiatic Turkey; irrespectively of any opposition to be encountered from the troops which would be assembled for their defence.

According to the Sultan's present organization, three

infantry regiments, two of cavalry, and one of artillery, or about 12,500 men, are placed under a general of division, or Feret. Two of these divisions constitute an Ordou, under a Mushir, or field marshal. Were they completed, the six *corps d'armée* which are in progress of formation, would give 150,000 men; and the Redif, or militia, as many more. At the lowest estimate, the actual effective of both together can scarcely be less than 160,000 men.

Since the time of General Andreossi, the artillery has always received more care from the Turks than the other two arms, and particular attention has been paid to it by the authorities of late years. Its more immediate superintendence has been entrusted to Lieutenant Colonel Von Kuczkowski, who is better known as Mucklis Bei. This officer formerly served in the Prussian army, and he has been employed of late in organizing six regiments of artillery, one for each Ordou.

According to his system, a regiment or park of artillery is composed of twelve batteries, viz., two 12-pounder, and four 8-pounder batteries on foot; two 7-pounder howitzer batteries; three flying or horse artillery batteries armed with light howitzers; and a very light howitzer battery, intended for mountain service. The personnel of a battery consists of one captain, three lieutenants, and six inferior officers, with 109 gunners. In time of peace there are four, and on the war footing six guns. The staff for the twelve batteries of a regiment consist of one Liva, pasha, or major general; two oberston, or colonels; two lieutenant colonels; six majors; and six kotasis, or second majors, with 1,336 non-commissioned officers and gunners. The soldier-like bearing of the men, and their conduct in the field, show that a considerable efficiency has been attained by the artillery service. This is a most important point; and, if the author be not misinformed, the rapid advance made by the Turkish artillery of late, has been fully appreciated in a very high quarter. For when its state was described to the Emperor Nicholas previous to the declaration of war, his Majesty remarked, "This will be a hard nut to crack."

With the addition of the Albanian, Kurdish, and Egyptian contingents, there must be a mixed force of fully 240,000* men to meet the enemy on both sides of the Euxine, irrespectively of their well-served and efficient artillery.

The irregular Turkish troops of the present day might remind us of the followers of Xerxes or Darius; with this difference, that a royal mandate assembled the latter, while the invasion of their country has been sufficient to cause the Albanian, the Kurd, and the Turcoman to leave their

* Ubicini (Lettres sur la Turquie, &c., p. 474) gives a force of:—

The Regular effective army,	148,680 men.
The Regular reserve	148,680 "
Auxiliary contingents	121,000 "
Irregular troops	87,000 "
	505,360 men.

flocks, and the peasant to quit his fields, and after taking down his arms and saddling his horse, to hasten to the frontiers. One may almost imagine the animating picture presented by the flowing dress of the Kurds, mixed with the tartan-like stripes of the Albanians, the projecting turban and ample garments of the Turk of Asia Minor, with his yatagan and huge pistols in front of his person, contrasted with the simple cloak and close fitting kefiyeh of the Arab, with a long spear in his hand. All these tribes were born and have been bred to an irregular military life, tending to foster that sort of pride which induces each to imagine that the success of the coming campaign against the "Father of the Russians," will depend upon his individual exertions in the cause. It must be admitted that, to a certain extent, their personal qualities entitle them to this claim.

A circumstance, related to the author by a Russian officer, may here be mentioned as showing the spirit that actuates this portion of the Sultan's people.

During one of the intervals which occurred between the attacks made during the battle of Kulewtscha, a Turk who was on the opposite side of a ravine, but within musket range of his opponents, deliberately walked along parallel to a Russian battalion, making insulting grimaces. A dropping fire was kept up the whole time, nearly from one end of the line to the other; which, strange to say, failed to bring him down.

Physically, the Turks are a fine race of men, and excellent soldiers. If Turkey should be spared in quiet for a few years, her Redif or Landwehr will have taken the place of the irregular levies just described: as in fact it has already done in part.

We have seen what resistance was offered to the Russian army by an untrained force in 1828 and 1829; not only in the open field, but also in defending towns, as it were, but half fortified. The speed with which defensive works were added during sieges, under the fire of the enemy, and above all the rapidity with which the Turks cover an army with intrenchments, are examples which might be followed by ourselves and other nations with advantage. Nor is this all, for it appears that the first regular approaches against a fortress were introduced by this people.

It is stated in a well-known work, that when the son of the Grand Vizír, who was entrusted with the siege of Candia, found himself unable to make approaches against that town, he despatched an engineer to his father, requesting instructions from him. The Grand Vizír, after listening patiently to his son's messenger, desired him to approach the divan on which he was seated, without putting his feet on the carpet stretched before it; and the Vizír, making a signal for the purpose, two attendants rolled the carpet onwards. "Advance now without fear," said he to the engineer, "and let this be the answer you carry to my son."*

* Essai Général de Fortification et d'attaque et défense des places, &c. Dédié au Roi de Prusse, par M. de Bousmard, Ingénieur Français. Tome 1, p. 61.

Another important warlike accessory, hot-shot, appears, as far as the author is aware, to be also of Turkish origin; it goes back at least to the siege of Vienna, in 1683. The historian of John Sobieski, when speaking of the other means of attack used on that occasion, goes on to say: "L'artillerie turque était plus à craindre que tous ces phantômes. On s'occupait sans cesse à éteindre le feu que les bombes et les boulets rouges portaient dans la ville, tandis que les dehors tombaient en éclats. La demi-lune souffrait déjà beaucoup."*

The so-called Paixhans, or howitzer gun, is likewise derived from the Turks. A piece of this kind may be seen at Woolwich. It is one of those cast by order of Sultan Sultan, in and previously to 1805. This piece appears to have been adopted by the Russians, and was first used by them under the name of unicorns, at the battle of Smolensko. On this occasion its long range attracted Napoleon's attention, and the introduction of an improved gun has resulted from it. The horizontal shell-firing, which was the chief agent in sending the Turkish vessels to the bottom at Sinope, was thus originally introduced by the Turks.

The works raised at Kurtesse and Schumla in 1828, and those constructed more recently at Oltenitza and Khalafat, are sufficient to give us examples. The celerity and suc-

* Histoire de Jean Sobieski, Roi de Pologne, par M. L'Abbé Coyer tome 2, pp. 275, 276, 1853.

cess with which the operative part of this branch of the art of war is executed by the Turk, combined with the more general qualifications of valour, obedience, and temperance, which he possesses in an eminent degree, offer the best materials for the formation of an army.

It should be borne in mind, however, that it is but a short time since a regular organization of the Sultan's army has been commenced, and that there is in consequence a serious deficiency of battalion officers, as well as of the higher organization of the army : which is also but little accustomed to warlike operations.

The want of commanding officers acquainted with their duty, was the greatest evil with which Turkey had to contend in the former war. The brave, but desultory efforts of the Pashas, require to be brought into one combined system of authority. In almost every case, the want of military experience in the Turkish commanders was the cause of the disadvantages experienced in the preceding campaigns ; and it is the author's belief that much remains to be done at present to remedy this defect. A regular gradation of ranks appears to prevail in the force on the banks of the Danube, under the talented Omar Pasha ; who has already done much, and probably will yet accomplish much more in this respect. But many such men are required for various commands at such a juncture as the present one.

Gradations of authority, from the commander-in-chief

down to the common soldier, are absolutely necessary to the well-being of an army. These advantages were sadly wanting during the invasion of Turkey in 1828 and 1829, as well as numerical strength. The latter has now been supplied, with a much greater degree of discipline among the troops; consequently, all that is now wanting are combination, and a directing power, in addition to the gradation of ranks already mentioned.

The Sultan's fleet comprises six line-of-battle ships, four frigates (six having been destroyed at Sinope), five corvettes (one having been lost at Sinope), five steamers (one having been lost at Sinope), and forty-two small steamers, brigs, and cutters. Numerical strength is, therefore, on the side of Russia; but a judicious outlay in Europe might so augment the steam flotilla, as to render the Turkish and Egyptian fleets capable of accomplishing the all-important object of regaining the command of the Black Sea. At all events they might thus be enabled to prevent all hostile movements by water, and render abortive any attempt of the enemy to land a force south of the Balkan, as was done in 1829; thus obliging the hostile operations to take place by land.

The difficulty of manning these additional steamers would not be so great as may at first be supposed, since artillerymen, with a small proportion of seamen, would (as might be done with our own mercantile steamers in case of sudden hostilities) give the requisite degree of efficiency to these vessels.

The turn of events has put Russia in possession of Moldavia and Wallachia, with the supplies to be drawn from those provinces to carry on the war. She has the additional advantage at this season of crossing the Danube on the ice. But setting aside this possibility, we may consider an invasion as taking place under ordinary circumstances, when the Danube is open. The destruction of the *têtes-de-ponts* after the peace of 1829, and the possession of the left bank of the river, with the exception of Khalafat, have again given the invaders many advantages. These may, however, be counterbalanced in a great measure, if an Ordou of some 20,000 men be posted behind the upper part of the Danube, another near the centre about Silistria, and a third lower down in the Dobrudscha. Here, owing to the sweep of the river, troops placed behind it necessarily outflank an enemy when occupying the left bank of the Danube ; as is the case also in the higher part of that river in the neighbourhood of Khalafat.

It may here be observed that a defensive war behind the Danube would be in favour of the Turks; who would lose their river barrier and other advantages, if they were to cross into Wallachia and endeavour to oppose a mass of troops to those of the enemy. Such a course does not seem, therefore, by any means advisable. Yet, with due caution, daring and possibly successful operations may be carried out by Omar Pasha. By taking advantage of the northerly bend of the Danube, a force might cross the river, almost at the banks of the Pruth ; and as the movement thus made would be on the left flank and rear of the Russians, it might, considering the long line occupied, be fatal to them; unless they had time to prepare for it by changing front and concentrating their troops. The worst, probably, that could happen to the Turkish force in that case would be the necessity of retiring to the right bank; and it would then be open to them to endeavour, by means of another Turkish force, either to break through the centre of the enemy's line, or to threaten his right: as is now being done in the neighbourhood of Khalafat.

Presuming that it would be injudicious on the part of the Turks to expose the mass of their troops to those of the Russians, when concentrated in the plains of Wallachia, let us confine our observations to the defence of Bulgaria and Roumelia.

In the present case the defence of these provinces may be said to begin with the Danube. The judicious use of some gun-boats and small steamers to ascertain the movements of the Russians, would render the passage of a wide and rapid river, in the face of an army favoured by its commanding banks, a tedious and perilous operation. But supposing this to have been at length accomplished, and the Turks to have taken up a suitable position in the rear with the view of covering the fortresses, the invaders would have the choice of two modes of operation. Either of continuing to advance with much risk after masking certain fortresses, or of endeavouring to secure their line of marcn more effectually by besieging those places likely to operate on their rear. In the latter case, as the fortresses attacked would naturally be supported by the Turkish field force, considerable time must be consumed before the hostile army could advance into the country. In the former case, the Turks would dispute every inch of ground as they retreated.

On reaching the second line of defence, which is formed by the fortress of Varna, and the strong posts of Pravadi, Schumla, and Tirnova, the invaders would again be reduced to the same alternative as after crossing the Danube. They must either continue their march, after masking these places, or they must besiege one or two of them. If the latter, the Turkish army could operate with great advantage by debouching on their rear ; and even if their efforts to raise these sieges or blockades should fail, their invaders would be delayed at the foot of the Balkan; where, in case of failing to force a passage, they must soon suffer from the want of supplies.

If, on the other hand, the enemy followed the more daring course of passing the fortresses with such a body of troops as might be sufficient to force the mountain defiles, and yet not too numerous to carry supplies during his *coup-de-main* march against Constantinople, difficulties would still assail him. Even supposing everything to have favoured the advance of the invaders, they would at length find themselves in front of the formidable position of

Buyuk Checkmedgé. An attack on this position, in the face of an army, could only be undertaken advantageously after bringing up heavy artillery to carry on their operations; and these, both here and at Kuchuk Checkmedgé would probably be attended with such serious loss as to render any ulterior operations impracticable.

It need scarcely be observed that an invading army, after having risked everything by such a daring march, would be placed in a most critical situation. The fleet, even if it had the entire command of the Black Sea, could not land supplies without securing one or more suitable harbours on its shores; and all means of communication with the Russian base of operations beyond the Danube could be entirely cut off by the various garrisons in the rear.

It has been supposed that an enemy might divert the attention of the Turkish general, either by a flank march through Servia, or by endeavouring to cross the Balkan at two points; one column advancing, as in 1829, in the direction of Aidos, and the other by a more western route: that of Shipka for instance.

Under ordinary circumstances, the use of a second or third line of march would increase the chances of success.

But, as Servia is neutral territory, the alternative of the tedious and difficult routes across the Balkan seems to make a surprise on the part of the invaders almost impossible. Indeed, the separation and consequent weakness of the divisions, would have the manifest disadvantage of two lines of communication; which would thus permit the mass of the Turkish force to overwhelm either, or perhaps both, in turn.

The fate of war is proverbially uncertain; but if the necessary intrenchments have, as we have been told, been constructed in certain passes of the mountains, such as the Kamtchik and Bairam Ovo; and if the Turkish army retires, to occupy them with troops and artillery, without previously risking a battle excepting under the most palpable advantages; it is not going too far to predict that the enemy will not penetrate beyond the northern slopes of the Balkan, should the present state of hostilities lead to the continuance of the Russian campaign in Turkey.

THE END.

APPENDIX.

I.

Note verbale (3e) *remise par le prince Menschikoff au ministre des affaires étrangères de la Sublime-Porte.*

Péra, le 23 avril (5 mai) 1853.

Le soussigné ambassadeur de Russie, a eu l'honneur de remettre à Son Excellence le ministre des affaires étrangères de la Sublime-Porte, le 10 (22) mars, une communication confidentielle qui accompagnait le projet d'un acte devant offrir au gouvernement de Sa Majesté l'Empereur des garanties solides et inviolables pour l'avenir, dans l'intérêt de l'église orthodoxe d'Orient.

L'ambassadeur croyait pouvoir s'attendre à rencontrer, de la part du gouvernement de la Sublime-Porte, un désir empressé à renouer, sur cette base, des relations de bonne et franche amitié avec la Russie. Il doit l'avouer avec un profond regret, il a été ébranlé dans cette conviction qui, dès son début, lui avait été inspirée par l'accueil gracieux de Sa Majesté le Sultan.

Animé, néanmois, de cet esprit de conciliation et de bienveillance qui forme le fond de la politique de son auguste maître, l'ambassadeur ne rejeta point les observations confidentielles et préalables qui lui furent faites par Son Excellence Rifa'at pacha, tant sur la forme de l'acte précité, que sur la teneur de quelques-uns des articles qui devaient en faire partie.

Quant à la forme, l'ambassadeur maintient sa déclaration : qu'une longue et pénible expérience du passé exige, pour prévenir toute froideur et toute méfiance entre les deux gouvernements à l'avenir, un engagement solennel ayant force de traité.

Pour le contenu et la rédaction des articles de cet acte, il demandait une entente préalable, et voyant avec peine les retards qu'y apportait le cabinet ottoman et son désir évident d'éluder la discussion, il se vit obligé, par sa note verbale du 7 (19) avril, de récapituler ses demandes, et de les formuler de la manière la plus pressante.

Ce n'est qu'aujourd'hui que la note de Son Excellence le ministre des affaires étrangères, en date du 26 redjeb (23 avril—5 mai), accompagnant les copies vidimées des deux orders souverains sur les sanctuaires de Jérusalem et la coupole du Saint-Sépulcre, est parvenue à l'ambassadeur. Il considère cette communication comme une suite donnée aux deux premières demandes contenues dans sa note du 7 (19) avril, et se fera un devoir de placer ces documents sous les yeux de son gouvernement.

Mais, n'ayant obtenu jusqu'ici aucune réponse au troisième et plus important point qui réclame des garanties pour l'avenir, et ayant tout récemment reçu l'ordre de redoubler l'insistance pour arriver à la solution immédiate qui forme le principal objet de la sollicitude de Sa Majesté l'Empereur, l'ambassadeur se voit dans l'obligation de s'adresser aujourd'hui à Son Excellence le ministre des affaires étrangères, en renfermant, cette fois, ses réclamations dans les dernières limites des directions supérieures.

Les bases de l'arrangement qu'il est chargé d'obtenir restent, dans leur fond, les mêmes.

Le culte orthodoxe d'Orient, son clergé et ses possessions, jouiront dans l'avenir, sans aucune atteinte, sous l'égide de Sa Majesté le Sultan, des priviléges et immunités qui leur sont assurées *ab antiquo*, et, dans un principe de haute équité, participeront aux avantages accordés aux autres rites chrétiens.

Le nouveau firman explicatif sur les Saints-Lieux de Jérusalem aura la valeur d'un engagement formel envers le gouvernement impérial.

A Jérusalem, les religieux et les pèlerins russes seront assimilés aux prérogatives des autres nations étrangères.

Les points indiqués ici sommairement formeront l'objet d'un *sened* qui attestera la confiance réciproque des deux gouvernements.

Dans cet acte, les objections et difficultés exprimées à plusieurs reprises par Son Excellence Rifa'at pacha et quelques-uns de ses collègues, ont été prises en considération, comme Son Excellence le verra par la minute d'un sened que l'ambassadeur a l'honneur de joindre à la présente note.

L'ambassadeur se flatte de l'espoir que, désormais, la juste attente de son auguste maître ne sera pas trompée, et que, mettant de côté tout hésitation et toute méfiance dont sa dignité et ses sentiments généreux auraient à souffrir, la Sublime-Porte ne tardera pas à transmettre à l'ambassade impériale les décisions souveraines de Sa Majesté le Sultan, en réponse à la présente notification.

C'est dans cette espérance que l'ambassadeur prie Son Excellence Rifa'at pacha de vouloir bien lui faire parvenir cette réponse jusqu'à mardi prochain, 28 avril (10 mai.) Il ne pourrait considérer un plus long délai que comme un manque de procédés envers son gouvernement, ce qui lui imposerait les plus pénibles obligations.

L'ambassadeur offre à Son Excellence l'assurance, etc.

Signé : MENSCHIKOFF.

(Annexé.)

Projet de sened, joint à la note précédente.

Sa Majesté l'Empereur et Padichah des Ottomans et Sa Majesté l'Empereur de toutes les Russies, dans le désir commun de maintenir la stabilité du culte orthodoxe gréco-russe professé par la majorité de leurs sujets chrétiens, et de garantir ce culte de tout empiétement à l'avenir ont désigné:

Sa Majesté l'Empereur des Ottomans . . . . et Sa Majesté l'Empereur de toutes les Russies . . . . lesquels, après s'être expliqués, sont convenus de ce qui suit:

I. Il ne sera apporté aucun changement aux droits, priviléges et immunités dont ont joui ou sont en possession *ab antiquo* les églises, les institutions pieuses et le clergé orthodoxe dans les Etats de la Sublime-Porte Ottomane, qui se plaît à les leur assurer à tout jamais, sur la base du *statu quo* strict existant aujourd'hui.

II. Les droits et avantages concédés par le gouvernement ottoman, qui le seront à l'avenir aux autres cultes chrétiens par traités, conventions ou dispositions particulières, seront considérés comme appartenant aussi au culte orthodoxe.

III. Etant reconnu et constaté par les traditions historiques et par le nombreux documents que l'église grecque orthodoxe de Jérusalem, que son patriarcat et les laïques qui lui sont subordonnés ont été de tout temps, depuis l'époque des califes et sous les règnes successifs de tous les empereurs ottomans, particulièrement protégés, honorés et confirmés dans leurs anciens droits et immunités, la Sublime Porte, dans sa sollicitude pour la conscience et les convictions religieuses de ses sujets de ce culte, ainsi que de tous les chrétiens qui le professent, et dont la piété a été alarmée par divers événements, promet de maintenir et de faire respecter ces droits et ces immunités, tant dans la ville de Jérusalem qu'au dehors, sans préjudice aucun pour les autres communautés chrétiennes d'indigènes, rayas ou étrangers admis à l'adoration du Saint-Sépulcre et des autres sanctuaires, soit en commun avec les Grecs, soit dans leurs oratoires séparés.

IV. Sa Majesté le Sultan, aujourd'hui glorieusement régnant, ayant jugé nécessaire et équitable de corroborer et d'expliquer son firman souverain, revêtu du khatti-humayoun, au milieu de la lune de *rebiul-akhir* 1268, par son firman souverain de . . . . et d'ordonner en sus par un autre firman, en date de . . . ., la réparation de la grande coupole du temple du Saint-Sépulcre, ces deux firmans seront textuellement exécutés et fidèlement observés pour maintenir à jamais le *statu quo* strict des sanctuaires possédés par les Grecs exclusivement ou en commun avec d'autres cultes.

Il est convenu que l'on s'entendra ultérieurement sur la régularisation de quelques points de détail qui n'ont pas trouvé place dans les firmans précités.

V. Les sujets de l'empire de Russie, tant séculiers qu'ecclésiastiques, auxquels il est permis, suivant les traités, de visiter la sainte ville de Jérusalem et autres lieux de dévotion, devant être traités et considérés à l'égal des sujets des nations les plus favorisées, et celles-ci, tant catholiques que protestantes, ayant leurs prélats et leurs établissements ecclésiastiques particuliers, la Sublime Porte s'engage, pour le cas où la cour impériale de Russie lui en fera la demande, d'assigner une localité convenable dans la ville de Jérusalem ou dans les environs pour la construction d'une église consacrée à la célébration du service divin par des ecclésiastiques russes, et d'un hospice pour les pèlerins indigents ou malades, lesquelles fondations seront sous la surveillance du consulat général de Russie en Syrie et en Palestine.

VI. Il est entendu que, par le présent acte motivé par des circonstances exceptionnelles, il n'est dérogé à aucune des stipulations existantes entre les deux cours, et que tous les traités antérieurs, corroborés par l'acte séparé du traité d'Andrinople, conservent toute leur force et valeur.

Les six articles qui précèdent ayant été arrêtés et conclus, notre signature et le cachet de nos armes ont été apposés au présent acte, qui est remis à la Sublime-Porte Ottomane en échange de celui qui nous est remis par . . . . précités.

Fait à . . . . le . . . . 1853 et de l'hégire . . . .

Signé : . . . .

Ambassadeur extraordinaire et ministre plénipotentiaire de S. M. l'Empereur de toutes les Russies près la Sublime-Porte Ottomane.

II.

Note (2e) *de la Sublime-Porte à Son Excellence le prince Menschikoff, en date du* 2 *chaban* 1269 (10 *mai* 1853).

J'ai reçu la note que Votre Excellence m'ai fait l'honneur de m'adresser le 5 du mois de mai *à la franque*,* et j'ai lu avec attention les différentes pièces qui y sont relatives. Comme le gouvernement ottoman veut maintenir et accroître les liens d'amitié sincère et les relations d'affectueuse entente qui existent entre la Sublime-Porte et la Russie, et que Sa Majesté Impériale, surtout, désire ardemment et veut sincèrement consolider et raffermir de plus en plus les bases de l'amitié intime et sincère qui, depuis longtemps, sont heureusement

* C'est-à-dire d'après la manière de compter des Francs. La supputation des années, a Constantinople, se fait de trois manières : *à la franque*, d'après le calendrier grégorien ; *à la grecque*, d'après le calendrier gréco-russe ; *à la turque*, d'après le calendrier musulman.

établies entre elle et Sa Majesté l'Empereur, le gouvernement ottoman est dans la ferme intention de régler conformément aux rapports de bon voisinage et aux liens d'une amitié sincère et fidèle dans ses engagements, toutes les demandes de la Russie qui ne porteront ni tort, ni dommage, ni danger, aux droits d'indépendance souveraine de la Sublime-Porte et à ses intérêts légitimes.

En se trouvant dans la nécessité de répondre catégoriquement aux différents points contenus dans la pièce jointe à la note de Votre Excellence, le gouvernement s'empresse de lui soumettre cette réponse, et il espère que Votre Excellence voudra bien lire avec bienveillance les considérations ci-après. La Sublime-Porte ne se refuse nullement à acquiescer et à confirmer la décision qui sera prise, à la suite des conférences *ad hoc*, sur les demandes relatives aux moines et pèlerins russes, ainsi qu'à l'église et à l'hôpital demandés à Jérusalem, pourvu que cette décision ne porte nullement atteinte à ses droits souverains.

De tout temps, le gouvernement de la Sublime-Porte et celui de Sa Majesté Impériale en particulier, par suite des sentiments de sollicitude dont il est animé pour ses sujets, s'est toujours fait un devoir de maintenir intégralement les priviléges religieux que ses sujets chrétiens ont obtenus et dont ils ont la jouissance; cependant la Russie a conçu quelques doutes à l'égard des priviléges religieux des Grecs, sujets ottomans, et elle a demandé qu'il lui fût donné des garanties à cet égard. Or, comme Sa Majesté Impériale compte au nombre de ses devoirs le plus sacrés le maintien pérpétuel des anciens priviléges des Grecs ses sujets et de toutes les autres classes de sujets de son empire, et qu'elle n'est pas dans l'intention de jamais détruire ces priviléges religieux, le gouvernement s'applique sans cesse et met constamment ses soins à en assurer fermement le maintien. Mais, quels que soient les sentiments d'amitié qui existent entre la Sublime-Porte et la Russie, il est constant pour tout le monde que, si un gouvernement, pour une question aussi grave que celle-ci, qui annulerait et détruirait les bases de son indépendance, signait un engagement avec un autre gouvernement, il ferait un acte entièrement contraire aux droits des nations entre elles, et il effacerait totalement le principe de son indépendance.

Les dangers immenses et l'impossibilité réelle de ce point seront admis par tout le monde, et principalement par Sa Majesté l'Empereur, dont la loyauté est universellement reconnue.

La Sublime-Porte a su maintenir fidèlement, depuis les temps les plus reculés jusqu'à ce jour, tous le priviléges religieux qu'elle a accordés et octroyés, de son libre arbitre, à ses sujets chrétiens et surtout à la nation grecque et à ses religieux, et elle s'appliquera, dans l'exercice de ses droits souverains, à les maintenir et à les conserver encore, comme il convient, dans l'avenir.

En proclamant une fois de plus, et d'une manière toute spéciale, devant le monde entier, sa résolution sincere et ses intentions inaltérables, le gouvernement de la Sublime-Porte veut constater formellement les sentiments de haute sollicitude qui l'animent pour ses sujets, et il ne restera à personne le moindre doute sur la pureté de ses intentions.

Conformément aux ordres de Sa Majesté Impériale, j'ai l'honneur de transmettre la présente à Votre Excellence, et je la prie d'agréer l'assurance, etc.

Signé: RIFA'AT.

III.

Note (4e) remise par le prince Menschikoff au ministre des affaires étrangères de la Sublime-Porte.

Buyukdéré, le 29 avril (18 mai) 1853.

Le soussigné, ambassadeur de Russie, a eu l'honneur de recevoir la note de Son Excellence le ministre des affaires étrangères de la Sublime-Porte en date du 28 avril (10 mai). C'est avec un contentement profond qu'il s'est plu à y trouver l'expression des sentiments d'amitié qui animent Sa Majesté le Sultan pour l'Empereur, son auguste allié, ainsi que des assurances sur le désir sincère du cabinet ottoman de reserrer les anciens liens qui l'unissent au gouvernement impérial. Mais l'étonnement que le soussigné a ressenti n'en a été que plus pénible lorsqu'il a dû, en même temps, relever dans cette communication la méfiance avec laquelle le gouvernement de la Sublime-Porte accueillait les démarches franches et loyales qu'il avait à formuler au nom de l'Empereur. Cetts méfiance se fait jour dans l'interprétation que la Sublime-Porte veut donner aux intentions de Sa Majesté Impériale, en y cherchant la pensée, inadmissible et contraire à sa politique généreuse et conservatrice, de vouloir obtenir un droit nouveau au détriment l'indépendance et de la souveraineté de la Sublime-Porte. Le soussigné se croit en devoir de faire remarquer à Son Excellence que ce doute est émis lorsque avec un épanchment affectueux l'Empereur fait un appel à l'amitié de son auguste allié, et ne lui demande, sans prejudice aucun du pouvoir sacré et inviolable de Sa Majesté le Sultan, qu'une preuve ostensible de sa sollicitude pour le culte orthodoxe grec, qui est celui de la Russie, et dont l'Empereur est le défenseur naturel.

Le soussigné croit inutile de rappeler ici les faits regrettables qui ont éveillé les appréhensions si justes de son auguste maître pour l'avenir du culte chrétien d'Orient. Ce n'est qu'un acte émanant de la volonté souveraine du Sultan, un engagement libre, mais solennel, qui peut effacer le souvenir pénible des fautes commises par quelques conseillers malveillants, et inhabiles de sa Majesté le Sultan. Le soussigné est chargé de négocier ce témoignage d'égards pour les convictions religieuses de l'Empereur ; mais si les principes qui en forment la bas sont rejetés, ainsi qu'il ressort de la note de Son Excellence le ministre des affaires étrangères du 28 avril (10 mai), si, par une opposition systématique, la Sublime-Porte persiste à lui fermer toutes les voies d'une entente intime et directe comme elle doit l'être dans un différend à régler entre deux puissances amies ; le soussigné déclare avec peine qu'il devra considérer sa mission comme terminée, interrompre ses relations avec le cabinet de Sa Majesté le Sultan, et rejeter sur la responsibilité de ses ministres toutes les conséquences qui pourraient en résulter. Le soussigné se flatte de l'espoir que ces considérations fixeront l'attention la plus sérieuse de la Sublime-Porte, et que Son Excellence le ministre des affaires étrangères, pénétré de leur haute importance, ainsi que de l'esprit de conciliation qui les dicte, voudra bien apprécier en même temps les motifs qui ne permettent point à l'ambassadeur d'accepter la note du 28 avril (10 mai), comme une réponse conforme à la dignité de son souverain.

Il ne reste au soussigné qu'à prier Son Excellence de vouloir bien lui répondre concernant la présente communication jusqu'à samedi prochain 2 (14) mai. Il croit ainsi donner le temps nécessaire à la reflexion que demande la gravité même de la question.

L'ambassadeur saisit, etc.

Signé : MENSCHIKOFF.

IV.

Note (3e) *de la Sublime-Porte à Son Excellence le prince Menschikoff, en date du* 7 *chaban* 1269 (15 *mai* 1853).

La Sublime-Porte a pris connaissance de la dernière note de Son Excellence le prince Menschikoff. Ainsi que Son Excellence le prince Menschikoff en a été déjà informé, tant en personne que par intermédiaire, il est impossible, par suite des changements survenus dans le ministère, de donner une réponse explicite sur une question aussi délicate que celle des priviléges religieux avant de les examiner avec soin.

Mais comme le maintien des relations amicales avec l'auguste cour de Russie est l'objet de la plus vive sollicitude de la part de Sa Majesté le Sultan, il s'ensuit que la Sublime-Porte désire sincèrement trouver un moyen de garantie de nature à satisfaire les deux parties. En informant Son Altesse le prince Menschikoff qu'un délai de cinq jours suffira, et que l'on s'efforcera d'arriver, s'il est possible, à une plus prompte solution dans la question.

J'ai l'honneur, etc.

Signé : RÉCHID.

V.

Note (6e) du prince Menschikoff au ministre des affaires étrangères de la Sublime-Porte.

Buyukdéré, le 9 (21) mai.

Au moment de quitter Constantinople, le soussigné, ambassadeur extraordinaire de Sa Majesté l'Empereur de toutes les Russies, a appris que la Sublime-Porte manifestait l'intention de proclamer une garantie pour l'exercice des droits spirituels dont se trouve investi le clergé de l'Eglise d'Orient, ce qui, de fait, rendrait douteux le maintien des autres priviléges dont il jouit.

Quel que puisse être le motif de cette détermination, le soussigné se trouve dans l'obligation de faire connaître à Son Excellence le ministre des affaires étrangères qu'une déclaration ou tel autre acte qui tendrait, tout en maintenant l'intégrité des droits purement spirituels de l'Eglise orthodoxe d'Orient, à invalider les autres droits, priviléges et immunités accordés au culte orthodoxe et à son clergé depuis les temps les plus anciens, et dont ils jouissent encore actuellement, serait considérée par le cabinet impérial comme un acte hostile à la Russie et à sa religion.

Signé : MENSCHIKOFF.

VI.

Firman remis aux chefs spirituels des quatre communautés.

KHATTI CHÉRIF (CHIFFRE IMPERIAL).

*Qu'il soit fait toujours continuellement attention à exécuter sans changement les décrets contenus dans mon ordre supérieur, et qu'on s'abstienne d'y contrevenir.**

TEXTE.

A l'arrivée de mon ordre impérial adressé à toi (*ici le nom du patriarche de la communauté*), honneur et élu de la nation chrétienne, des chefs de la communauté du Christ (que ton rang soit de longue durée) ; tu sauras que, comme le Seigneur très-juste, le donateur absolu des biens, ayant élevé mon august personne impériale à la

* Cette formule, placée en tête du firman, est écrite de la propre main du Sultan, d'où son nom de *khatti cherif* ou *khatti humaïoun* (*écriture auguste* ou *impériale*).

gloire du sultanat et du commandement, et m'ayant fait parvenir au haut poste d'Empereur et de califat, suivant sa bonté divine et sa clémence infinie (grâce et reconnaissance à lui), a remis tant de royaumes, de villes, de diverses classes de sujets, de nations et de serviteurs, entre les mains pleines de justice de mon califat, comme un dépôt divin tout particulier, d'après ce qui est nécessaire à la bonté requise du califat et de l'empire, et ainsi qu'il convient à la haute habitude du sultanat et de la souveraineté, j'ai toujours, depuis que, secouru par les bontés divines et assisté de la clémence céleste, je me suis assis sur mon trône impérial, employé généreusement ma sollicitude active, et mon gouvernement impérial a continuellement témoigné de sa bienveillance pour que toutes les classes des sujets de mon empire jouissent d'une protection parfaite, et que, en particulier, ainsi que cela se pratiquait dès le principe, ils possèdent sans exception une tranquillité complète dans l'exercice de leur culte et dans leurs affaires spirituelles, suivant mes intentions sincères et bienveillantes et ma volonté formelle.

Comme les bons effets et les utiles résultats de ces dispositions sont évidents et appréciés, c'est le but de mes désirs impériaux d'éloigner et d'anéantir complétement, de manière qu'ils ne puissent jamais se renouveler, certains abus qui ont pu avoir lieu par négligence ou par paresse. Ainsi, je veux et je tiens à ce que soient toujours conservés intacts les priviléges spirituels particuliers des églises et des couvents qui existent dans mes Etats impériaux, ainsi que des terres, des propriétés, immeubles et autres endroits religieux qui dépendent de ces églises et couvents; les immunités et les droits propres à de pareils établissements de prières et aux ecclésiastiques, les priviléges et concessions semblables, écrits et contenus dans les berats qui renferment les conditions anciennes des patriarches et de leurs fondés de pouvoirs, priviléges, immunités et concessions donnés aux ecclesiastiques des sujets fidèles de mon empire qui se trouvent dans la nation (*ici le nom de la communauté*), par mes illustres et magnanimes ancêtres, et reconnus et admis par moi.

En confirmante de nouveau et annonçant ma haute volonté impériale, cet *iradé* décisif et plein de justice a été émané pour qu'on s'y conforme et qu'on sache que ceux qui agiront contrairement seront exposés à ma colère impériale. Les employés nécessaires en ont été informés pour qu'il n'y ait point lieu d'excuse au cas où ils commettraient quelque négligence. L'exécution complète et exacte en étant mon haut but souverain, afin de le confirmer et annoncer, mon firman supérieur a été émané de mon Divan impérial. Et toi qui es ce patriarche, quand tu en auras pris connaissance, tu agiras et tu te conduiras toujours suivant mon ordre supérieur, et tu t'abstiendras d'agir contrairement. S'il arrive rien qui soit contraire à ce décret décisif, tu te hâteras d'en faire part immédiatement à ma Sublime-Porte. Sache-le ainsi, et ajoute foi à mon chiffre impérial.

Ecrit vers la fin de chaban 1269 (6 juin 1853), dans cette capitale de Constantinople.

VII.

Lettre du comte de Nesselrode à Réchid pacha.

Saint-Pétersbourg, le 19 (31) mai 1853.

Monsieur,

L'Empereur mon auguste maître vient d'être informé que son ambassadeur a dû quitter Constantinople à la suite du refus péremptoire de la Porte de prendre vis-à-vis de la cour impériale de Russie le moindre engagement propre à la rassurer sur les intentions protectrices du gouvernement ottoman à l'égard du culte et des églises orthodoxes en Turquie.

C'est après un séjour infructueux de trois mois, après avoir épuisé de vive voix et par écrit tout ce que la vérité, la bienveillance et l'esprit de conciliation pouvaient lui dicter; c'est enfin après avoir cherché à ménager tous les scrupules de la Porte par les modifications successives auxquelles il avait consenti dans les termes et la forme des garanties qu'il était chargé de demander, que le prince Menschikoff a dû prendre la détermination que l'Empereur apprend avec peine *mais que Sa Majesté n'a pu qu'approuver pleinement.*

Votre Excellence est trop éclairée pour ne pas prévoir les conséquences de l'interruption de nos relations avec le gouvernement de Sa Hautesse. Elle est trop dévouée aux intérêts véritables et permanents de son souverain et de son empire, pour ne pas éprouver un profond regret en prévision des événements qui peuvent éclater et dont la responsabilité pèsera tout entière sur ceux qui les provoquent.

Aussi, en adressant aujourd'hui cette lettre à Votre Excellence, je n'ai d'autre but que de la mettre à même, tant qu'elle le peut encore, de rendre un très-important service à son souverain. Mettez encore une fois, monsieur, sous les yeux de Sa Hautesse, la situation réelle des choses, la modération et la justice des demandes de la Russie, la très-grande offense que l'on fait à l'Empereur en opposant à ses intentions si constamment amicales et généreuses une méfiance sans motif et des refus sans excuse.

La dignité de Sa Majesté, les intérêts de son empire, la voix de sa conscience, ne lui permettent pas d'accepter des procédés pareils en retour de tous ceux qu'elle a eus et qu'elle désire encore avoir pour la Turquie. Elle doit chercher à en obtenir la réparation et à se prémunir contre leur renouvellement à l'avenir.

Dans quelques semaines, les troupes recevront l'ordre de passer les frontières de l'empire, non pas pour faire la guerre qu'il répugne à Sa Majesté d'entreprendre contre un souverain qu'elle s'est toujours plu à considérer comme un allié sincère, mais pour avoir des garanties matérielles jusqu'au moment où, ramené à des sentiments plus équitables, le gouvernement ottoman donnera à la Russie les sûretés morales qu'elle a demandées en vain depuis deux ans par ses représentants à Constantinople, et en dernier lieu par son ambassadeur. Le projet de note que le prince Menschikoff vous a remis se trouve entre vos mains ; que Votre Excellence se hâte, après avoir obtenu l'assentiment de Sa Hautesse le Sultan, de signer cette note *sans variantes* et de la transmettre au plus tôt à notre ambassadeur à Odessa, où il doit se trouver encore.

Je souhaite vivement que, dans se moment décisif, le conseil que j'adresse à Votre Excellence, avec la confiance que ses lumières et son patriotisme m'inspirent, soit appréciée par elle comme par ses collègues du Divan, et que, dans l'intérêt de la paix, que nous devons être tous également désireux de conserver, il soit suivi sans hésitation ni retard.

Je prie Votre Excellence, etc.

Signé : NESSELRODE.

VIII.

Réponsé de Réchid pacha à la lettre du comte de Nesselrode.

Constantinople, le 16 juin, 1853.

Monsieur,

Je me suis empressé de mettre sous les yeux de Sa Majesté le Sultan, mon auguste maître, la dépêche que Votre Excellence m'a fait l'honneur de m'adresser le 19 (31) mai dernier.

Sa Majesté le Sultan a toujours montré, en toute occasion, le plus grands égards pour Sa Majesté l'Empereur de Russie, qu'il considère comme son allié sincère et comme un voisin bien intentionné. La Sublime-Porte, ne mettant nullement en doute les intentions généreuses de l'Empereur, a ressenti un profond chagrin de l'interruption des relations, survenue malheureusement parce qu'on n'a pas bien compris peut-être l'impossibilité réelle où elle se trouvait, à propos de la question soulevée par M. le prince Menschikoff, de consigner, dans un engagement diplomatique, les priviléges religieux accordés au rite grec. Toutefois, elle éprouve la consolation de voir que, pour sa part, elle n'a nullement contribué à amener un semblable état de choses. En effet, le gouvernement ottoman a montré, dès le principe, les meilleures dispositions et toutes les facilités relativement à toutes les questions que M. le prince Menschikoff était chargé de régler, d'après les ordres de l'Empereur ; et même, dans une question aussi délicate que celle des priviléges religieux de l'Eglise grecque, s'inspirant encore de ses sentiments pacifiques, et ne refusant pas les assurances qui pouvaient faire disparaître et réduire à néant tous les doutes qui auraient pu s'élever à cet égard, la Porte espérait surtout de la sagesse reconnue du prince Menschikoff que cet ambassadeur se montrerait satisfait du projet de note qui lui avait été transmis en dernier lieu, et qui contenait toutes les assurances demandées. Quoi qu'il en soit, ce fait regrettable s'est produit.

Il est vrai que Son Altesse le prince Menschikoff a, la seconde fois, abrégé la minute du sened qu'il avait donnée d'abord, et, en donnant à la fin un projet de note, il a fait quelques changements, soit dans les termes, soit dans la rédaction et le titre de la pièce ; mais le sens d'un engagement s'y trouvait toujours, et comme cet engagement diplomatique ne peut s'accorder, ni avec l'indépendance du gouvernement ottoman, ni avec les droits de son autorité souveraine, on ne pouvait donner aux motifs d'impossibilité réelle présentés sur ce point par la Porte le nom de refus, et faire de cela une question d'honneur pour Sa Majesté l'Empereur de Russie. De plus, si l'on se plaint de cette impossibilité, en l'attribuant à un sentiment de défiance, la Russie, en ne tenant aucun compte de toutes les assurances offertes de la manière la plus solennelle par la Sublime-Porte, et en déclarant qu'il était indispensable de les consigner dans un acte ayant force d'engagement, ne donne-t-elle pas plutôt une preuve patente de son manque de confiance envers le gouvernement ottoman, et celui-ci n'a-t-il pas à son tour, le droit de s'en plaindre?

Toutefois, il s'en remit, pour répondre sur ces deux points à la haute justice si connue de l'Empereur de Russie, ainsi qu'à la haute raison et aux sentiments éminemment pacifiques de Votre Excellence, que chacun, d'ailleurs, a pu connaître et apprecier.

Sa Majesté le Sultan, par un firman impérial, revêtu de son auguste *khatti-cherif*, vient de confirmer de nouveau les priviléges, droits et immunités dont les religieux et let églises du rite grec jouissent *ab antiquo*. La Sublime-Porte n'hésitera jamais à maintenir et à donner les assurances contenues et promises dans le projet de note remis au prince Menschikoff peu avant son départ.

La dépêche reçue de la part de Votre Excellence parle de faire passer les frontières aux troupes russes. Cette déclaration est incompatible avec les assurances de paix et de bon vouloir de Sa Majesté l'Empereur. Elle est, en vérité, si contraire à ce que l'on est en droit d'attendre de la part d'une puissance amie, que la Porte ne saurait comment l'accepter. Les préparatifs militaires et les travaux de défense ordonnés par la Porte, ainsi qu'elle l'a déclaré officiellement aux puissances, ne sont donc necessités que par les armements considérables de la Russie. Ils ne constituent qu'une mesure purement défensive. Le gouvernement du Sultan, n'ayant aucune intention hostile contre la Russie, exprime le désir que les anciennes relations que Sa Majesté regarde, d'ailleurs, comme si précieuses, et dont les nombreux avantages sont manifestes pour les deux parties, soient rétablies dans leur état primitif. J'espère que la cour de Russie appréciera avec un sentiment de confiante considération les intentions sincères et loyales de la Sublime-Porte, et tiendra compte de l'impossibilité réele où elle se trouve de déférer aux désirs qui lui ont été exprimés. Que cette impossibilité soit appréciée comme elle mérite de l'être, et la Sublime-Porte, je puis l'assurer à Votre Excellence, n'hésitera pas à charger un ambassadeur extraordinaire de se rendre à Saint-Petersbourg pour y renouer les négociations, et chercher, de concert avec le gouvernement de Sa Majesté l'Empereur de Russie, un accommodement qui, tout en étant agréable à Sa Majesté, serait tel, que la Porte pourrait l'accepter sans porter aucune atteinte, soit aux bases de son indépendance, soit à l'autorité, souveraine de Sa Majesté le Sultan.

Votre Excellence peut tenir pour certain que, pour ma part, j'appelle ce résultat de tous mes vœux; j'aime a croire que, de son côté, il en est de même.

Je prie Votre Excellence, etc., etc.

Signé: Réchid.

IX.

Manifeste (1er) *de l'Empereur de Russie.*

Par la grâce de Dieu, nous, Nicolas 1er, Empereur et autocrate de toutes les Russies, etc., etc., etc.

Savoir faisons:

Il est à la connaissance de nos fidèles et bien aimés sujects que, de temps immémorial, nos glorieux prédécesseurs ont fait vœu de défendre la foi orthodoxe.

Depuis l'instant où il a plu à la divine Providence de nous transmettre le trône héréditaire, l'observation de ces devoirs sacrés qui en sont inséparables a constamment été l'objet de nos soins et de notre sollicitude. Basés sur le glorieux traité de Kaïnardji confirmé par les transactions solennelles conclues postérieurement avec la Porte Ottomane, ces soins et cette sollicitude ont toujours eu pour but de garantir les droits de l'église orthodoxe.

Mais, à notre profonde affliction, malgré tous nos efforts pour défendre l'intégrité des droits et priviléges de notre Eglise orthodoxe, dans ces derniers temps de nombreux actes arbitraires du gouvernement ottoman ont porté atteinte à ces droits et menaçaient enfin d'anéantir complétement tout l'ordre de choses sanctionné par les siècles, et si cher à la foi orthodoxe.

Nos efforts pour détourner la Porte d'actes semblables sont restés infructueux, et même la parole solennelle que le Sultan nous avait donnée en cette occasion n'a pas tardé à être violée.

Après avoir épuisé toutes les voies de la persuasion et tous les moyens d'obtenir à l'amiable la satisfaction due à nos justes réclamations, nous avons jugé indispensable de faire entrer nos troupes dans les principautés danubiennes, afin de montrer à la Porte où peut la conduire son opiniâtreté. Toutefois, même à présent, notre intention n'est point de commencer la guerre; par l'occupation des principautés, nous voulons avoir entre les mains un gage qui nous répondre en tout état de cause du rétablissement de nos droits.

Nous ne cherchons point de conquêtes; la Russie n'en a pas besoin. Nous demandons qu'il soit satisfait à un droit légitime si ouvertement enfreint. Nous sommes prêts, même dès à présent, à arrêter le mouvement de nos troupes, si la Porte Ottomane s'engage à observer religieusement l'intégrité des priviléges de l'Eglise orthodoxe. Mais, si l'obstination et l'aveuglement veulent absolument le contraire, alors, appelant Dieu à notre aide, nous nous en remettrons à lui du soin de décider de notre différend, et plein d'espoir en sa main Toute-Puissante, nous marcherons à la défense de la foi orthodoxe.

Donné à Peterhoff, le quatorzième jour (26) du mois de juin de l'an de grâce 1853, et de notre règne le vingt-huitième.

Signé: NICOLAS.

X.

Protestation de la Porte contre l'entrée des troupes russes en Moldavie.

La Sublime Porte vient d'apprendre officiellement que l'armée russe a passé le Pruth et qu'elle est entrée dans la Moldavie avec l'intention d'occuper aussi la Valachie. Ce mouvement, opéré sans son concours sur une partie intégrante de son Empire, a dû lui causer autant de peine que de surprise. Il lui est pénible de voir les habitants de ces provinces loyales et tranquilles exposés à toutes les chances d'une occupation militaire. Il lui est difficile de concilier une telle agression avec les déclarations pacifiques et les assurances amicales que le cabinet de Saint-Pétersbourg a tant de fois réitérées. Il lui est encore plus difficile de ne pas s'étonner d'une opération qui porte atteinte aux principes établis dans le traité de 1841.

La Sublime Porte, en exprimant les sentiments que cet événement lui fait éprouver, ne peut se dispenser de mettre dans leur vrai jour quelques circonstances auxquelles les ministres de Sa Majesté Impériale se sont efforcés en vain de donner une conclusion telle que leur amour de la justice et de la tranquillité la leur faisait désirer.

Les négociations qui furent entamées de concert avec le prince Menschikoff se bornaient d'abord aux points qui souffraient des difficultés relativement à la question des Lieux-Saints, et les différends qui en étaient les objects principaux ne tardèrent pas à recevoir une solution propre à satisfaire toutes les parties intéressées.

Nous avons consenti, en outre, à la construction d'une église et d'un hôpital à Jérusalem pour le service spécial des Russes, en sorte que les concessions demandées en faveur des prêtres et pèlerins de la même nation n'ont pas été refusées non plus.

Après l'heureuse conclusion de la partie des négociations qui avait trait au seul objet ostensible de la mission extraordinaire du prince Menschikoff, cet ambassadeur s'est empressé avec les plus vives instances de faire accepter une autre demande dont les conséquences, si elle avait été admise par le gouvernement de Sa Majesté le Sultan, n'aurait pas manqué de porter une grande atteinte aux intérêts de l'empire, et de compromettre les droits souverains qui en sont lest ornements et les soutiens.

On a vu par les communications officielles que la Sublime-Porte a faites en temps et lieu aux hautes puissances, qu'elle n'hésite point à donner des assurances suffisantes capables de dissiper les doutes qui ont amené les discussions relatives aux droits, aux priviléges spirituels et à d'autres immunités qui s'y rattachent, et dont les églises grecques et les prêtres grecs sont en possession de la part de Sa Majesté le Sultan. Loin de songer à retirer une partie quelconque de ces priviléges, ou même à en restreindre la jouissance consacrée par leur utilité, Sa Majesté Impériale se fait une glorie de les confirmer publiquement, et, fidèle aux maximes de la justice et de la clémence, de les mettre à l'abri de tout préjudice au moyen d'un acte solennel revêtu de son khatti-chérif, et qui a été porté à la connaissance de tous les gouvernements amis. Tel étant les cas, ce serait une chose oiseuse que d'encombrer cette question de détails inutiles. Il suffit ici de constater que, d'une côté, la demande de l'ambassadeur russe, nonobstant certaines modifications, soit dans les termes, soit dans la forme, demeurait à la fin inadmissible à cause de ce qui vient d'être expliqué; tandis que, de l'autre côté, elle devenait sans objet réelle par suite des garanties solennelles données spontanément par le souverain lui-même à la face du monde entier. Ces faits incontestables suffisent pour dégager la Sublime-Porte de toute obligation de s'excuser davantage au sujet des priviléges religieux. Il est d'une évidence incontestable que l'indépendance d'un Etat souverain est nulle, si parmi ses attributions il n'existe pas celle de refuser sans offense une demande que les traités n'autorisent point, et dont l'acceptation serait en même temps superflue quant à son object ostensible, et non moins humiliante que nuisible à la haute partie qui s'en excuse.

Néanmoins, la Sublime-Porte ne se désiste en rein de son désir amical et profondément sincère, non, non-seulement de remplir tous ses engagements envers la Russie avec la plus scrupuleuse exactitude, mais, en outre, de lui donner toute nouvelle preuve de ses dispositions cordiales qui soit compatible avec les droit sacrés de la souveraineté et avec l'honneur et les intérêts fondamentaux de son empire.

Elle est toujours prête à réitérer les assurances promises dans la lettre du 4 (16) juin, écrite en réponse à celle de Son Excellence le comte de Nésselrode, portant la date du 19 (31) mai, et elle est encore disposée, pour peu que l'on veuille s'arrêter à un arrangement propre à satisfaire la cour de Russie, sans préjudice pour les droits sacrés du Sultau, à envoyer un ambassadeur extraordinaire à Saint-Pétersbourg pour chercher, de concert avec le cabinet russe, les moyens de parvenir à ce but.

Quant au passage de la lettre de Son Excellence le comte de Nessel rode, relatif à l'invasion eventuelle du territoire ottoman, la Sublime-Porte a déjà déclaré qu'elle ne saurait l'accepter, et puisque cette lettre ainsi que la réponse du ministère ottoman on été sur-le-champ communiquées aux puissances signataires du traité du 1841, il devient évidemment inutile de se répandre en détails sur une question aussi pénible.

A la suite de ces circonstances, et en vertu de ces considérations, le gouvernement de Sa Majesté avait lieu d'espérer que les motifs fondés qu'il n'a cessé d'alléguer pour justifier le refus de son consentement, l'impossibilité dans laquelle il se trouve de l'accorder, et le désir sincère qu'il a exprimé à plusieurs reprises de voir renouer les relations des deux hautes parties, seraient enfin appréciés, et que la cour de Russie reviendrait à des sentiments plus équitables à son égard. La Sublime-Porte éprouve d'autant plus de douleur en se voyant deçue dans cet espoir, que les qualités éminentes de l'Empereur de Russie, sa modération et sa justice connues, ne lui permettent pas de supposer que sa Majesté serait capable de vouloir fonder ses demandes sur d'autres bases que celles de la raison et du bon droit, et qu'elle a tout récemment donné, soit au Sultan lui-même, soit aux puissances européennes, des assurances positives de son désir de respecter la dignité et de maintenir l'indépendance de l'empire ottoman.

Voilà dans quel état de choses la Sublime-Porte vient de recevoir l'avis officiel que les troupes russes ont franchi la frontière.

Si la cour de Russie persist à fonder la demande de consacrer par un document obligatoire envers elle les priviléges religieux dont il est question sur le traité de Kaïnardji, il est à remarquer que la promesse contenue dans la première partie de l'article 7 de ce traité, relativement à la protection de la religion chrétienne et de ses églises, est une généralité, et l'on ne peut guère y voir le degré de force que la Russie lui attribue, et encore moins une spécialité en faveur de la religion grecque.

Quoi qu'il en soit, si la Sublime-Porte manquait de proteger la religion et les églises chrétiennes, c'est alors seulement qu'il faudrait lui rappeler sa promesse en citant le susdit traité; et il n'est pas moins clair que cette nouvelle proposition ne saurait être fondée sur ce traité, attendu que les priviléges et les immunités de la religion grecque ont été octroyés par la Sublime-Porte sans la demande ni l'intervention de qui que ce soit. C'est, en effet, un point d'honneur pour elle de les maintenir à présent et à l'avenir, et un devoir que lui impose son système plein de sollicitude pour ses sujets. Les firmans qui viennent d'être promulgués, et qui confirment les priviléges et les immunités de toutes les religions, témoignent publiquement des fermes intentions de la Sublime-Porte à cet égard; de manière que, sans le moindre doute, une intervention étrangère n'est point du tout nécessaire à cet effet. Seulement, puisque la cour de Russie a conçu, quel qu'en puisse être le motif, des soupçons par rapport à ces privilèges religieux, et que la religion grecque est celle de l'auguste Empéreur et d'une grande partie de ses sujets, la Sublime-Porte, mue par ces considérations, comme aussi par déférence pour les relations amicales qui existent encore entre les deux puissances, ne recule pas devant la résolution de donner, à ce sujet, des assurances suffisantes. Mais, si un gouvernement contractait sur les droits et les privilèges qu'il a, de son propre mouvement, accordés aux églises et aux prêtres d'une nation de tant de millions d'âmes soumise à son autorité, des obligations exclusives avec un autre gouvernement, ce serait partager son autorité avec ce gouvernement, ce serait anéantir sa propre indépendance.

Les traités conclus entre la Sublime-Porte et la cour de Russie, concernant les deux principautés, n'autorisent en aucune manière l'envoi de la part de la Russie de troupes dans ces deux pays, et l'article y relatif qui se trouve dans le sened de Balta-Liman est subordonné au cas où des troubles internes éclateraient;* ce qui n'est nullement le cas dans circonstance actuelle.

Le fait est que ce procédé aggressif de la part de la Russie ne saurait être, en principle, considéré autrement que comme une déclaration de guerre, donnant à la Sublime-Porte le droit incontestable d'employer en revanche la force militaire. Mais la Sublime-Porte est loin de vouloir pousser ses droits à l'extrême.

Forte de la justice qui règle sa politique envers les puissances, elle préfère les réserver, dans l'attente du retour spontané de la Russie à une manière d'agir plus conforme à ses déclarations. C'est dans le but d'écarter tout obstacle à ce retour, qu'elle se borne, pour le moment, à protester contre l'agression dont elle a bien le droit de se plaindre. Elle croit offrir, par ce moyen, au monde entier une nouvelle preuve de la modération du système qu'elle a adopté dès le commencement de cette affaire. Elle s'abstient de tout acte hostile; mais elle déclare qu'elle ne consent en aucune manière à ce que l'on fasse entrer de temps en temps des troupes dans les provinces de Moldavie

* *Art 4 de la convention de Balta-Liman*:—"Les troubles qui viennent d'agiter si profondément les Principautés ayant démontré la nécessité de prêter à leurs gouvernements l'appui d'une force militaire capable de réprimer promptement tout mouvement insurrectionnel et de faire respecter les autorités établies, les deux cours impériales sont convenues de prolonger la présence d'une certaine partie des troupes russes et ottomanes qui occupent aujourd'hui le pays, et notamment pour préserver la frontière de Valachie et de Moldavie des accidents du dehors, il a été décidé qu'on y laisserait, *pour le moment*, de vingt-cinq à trente-cinq mille hommes de chacune des deux parts. Après le rétablissement de la tranquillité des dites frontières, il restera dans les deux pays dix mille hommes de chaque côté, jusqu'à l'achèvement des travaux d'amélioration organique et la consolidation du repos intérieur des deux provinces. Ensuite, les troupes des deux puissances évacueront complétement les Principautés, mais resteront encore à portée d'y rentrer immédiatement, dans le cas où des circonstances graves, survenues dans les principautés, réclameraient de nouveau l'adoption de cette mesure. Indépendamment de cela, on aura soin de compléter sans retard la réorganisation de la milice indigène, de manière qu'elle offre, par sa discipline et son effectif, une garantie suffisante pour le maintien de l'ordre légal."

et de Valachie, qui sont parties intégrantes de l'empire ottoman, en les regardent comme une maison sans maître.

Elle proteste donc formellement et ouvertement contre cet acte, et, dans la conviction que les puissances signataires du traité de 1841, ne donneraient pas leur assentiment à une pareille agression, elle leur a fait un exposé des circonstances, et garde, en attendant, une attitude armée pour sa défense.

Pour en venir à la conclusion, elle répète que Sa Majesté le Sultan est toujours désireux d'aller au-devant de toute réclamation fondée de la cour de Russie, ce dont il a déjà donné maintes preuves, et est prêt à redresser tout grief concernant les affaires religieuses dont ses sujets grecs pourraient encore avoir à se plaindre; que réparation a été faite par rapport aux Lieux-Saints; que cette question a été résolue à la satisfaction de la Russie, et que la Sublime-Porte n'hésite pas à offrir des assurances plus explicites, afin de confirmer l'arrangement qui a été fait au gré de toutes les parties.

XI.

Circulaire du gouvernement de l'Empereur en réponse à la circulaire (2e) du comte de Nesselrode.

Paris, le 15 juillet 1853.

Monsieur,

La nouvelle dépêche de M. le comte de Nesselrode que le *Journal de Saint-Pétersbourg* publiait le lendemain du jour où elle était expédiée à toutes les légations de Russie, a produit sur le gouvernement de l'Empereur une impression que Sa Majesté Impériale m'a ordonné de vous faire connaître sans détour.

Nous ne pouvons que déplorer de voir la Russie, au moment même où les efforts de tous les cabinets pour amener une solution satisfaisante des difficultés actuelles, témoignent si hautement de leur modération, prendre une attitude qui rend le succès de leurs négociations plus incertain, et impose à quelques-uns d'entre eux le devoir de repousser la responsabilité que l'on essayerait vainement de faire peser sur leur politique.

Je ne voudrais pas, monsieur, revenir sur une discussion épuisée; mais, comme M. le comte de Nesselrode allègue toujours, à l'appui des prétentions de Saint-Pétersbourg, l'offense que la Porte aurait commise à son égard en ne tenant pas compte des promesses qu'elle aurait faites à la légation de Russie à l'époque du premier réglement de la question des Lieux-Saints, en 1852, je suis forcé de répéter que les firmans rendus par le Sultan, à la suite de la mission de M. le prince

Menschikoff, ont ôté tout fondement à cet unique grief, et que, s'il est un gouvernement autorisé à élever des plaintes légitimes, ce n'est pas celui de Sa Majesté l'empereur Nicolas.

En effet, à la date du 10 mai dernier, M. le comte de Nesselrode, qui venait de recevoir des dépêches de M. l'ambassadeur de Russie à Constantinople, se félicitait, avec M. le général de Castelbajac, d'un résultat qu'il considerait comme une heureuse conclusion de l'affaire des Lieux Saints; M. Kisseleff, à Paris, me faisait une semblable déclaration, et partout les agents du cabinet de Saint-Pétersbourg tenaient le même langage.

Les demandes formulées postérieurement par M. le prince Menschikoff, quand l'objet principal de sa mission était atteint, quand on annonçait déjà son retour, ne se rattachaient donc par aucun lien à celles qu'il avait fait accueillir par la Porte; et c'était bien une nouvelle question, une difficulté plus grave, qui surgissait à Constantinople, alors que l'Europe, un instant alarmée, état invitée, par la Russie elle-même, à se rassurer complétement.

Pris, en quelque sorte, au dépourvu par des exigences qu'ils n'avaient pas dû soupçonner, les représentants de la France, de l'Autriche, de la Grande-Bretagne et de la Prusse à Constantinople ont loyalement employé leurs efforts pour empécher une rupture dont les conséquences pouvaient être si fatales. Ils n'ont pas conseillé à la Porte une résistance de nature à l'exposer aux dangers les plus sérieux; et, reconnaissant à l'unanimité que les demandes de la Russie touchaient de trop près à la liberté d'action et à la souveraineté du Sultan pour qu'ils pussent se permettre un avis, ils ont laissé aux seuls ministres de Sa Hautesse la responsabilité du parti à prendre. Il n'y a donc eu de leur part ni pression d'aucun genre, ni ingérence quelconque; et, si le gouvernement ottoman, livré à lui-même, n'a pas voulu souscrire aux conditions que l'on prétendait lui imposer, il faut qu'il les ait trouvées entièrement incompatibles avec son indépendance et sa dignité.

C'est dans de telles conjonctures, monsieur, que M. le prince Menschikoff a quitté Constantinople, en rompant toute relation diplomatique entre la Russie et la Porte, et que les puissances engagées par leurs traditions et leurs intérêts à maintenir l'intégrité de la Turquie ont eu à se tracer une règle de conduite.

Le gouvernement de Sa Majesté Impériale, d'accord avec celui de Sa Majesté Britannique, a pensé que la situation était trop menaçante pour ne pas être surveillée de près, et les escadres de France et d'Angleterre reçurent bientôt l'ordre d'aller mouiller dans le baie de Bésika, où elles arrivèrent au milieu du mois de juin. Cette mesure, toute de prévoyance, n'avait aucun caractère hostile à l'égard de la Russie; elle était impérieusement commandée par la gravité des circonstances, et amplement justifiée par les préparatifs de guerre qui, depuis plusieurs mois, se faisaient en Bessarabie et dans la rade de Sébastopol.

Le motif de la rupture entre le cabinet de Saint-Pétersbourg et la Porte avait, pour ainsi dire, disparu; la question qui pouvait se poser à l'improviste à Constantinople, c'était celle de l'existence même de l'Empire ottoman, et jamais le gouvernement de Sa Majesté impériale n'admettra que de si vastes intérêts se trouvent en jeu sans revendiquer aussitôt la part d'influence et d'action qui convient à sa puissance et à son rang dans le monde.

A la présence d'une armée russe sur les frontières de terre de la Turquie, il avait le droit et le devoir de répondre par la présence de ses forces navales à Bésika, dans une baie librement ouverte à toutes les marines, et située en deçà des limites que les traités défendent de franchir entemps de paix.

Le gouvernement de Russie, du reste, devait bientôt se charger d'expliquer lui-même la nécessité du mouvement ordonné aux deux escadres.

Le 31 mai, en effet, quand il était impossible de connaître à Saint-Pétersbourg, où la nouvelle n'en parvint que le 17 juin, les résolutions auxquelles pourraient s'arrêter la France et l'Angleterre, M. le comte de Nesselrode envoyait à la Porte, sous forme d'une lettre à Réchid pacha, un dernier ultimatum à bref délai, et qui contenait très-clairement exprimée la menace d'une prochaine occupation des principautés du Danube.

Lorsque cette décision était prise avec une solennité qui ne permettait plus un gouvernement jaloux de sa dignité de la modifier, lorsque, par une circulaire datée du 11 juin, Sa Majesté l'empereur Nicolas la faisait annoncer à l'Europe comme pour en rendre l'exécution plus irrévocable, notre escadre était encore à Salamine, et celle de l'Angleterre n'était pas sortie du port de Malte.

Ce simple rapprochement de date suffit, monsieur, pour indiquer de quel côte est partie cette initiative que l'on s'efforce aujourd'hui de décliner en rejetant la responsabilité sur la France et l'Angleterre; il suffit également pour prouver que, entre la communication faite à Paris et à Londres de la démarche tentée directement par M. le comte de Nesselrode à Constantinople, et le rejet de cet ultimatum, le temps a manqué matériellement aux gouvernement de Sa Majesté Impériale et de Sa Majesté Britannique pour exercer dans un sens quelconque leur influence à Constantinople. Non, monsieur, je le dis avec toute la puissance de la conviction, le gouvernement français, dans ce grave débat, n'a nul reproche à se faire, et, fort de sa modération, en appelle sans crainte, à son tour, au jugement des cabinets. Sauf le but si différent des deux démonstrations, il y avait peut-être une sorte d'analogie dans les situations respectives quand l'armée russe se tenait sur la rive gauche du Pruth, et que les flottes de France et d'Angleterre jetaient l'ancre à Bésika. Cette analogie a disparu depuis le passage de la rivière qui forme les limites de l'empire russe et de l'empire ottoman. M. le comte de Nesselrode, d'ailleurs, semble le reconnaître quand il suppose déjà les escadres en vue même de Constantinople, et représente comme une compensation nécessaire à ce qu'il appelle notre *occupation maritime* la position militaire prise par les troupes russes sur les bords du Danube.

Les forces anglaises et françaises ne portent, par leur présence en dehors des Dardanelles, aucune atteinte aux traités existants. L'occupation de la Valachie et de la Moldavie, au contraire, constitue une violation manifeste de ces mêmes traités. Celui d'Andrinople, qui détermine les conditions du protectorat de la Russie, pose implicitement le cas où il serait permis à cette puissance d'intervenir dans les Principautés; ce serait si leurs priviléges étaient méconnus par les Turcs.

En 1848, quand ces provinces ont été occupées par les Russes, elles se trouvaient en proie à une agitation révolutionnaire que menaça t leur sécurité, celle de la puissances souveraine et celle de la puissance protectrice. La convention de Balta-Liman, enfin, a admis que, si des événements semblables venaient à se renouveler dans une période de sept années, la Russie et la Turquie prendraient en commun les mesures les plus propres à rétablir l'ordre.

Les priviléges de la Moldavie et de la Valachie sont-ils menacés? Des troubles révolutionnaires ont-ils éclaté sur leur territore? Les faits répondent d'eux-mêmes qu'il n'y a lieu, pour le moment, à l'application, ni du traité d'Andrinople, ni de la convention de Balta-Liman. De quel droits les troupes russes ont-elles donc passé le Pruth, si ce n'est du droit de la guerre, d'une guerre, je le reconnais, dont on ne veut pas prononcer le vrai nom, mais qui dérive d'un principe nouveau, fécond en conséquences désastreuses, que l'on s'étonne de voir pratiquer pour la première fois par une puissance conservatrice de l'ordre européen à un degré aussi éminent que la Russie, et que n'irait à rein moins qu'à l'oppression, en pleine paix, des états faibles par les états plus forts qui sont leurs voisons?

L'intérêt général du monde s'oppose à l'admission d'une semblable doctrine, et la Porte en particulier a le droit incontestable de voir un acte de guerre dans l'envahissement de deux provinces, qui, quelle que soit leur organisation spéciale, font partie intégrante de son Empire. Elle ne violerait donc pas plus que les puissances qui viendraient à son aide le traité du 13 juillet 1841, si elle déclarait les détroits des Dardanelles et du Bosphore ouverts aux escadres de France et d'Angleterre. L'opinion du gouvernement de Sa Majesté Impériale est formelle à cet égard; et, bien que, dans sa pensée, elle n'exclue pas la Russie et la Turquie, j'ai invité M. le général par le recherche d'un moyen efficace de conciliation de Castelbajac à faire connaître notre manière de voir à M. le comte de Nesselrode et à lui communiquer cette dépêche.

Agréez, monsieur, l'assurance de ma haute considération.

Signé: Drouyn de Lhuys.

XII.

The Earl of Clarendon to Sir G. H. Seymour.

Foreign-office, July 16, 1853.

Sir,—Baron Brunnow has communicated to me the circular despatch dated the 20th of June, (2nd of July), which Count Nesselrode has addressed to the Russian missions.

It is difficult to express the astonishment and regret with which her Majesty's Government have read in this despatch the declaration, that the Principalities have been invaded and occupied in consequence of England and France having disregarded the recommendations of the Russian Government, and having sent their fleets to the waters of Turkey.

The passages of the despatch which contains this extraordinary statement are the following:—

"En posant cet ultimatum à la Porte, nous avions plus particulièrement informé les grands Cabinets de nos intentions. Nous avions engagé nommément la France et la Grand Bretagne à ne pas compliquer par leur attitude les difficultés de la situation, à ne pas prendre trop tôt de mesures qui, d'un côté, auraient pour effet d'encourager l'opposition de la Porte; de l'autre, engageraient plus avant qu'ils ne l'étaient déjà dans la question l'honneur et la dignité de l'Empereur.

"D'autre part, les deux Puissances maritimes n'ont pas cru devoir déférer aux considérations que nous avions recommandées à leur sérieuse attention. Prenant avant nous l'initiative, elles ont jugé indispensable de dévancer immédiatement par un mesure effective, celles que nous ne leur avions annoucées que comme purement éventuelles, puisque nous en subordonnions la mise à effet aux résolutions finales de la Porte; et qu'au moment même où j'écris l'execution n'en a pas encore commencé. Elles ont sur-le-champ envoyé leurs flottes dans les parages de Constantinople. Elles occupent déjà les eaux et les ports de la domination ottomane à portée des Dardanelles. Par cette attitude avancée, les deux Puissances nous ont placés sous le poids d'une démonstration comminatoire, qui, comme nous le leur avions fait pressentir, devait ajouter à la crise de nouvelles complications.

"En présence du refus de la Porte, appuyé par la manifestation de la France et de l'Angleterre, il nous devient plus que jamais impossible de modifier les résolutions qu'en avait fait dépendre l'Empereur.

"En conséquence, Sa Majesté Impériale vient d'envoyer au corps de ses troupes stationné en ce moment en Bessarabie l'ordre de passer la frontière pour occuper les Principautés."

With respect to the first passage, I have to observe that Count

Nesselrode's despatch of June 1 to Baron Brunnow was not communicated to Her Majesty's Government till June 8, and, therefore, the order sent a week before to Admiral Dundas to proceed to the neighborhood of the Dardanelles was not issued in disregard, as Count Nesselrode's circular affirms, of considerations brought to the knowledge of the British Government. But, even if the case had been otherwise, and no orders had been issued, it was impossible for her Majesty's Government to suppose that the threat to occupy the Principalities would be rendered null by the Porte accepting the terms which a a few days before it had unhesitatingly rejected; and on the 8th of June, therefore, her Majesty's Government were compelled to consider the occupation of the Principalities inevitable; and they conclude that the Cabinet of St. Petersburg is not now prepared to admit that the note of Count Nesselrode to Redschid Pasha contained an empty menace, the execution of which was never seriously contemplated. But, in fact, Count Nesselrode's note of May 31, communicating the hostile intentions of Russia, would of itself have been sufficient to justify her Majesty's Government in taking measures for the protection of Turkey.

I shall now proceed to place on record at what time and for what reasons the British fleet was sent to the Turkish waters.

Prince Menschikoff, acting, it must be assumed, on the orders of his Government, stated in his note of the 5th of May, of which a copy was received in London on the 18th May, that any further delay in answering his proposals respecting the Greek church could only be considered by him as "un manque de procédés envers son Gouvernement, ce qui lui imposerait les plus pénibles obligations.

Again, in his note of the 11th of May, a copy of which was received in London on the 30th of May, Prince Menschikoff says, that in case of an unsatisfactory decision on the part of the Porte, "si les principes que en forment la base [of the articles he was negotiating] sont rejetés, si par une opposition systématique la Sublime Porte persiste à lui fermer jusqu'aux voies d'une entente intime et directe, il devra considérer sa mission comme terminée, interrompre les relations avec le Cabinet de Sa Majesté le Sultan, et rejeter sur la responsabilité de ses Ministres toutes les conséquences qui pourraient en résulter." And lastly, in his note of the 15th of May, received in London June 1, Prince Menschikoff concludes:—"Il appartient à la sagacité de votre Altesse de péser les suites incalculables et les grandes calamités qui pourraient en résulter, et qui retomberaient de tout leur poids sur la responsabilité des Ministres de Sa Majesté le Sultan."

This succession of menaces, addressed to a power whose independence Russia had declared her determination to uphold, and in support of claims so much at variance with the assurances given to her Majesty's Government, together with the vast military and naval armaments which for months had been preparing on the very confines of Turkey, left no doubt on the mind of her Majesty's Government of the imminent danger in which the Sultan was about to be placed.

They deeply lamented that this danger should arise from acts of the Russian Government, which was a party to the treaty of 1841; but, as her Majesty's Government adhere now, as firmly as in 1841, to the principles which that treaty records, and believe that the maintenance of European peace is involved in the maintenance of the Ottoman empire, they felt that the time had arrived when, in the interests of peace, they must be prepared to protect the Sultan; and, upon learning the abrupt departure of Prince Menschikoff, it was determined that the British fleet, which up to that time had not quitted Malta, should be placed at the disposal of her Majesty's Ambassador at Constantinople.

On the 1st of June a despatch was forwarded to Lord Stratford de Redcliffe, authorizing him in certain specified contingencies to send for the fleet, which would then repair to such place as he might point out. On the 2nd of June instructions were sent to Admiral Dundas to proceed at once to the neighborhood of the Dardanelles, and there to place himself in communication with her Majesty's Ambassador.

On the previous day we received a copy of Prince Menschikoff's note of May 18, announcing the determination of his mission, and that the refusal of the guarantee demanded " devra désormais imposer au Gouvernement Impérial la necessité de la chercher dans sa propre puissance."

The following is the reply of the four Ambassadors at Constantinople to Redschid Pasha, when consulted by him on the draught of the treaty which Prince Menschikoff had sent to the Divan:—

"*May* 21, 1853.

"The representatives of Great Britain, France, Austria, and Prussia, in reply to the desire expressed by his Excellency Redschid Pasha to learn their views on a draught of a note communicated by Prince Menschikoff, are of opinion that, on a question which touches so nearly the liberty of action and sovereignty of his Majesty the Sultan, his Excellency Redschid Pasha is the best judge of the course which ought to be adopted; and they do not consider themselves authorized, in the present circumstance, to give any advice on the subject.

(Signed) " REDCLIFFE.
" E. DE LA COUR.
" E. DE KLETZL.
" WILDENBRUCK."

On the 2nd of June I communicated to Baron Brunnow the measure taken by her Majesty's Government; it could not have been made known by him at St. Petersburg before the 7th or 8th, and consequently it could in no way influence the decision taken by the Russian Government; for Count Nesselrode's note to Redschid Pasha, announcing that "dans quelques semaines ses troupes recevront l'ordre de passer les frontières de l'empire," was dated the 31 of May; and his despatch to Baron Brunnow, in which he said that if the Porte did not sign Prince Menschikoff's note within a week after the arrival of the note to Redschid Pasha, the Emperor "ordonnera à ses troupes d'occuper les Principautés," was dated the 1st June.

It is thus clearly established that the British fleet was not sent to the waters of Turkey in disregard of considerations submitted to her Majesty's Government by the Cabinet of St. Petersburg, and that on the day before the instructions to Lord Stratford de Redcliffe left London, the decision to occupy the Principalities was taken by the Russian Government; and I say that decision was taken, because the Russian Government could never for one moment seriously have expected the submission of the Porte to the terms, "sans variante," that a regard for its own dignity and security had a few days before compelled it to decline. Yet Count Nesselrode, in his circular despatch of July 2, affirms that the presence of the English and French fleets in the Bay of Besika has mainly provoked and fully justifies the occupation of the Principalities; he insists that they are in sight of the capital, from which they are nearly 200 miles distant, and that their maritime occupation of the Turkish waters and ports can only be balanced by a military position on the part of Russia.

But her Majesty's Government must, in the strongest terms, protest against this assertion; and they deny that any resemblance exists between the position of the combined fleets in Besika Bay and that of the Russian armies in the Principalities. The fleets have the same right to anchor in Besika Bay as in any port in the Mediterranean. Their presence there violates no treaty and no territory; it infringes no international law; it is no menace to Turkish independence, and it assuredly ought to be no cause of offence to Russia; whereas by occupying the Principalities Russia does violate the territory of the Sultan and the special treaty which regards that portion of his dominion. It is an infraction of the law of nations, and an act of direct hostility against the Sultan, which he would be justified in meeting by a declaration of war, and by a requisition to the allied squadrons to come up to Constantinople for his defence; and, lastly, it is an act so dangerous as a precedent, and so violent on the part of a powerful State towards one whose very weakness should be its protection, that throughout Europe it has created feelings of alarm and reprobation. To admit that any similarity exists, or that any comparison can with truth be established, between the position of the English and French fleets outside the Dardanelles and that of the Russian armies within the Principalities, is manifestly impossible.

It is with deep regret that her Majesty's Government thus find themselves compelled to record their opinions upon the recent invasion of the Turkish territory; but they consider that the withholding of those opinions would be an abandonment of duty on their part, and might render it difficult for them hereafter to interfere in defence and support of treaties which constitute the international law of Europe, and which are the only effectual guarantees of general peace and of the rights of nations.

The sufferings which the occupation of the Principalities must entail upon the inhabitants will, doubtless, be much alleviated by the Russian Government taking upon itself the entire charge of that occupation.

As I have so often, and at such length, discussed the demands of Russia upon the Porte, it is hardly necessary for me to remark upon the other portions of Count Nesselrode's circular despatch, which, in fact, adduces no new fact or argument in support of those demands. I must, however, express the conviction of Her Majesty's Government that the Cabinet of St. Petersburg is altogether mistaken when it affirms that the Porte is indisposed to satisfy the just claims of Russia, or desires to shrink from its existing engagements with Russia. If this were correct, such influence as Her Majesty's Government may possess would be exercised to bring the Porte to a proper sense of its obligations; but they are as unaware of such breach of engagement on the part of the Porte as they are of those numerous arbitrary acts of the Ottoman Government, which, it is said, recently infringed the rights of the Greek church, and threatened utterly to annihilate the order of things sanctioned by ages, and so dear to the orthodox faith.

Russia claims for her "*co-religionnaires*" in the East the strict *status quo*, and the maintenance of the privileges they have enjoyed under the protection of their Sovereign; but Count Nesselrode entirely omits to show how that *status quo* has been disturbed, how those privileges have been curtailed, what complaints have been made, what grievances remain without redress. Her Majesty's Government know only of one offence committed by the Turkish Government against Russia, which, by the admission of Prince Menschikoff, was satisfactorily atoned for; while, on the other hand, the recent firman of the Sultan, confirming the privileges and immunities of the Greek church, has been gratefully acknowledged by the Patriarch of Constantinople.

Where, then, are the causes which Count Nesselrode, appealing to impartial Europe, assumes will justify the position now taken by Russia?

Count Nesselrode further says that Russia, by her position and by her treaties, virtually enjoys the right of protecting the Greek church in the East. If such be the case, and if that right, whatever its nature and extent may be, is undisturbed, it is Russia that throws doubt upon its existence or validity by endeavouring to force the Porte into fresh engagements. If ancient rights exist, and are observed by

Turkey, Russia has no cause of complaint against Turkey. But, if she seeks to extend those rights, then is Turkey justified in closely examining the nature of such fresh demands, and in refusing those from which her independence and dignity would suffer.

Her Majesty's Government receive with sincere satisfaction the renewed assurances that it is the policy of His Imperial Majesty and the interest of Russia to maintain the existing order of things in the East; and, as the interests of Turkey impose upon her the necessity of observing her engagements with Russia, Her Majesty's Government trust that Russia will not, by seeking at the present time to exact what the Porte ought not to yield, prolong a crisis that may render inevitable consequences which Europe is so deeply concerned in averting.

You will read this despatch to Count Nesselrode and furnish his Excellency with a copy of it.

I am &c.,

CLARENDON.

XIII.

Lettre du prince de Moldavie à Réchid pacha.

Jassy, 25 juin (7 julliet) 1853.

Altesse,

Je vou ai exposé hier les conséquences de l'occupation des provinces danubiennes par les troupes russes. Aujourd'hui j'ai la douleur de vous faire une communication que le consul russe vient de m'adresser. Les deux documents dont vous trouverez ci-inclus des copies vous donneront une idée de cette demande de Sa Majesté l'Empereur de Russie, qui m'ordonne d'interrompre mes relations avec la Sublime Porte et l'envoi du tribut, attendu que cela serait incompatible avec la présence de l'armée russe dans les Principautés.

J'ai eu une entrevue avec le prince Gortschakoff immédiatement après la réception de cette communication. J'ai cru devoir lui faire des observations à cette égard, et je lui ai déclaré que je me trouvais dans la nécessité d'en donner connaisance à la Sublime-Porte. Le général n'a pas élevé d'objection à ce sujet. Comme je sens combien il est au-dessus de mon pouvoir de toucher à des mesures dépendant de la décision des deux puissances, je me hâte, de mon côté, d'en faire un rapport à Votre Altesse, afin qu'elle résolve dans sa sagesse ce qu'elle jugera utile.

Agréez, etc. *Signé:* GHIKA.

PIÈCES ANNEXÉES A LA PRÉCÉDENTE.

1.

Lettre du consul général de Russie à Bucarest M. Khaltchinski, au prince de Moldavie.

Bucarest, le 23 juin (5 juillet) 1853.

J'ai l'honneur d'envoyer confidentiellement à Votre Altesse la copie ci-incluse d'une dépêche que M. le comte de Nesselrode, chancelier d'Etat, m'adresse en date du 3 juin. Vous y verrez, prince, les instructions les plus précises sur la conduite que vous devez suivre en raison de l'occupation des Principautés par les troupes impériales envers la Porte Ottomane, ainsi que les mesures que vous aurez à prendre pour retenir le tribut que la Moldavie a payé jusqu'à ce jour au gouvernement ottoman. En vous invitant à suivre les ordres de Sa Majesté Impériale contenus dans la dépêche que je vous envoie, j'ai l'honneur, etc.

Signé : KHALTCHINSKI.

2.

Dépêche de M. le comte de Nesselrode à M. Khaltckinski, consul général de Russie à Bucarest.

Saint-Pétersbourg, le 3 (15) juin 1853.

L'occupation militaire des Principautés danubiennes ne devra, comme je l'ai déjà dit, opérer aucun changement dans l'administration civile du pays et dans les attributions des fonctionnaires publics, à moins que les hospodars eux-mêmes ne jugent utile de remplacer des fonctionnaires, pour mettre la plus grande régularité dans les diverses branches du service public et dans celui de l'approvisionnement des troupes impériales.

Cependant il reste encore une question sur laquelle nous devons faire connaître aux deux hospodars notre opinion pour leur servir de guide.

Nous voulons parler de leur rapports avec Constantinople et le ministère ottoman. Il faudra que ces relations cessent le jour où nos troupes occuperont militairement les principautés, et où, par conséquent, toute influence et toute mesure de la puissance suzeraine devront temporairement rester suspendues.

On suspendra, en outre, le payement du tribut que les deux provinces doivent payer à la Porte Ottomane. Les sommes à encaisser devront rester à la disposition du gouvernement impérial, qui se réserve d'en faire l'usage qu'il jugera à propos. Vous communiquerez aux deux hospodars les ordres de l'Empereur que je viens de vous transmettre.

Signé : Nesselrode.

XIV.

Manifeste (2e) *de la Sublime-Porte adressé à la nation, en date du* 21 *chewal* 1269 (*juillet* 1853).

Le gouvernement de la Sublime-Porte et celui de Sa Majesté l'Empereur de Russie n'ayant pas pu tomber d'accord sur quelques questions qui existent entre eux, et le gouvernement russe ayant rompu ses relations officielles avec celui de la Sublime-Porte et rappelé de Constantinople son ambassade, en faisant de grands préparatifs de guerre sur terre et sur mer, le gouvernement impérial, dans un but de précaution et de conservation, s'est livré, de son côté, d'ordre de Sa Majesté le Sultan, à des préparatifs du même genre. Ces faits furent portés, il y a quelque temps, à la connaissance du public par le moyen du journal officiel le *Taqvimi-Vaqâi.*

Le véritable motif des discussions était celui-ci : le gouvernement russe voulait que les priviléges spirituels de l'Eglise et des moines grecs formassent l'argument d'un traité entre les deux puissances ; le gouvernement de la Sublime-Porte refusait d'entrer dans un pareil engagement.

En effet, ces priviléges, octroyés par Sa Majesté le Sultan Mohammed le Conquérant, ont été conservés et confirmés dans les siècles suivants par ses successeurs. Sa Majesté le Sultan actuel, en suivant les traces de ses glorieux ancêtres, leur a donné une nouvelle confirmation. Il ne saurait donc entrer dans la pensée de personne que des priviléges aussi anciens, spontanément accordés par l'autorité impériale, pussent nullement être retirés ou restreints. Le gouvernement impérial pouvait, là-dessus, donner des assurances à tout le monde.

Néanmoins, le gouvernement russe refusa d'accepter la forme d'assurance qui suffisait à effacer les soupçons accidentels formant l'objet de la question. Et comme il serait porté atteinte à l'indépendance d'une puissance et à ses droits souverains, si, sous couleur de traité ou cédant à la force, elle concédait à une puissance étrangère le droit de faire exécuter d'une manière régulière des priviléges religieux accordés à des millions de ses sujets, le gouvernement impérial déclara qu'il ne pouvait consentir à autre chose.

Or, le gouvernement russe, n'agréant pas la persévérance avec laquelle la Sublime-Porte lui déclara maintes fois, dans les terms les plus sincères et les plus amicaux, qu'elle ne pouvait pas se rendre à ses désirs, ce gouvernement persistant dans sa demande, et ayant tout récemment ordonné à ses troupes de franchir le Pruth dans le but de prendre momentanément possession des principautés de Moldavie et de Valachie, a causé un profond étonnement à Sa Majesté Impériale.

Ce passage des frontières étant contraire aux traités existants, le gouvernement impérial a dû, comme c'est d'usage parmi les nations, protester immédiatement contre un pareil acte, c'est-à-dire faire connaître à toutes les puissances, d'une manière légale et publique, qu'elle ne pouvait accepter une telle violation des traités existants.

Comme en conséquence des traités, il existe entre les puissances une espèce de solidarité quant aux matières qui touchent à la parfaite jouissance de leur souveraineté et de leur indépendance, et qu'il est d'usage en diplomatie, à l'apparition d'une question aussi importante, de prendre l'opinion des cabinets et de les informer des faits, le gouvernement russe a publiquement déclaré qu'il ne se proposait pas de faire la guerre à la Sublime-Porte, mais qu'il voulait seulement, par l'occupation de la Moldo-Valachie, s'assurer des garanties matérielles pour l'acceptation de sa demande. De son côté, le gouvernement de Sa Majesté Impériale, qui a reçu de toutes les puissances alliées, sans exceptions, et selon le grade de chacune, de hauts témoignages de sympathie et d'amitié; dont les représentants, en général, et ceux de l'Angleterre et de la France, en particulier, comme représentants de puissances maritimes, ont donné des preuves éclatantes de leur bon vouloir et de leur intention d'appuyer de toute leur force l'autorité de Sa Majesté Impériale, le gouvernement de la Sublime-Porte s'est aussi empressé, d'après les usages susmentionnés, de faire connaître publiquement que d'aucune façon il n'accepterait jamais quelque acte que ce soit pouvant porter atteinte à son indépendance et à ses droits de souveraineté, et que, en attendant de voir dans quelle phase sérait entrée la question, et dans le but de pourvoir, par des moyens de précaution, à sa propre conservation, il s'est déterminé à prendre une attitude armée sur le Danube et les frontières asiatiques, tout en ne discontinuant point de poursuivre la voie des négociations.

Telle est l'origine de la discussion qui existe entre les deux cabinets, et l'état actuel de la question. Le gouvernement de la Sublime-Porte s'empressant de faire toute sorte de préparatifs de guerre et de pourvoir du nécessaire ses troupes et ses places fortes, chaque sujet indistinctement de Sa Majesté Impériale, par le fait de vaquer aux affaires de son état ou de sa charge, de ne s'occuper que de ce qui le concerne, d'agriculture, d'industrie ou de commerce, sera censé exécuter les ordres de son gouvernement.

Il résulte de ce qui précéde que la discussion avec la cour de Russie porte sur le terrain des priviléges religieux des Grecs. Mais les chefs de la communauté grecque, et chacun de ses membres individuellement, ne sont nullement intervenus dans cette question. Ils professent, au contraire, des sentiments de parfaite soumission et de reconnaissance envers le gouvernement, et il est à la pleine connaissance de la Sublime-Porte qu'ils ont reçu de tout ceci une impression pénible. Il est donc parfaitement conforme à la nature de cette affaire qu'ils ne soient en rien molestés pour ce motif; que toute membre des communautés arméniennes, catholique, protestante ou juive, et sujet de notre auguste et bienfaisant maître le Sultan, soit considéré et respecté de même que les membres de la nation grecque. Il est du devoir de chacun d'observer envers les autres des procédés de bonne harmonie, de ne manifester aucun sentiment d'inimitié ou de haine. Les Musulmans, comme les autres sujets de la Sublime-Porte, doivent se tenir strictement dans la voie d'une loyale et parfaite union. Que personne ne s'occupe de discours hors de son état ou de sa charge, et ne cherche à semer la discorde, mais qu'il vaque uniquement et paisiblement à ses affaires.

Ces prescriptions ont été résolues dans un conseil tenu sous la présidence du grand vizir, et auquel ont assisté le cheikh-ul-islam, les ulémas, les membres du grand conseil, tous les ministres et hauts fonctionnaires de la Sublime Porte, d'après un ordre émané de Sa Majesté le Sultan. Celui qui ne s'y conformera pas et fera quelque acte en opposition aux avertissements qui y sont relatés, sera censé commettre le crime de rébellion, et puni en conséquence.

Suivent les signatures des personages qui ont approuvé et confirmé les résolutions et les dispositions du présent manifeste, en y apposant leur cachet, au nombre de soixant-deux, à savoir :

Moustafa-Naïli pacha, grand vizir.
Arif-Hikmet bey éfendi, cheikh-ul-islam.
Reouf pacha, ancien grand vizir, ministre sans portefeuille.
Izzet-Mehemet pacha, ancien grand vizir.
Khosrew-Mehemet pacha, ancien grand vizir.
A'ali pacha, ancien grand vizir.
Moustafa-Réchid, ministre des affaires étrangères.
Mehemet-Ali pacha, séraskier, ministre de la guerre.
Ahmed-Fethi pacha, grand maître de l'artillerie.
Rifa'at pacha, président du conseil d'état.
Mahmoud pacha, capitan-pacha (grand amiral), ministre de la marine.
Saïd pacha, ancien ministre de la guerre.
Riza pacha, ancien ministre de la guerre.
Mehemet-Ruchdi pacha, muchir de la garde impériale.
Ali-Ghalib pacha,* membre du conseil d'état.
Hassib pacha, ministre de l'hôtel impérial des monnaies.
A'arif pacha, ministre sans portefeuille.
Nafiz pacha, ancien ministre des finances.
Saffeti pacha,† ancien ministre des finances.
Namik pacha,‡ ministre du commerce.

* Fils de Réchid pacha, fiancé à la fille du Sultan, *Fatimé Sultane*, née le 2 novembre 1840.
† Actuellement de nouveau ministre des finances.
‡ Actuellement en mission à Paris.

Haïreddin pacha, ministre de la police.
Réchid pacha, ancien muchir de la garde impériale.
Izzet pacha, ancien ministre du commerce.
Mehemet pacha,* gouverneur général d'Andrinople.
Youssouf-Kiamil pacha, membre du conseil d'état.
Ismaïl pacha, gouverneur général de Smyrne.
Yacoub pacha, ex-gouverneur général de Salonique.
Salih pacha.
Ismet pacha.
Izzet pacha.
Khalil-Kiamili pacha,† ex-gouverneur général de Smyrne.
Aguiah pacha.
Ali-Riza pacha.
Sirri pacha.
Abdullak éfendi, kaziasker‡ en exercice.
Ibrahim éfendi, kaziasker, membre du conseil d'état.
Arif éfendi, kaziasker, membre du conseil d'état.
Taksin bey éfendi, kaziasker, membre du conseil d'état.
Ruchdi éfendi, kaziasker, membre du conseil d'état.
Izzet éfendi, kaziasker, membre du conseil d'état.
Ismet bey, kaziasker, membre du conseil de l'instruction publique.
Nafi éfendi, kaziasker, membre de la cour des comptes.
Chevket bey, conseiller du grand vizir.
Mouktar bey, ministre des finances.
Fuad éfendi, ex-ministre des affaires étrangères.
Husseïn bey, directeur de l'octroi.
Tevfik bey, intendant des dépenses.
Zuhdi bey, directeur de l'amirauté.
Ziver éfendi, ministre des fondations pieuses (*evkafs*).
Chefik bey, membre du conseil d'état.
Mazloum bey, ex-directeur des causes judiciaires.§
Eumer-Djemal éfendi, directeur des causes judiciaires.
Nafi éfendi, conseiller du ministre de la guerre.
Mahmoud bey, rapporteur du divan impérial.
A'afif bey, chancelier du divan impérial.
Nazif bey, maître des cérémonies du divan impérial.
Ali Riza éfendi, membre du conseil d'état.
Mumtaz éfendi, membre du conseil d'état.
Mouktar bey, membre du conseil d'état.

* Ancien ambassadeur à Londres (1849), ancien gouverneur d'Alep et commandant en chief de l'armée d'Arabie (1850).

† Beau-frère du Sultan.

‡ Le titre de kaziasker est le premier de l'ordre judiciaire, après le cheik-ul-islam ; il y a toujours deux kaziaskers en exercice, le kaziasker de Roumélie et le kaziasker d'Anatolie, qui sont les chefs de la magistrature, l'un en Europe, l'autre en Asie. Leurs fonctions, comme celles de tous les membres du corps judiciaire, sont annuelles.

§ Le directeur des causes judiciaires (*de' avi naziri*) remplit les fonctions de ministre de la justice.

Haïroullah éfendi, membre du conseil d'état.
Djemaleddin éfendi, directeur de l'école impériale de médecine.
Habab éfendi, chef du bureau de la correspondance du grand vizir.

XV.

Note explicative adressée par la Sublime-Porte aux représentants de France, d'Angleterre, d'Autriche, et de Prusse, avec le projet de Note modifié le 20 *août* 1853.

Le conseil des ministres a examiné attentivement le projet de Notre rédigé à Vienne, qui vient d'être transmis à la Sublime-Porte.

Le gouvernement ottoman a été profondément peiné de voir qu'au lieu de l'heureux résultat qu'il espérait du projet de Note antérieurement rédigé à Constantinople, dans une forme propre à aplanir le différend surgi entre lui et la cour de Russie, et communiqué aux grandes puissances, ce projet n'ait pas été pris en considération. Il n'est pas moins particulièrement affecté de se trouver obligé d'émettre quelques observations sur le projet de Note venu de Vienne, lequel, tout en prenant pour base, en ce qui concerne les privilèges religieux, le projet de Note précédemment rédigé par la Sublime-Porte pour être remis au prince Menschikoff, s'écarte cependant des limites du point en litige et contient des passages superflus, conçus dans un sens incompatible avec les droits sacrés de Sa Majesté Impériale.

Habitué de tout temps à recevoir de la part des grandes puissances, ses augustes alliées, des témoignages d'amitié, et infiniment reconnaissant, surtout, de la bienveillante sollicitude qu'elles n'ont cessé de lui montrer depuis le commencement de ces difficultés, le gouvernement impérial ne sait comment concilier la déférence toute particulière qu'il doit aux quatre grandes cours avec ses hésitations de souscrire à un arrangement qui a réuni leurs suffrages. Mais, malheureusement, la position difficile où il se trouve aujourd'hui n'est évidemment que la conséquence de ce fait, que, reconnu dès le principe comme seul juge compétent dans les questions relatives à ses droits et à son indépendance, son avis ne lui ait pas été demandé.

On pourrait alléguer, il est vrai, qu'on n'a pas non plus consulté l'opinion du cabinet de Saint-Pétersbourg pour la rédaction de ce projet de Note: mais ce que l'on s'efforçait de sauvegarder, c'étaient les droits de la Porte et c'est encore elle qui doit signer la Note à donner. Nous laissons à l'équité bien reconnue des hautes puissances à discerner, si, en cette occurrence, il était permis ou non de traiter les deux parties sur un pied égal, et nous jugeons à propos de ne pas nous étendre davantage là-dessus.

Le premier point qui fait hésiter la Sublime-Porte est le passage où il est dit :

"Si, à toute epoque, les empereurs de Russie ont témoigné leur active sollicitude pour le maintien des immunités et priviléges de l'église orthodoxe grecque dans l'empire ottoman, les Sultans ne se sont jamais refusés à les consacrer de nouveau par des actes solennels."

Que les empereurs de Russie témoignent leur sollicitude pour la prospérité de l'église orthodoxe et les splendeurs du culte qu'ils professent, rien de plus naturel. Mais, à en juger par la tournure de ce paragraphe, on dirait que les priviléges de cette église, dans l'empire ottoman, n'ont été concédés et maintenus, depuis Mohammed le Conquérant, de glorieuse mémoire, jusqu'à nos jours, sans la moindre ingérence de qui que ce soit. L'insertion de cette phrase dans la Note que la Sublime-Porte doit donner fournirait implicitement à la cour de Russie un prétexte de s'immiscer dans des affaires de cette nature. Il est donc évident que personne, en permettant une chose aussi nuisible au présent qu'à l'avenir, ne consentirait à s'exposer au blâme et au reproche des contemporains et de la postérité, et qu'aucun des serviteurs comblés de bienfaits de l'illustre dynastie d'Othman ne pourrait, ni n'oserait écrire des expressions qui sembleraient vouloir ravir aux glorieux Sultans précédents des monuments fondés et élevés par la seule impulsion de leur libéralité personelle et de leur bonté innée.

Le second point est le paragraphe du projet de Note relatif au traité de Kaïnardji.

Personne ne saurait nier que ce traité existe et qu'il est confirmé par celui d'Andrinople. Il est donc évident que toutes ses stipulations seront toujours fidèlement observées. Mais si, en insérant le paragraphe susmentionné, on a l'intention de considérer les priviléges religieux comme un resultat naturel de l'esprit commenté du traité de Kaïnardji, la disposition précise et réelle de ce traité est limitée à la seule promesse de la Sublime-Porte *de protéger elle même la religion chrétienne.* Le paragraphe que le Sublime-Porte pourrait, en ce qui concerne les priviléges religieux, insérer dans la Note qu'elle signera, ne devrait, comme il a été à toute époque déclaré, soit par écrit, soit verbalement, exprimer que des assurances propres à faire disparaître les doutes mis en avant par le gouvernement de Russie et qui ont fourni le sujet du différend actuel. Autrement, en fortifiant et en consolidant par de nouveaux liens l'analogie religieuse qui existe entre une très-grande communauté des sujets de la Sublime-Porte et une puissance étrangère, on motiverait les prétentions de la Russie à l'ingérence et au droit de surveillance en parielles matières, on partagerait, en quelque sorte, les droits souverains et l'on mettrait en péril l'indépendance du gouvernement. C'est à quoi la Sublime-Porte ne saurait jamais consentir de bon gré.

Si le but n'est que de faire renouveler les engagements dudit traité, la Sublime-Porte pourrait le faire par une Note séparée. A son avis, il est d'une très-haute importance que ce passage du projet débattu soit supprimé, ou que, s'il est maintenu, les deux points soient présentés d'une manière non équivoque, et que l'on distingue, du premier coup d'œil, que la promesse de protection contenue dans ledit traité et la question des priviléges religieux sont des choses tout à fait séparées.

Le troisième point concerne l'association du culte grec aux avantages accordés aux autres confessions chrétiennes.

Sans parler des avantages que, par un mouvement spontané de sa volonté, le gouvernement impérial à accordés aux autres cultes chrétiens professés par des communautés de ses propres sujets, la Sublime-Porte est à l'abri du reproche de vouloir jamais hésiter d'associer aussi le culte grec aux avantages qu'elle pourrait leur accorder par la suite. Il serait donc superflu de dire qu'elle est bien excusable de ne pouvoir consentir à l'emploi d'expressions obscures, telles que *conventions et dispositions particulières*, quand il s'agit d'une communauté considérable composée de tant de millions d'âmes, comme l'est celle des sujets grecs de l'Empire.

Tels sont les points qui, aux yeux de la Sublime-Porte, paraissent offrir des inconvénients, et tout en protestant de sa déférence absolue pour les conseils des grandes puissances ses alliées, et de son sincère désir de renouveler ses relations avec l'auguste cour de Russie, son amie et voisine, elle n'a pu s'empêcher de soumettre à leur équitable appréciation et à la balance de leur justice des observations qui concernent ses droits souverains et son indépendance.

En un mot, si le projet rédigé en dernier lieu par la Sublime-Porte est accepté, ou si celui venu de Vienne est modifié dans le sens voulu, le gouvernement impérial n'apportera aucun retard à la signature de l'un des deux, et à l'envoi immédiat d'un personnage en mission spéciale, sous la condition cependant que les deux principautés soient évacuées; mais il s'attend aussi à une garantie solide de la part des grandes puissances contre toute espèce d'ingérence ultérieure et contre de nouvelles et fréquentes expéditions de troupes en Valachie et en Moldavie.

Par toutes ces précautions, la Sublime-Porte n'a en vue que d'écarter tout ce qui, après la reprise de ses rapports avec le gouvernement de Russie, pourrait reproduire des discussions entre les deux cours.

Les passages du projet de Vienne relatifs à la question des Lieux-Saints et à la construction d'une église et d'un hôpital, ont été pleinement approuvés par la Sublime-Porte.

Je transmets à Votre Excellence, avec la présente, copie du projet de Note venu de Vienne avec les modifications que la Sublime-Porte a jugé à propos d'y faire. Bien que le gouvernement ottoman doive naturellement préférer celui qu'il avait lui-même rédigé, il veut donner aux grandes puissances signataires du traité de 1841 une nouvelle preuve de sa déférence particulière, en se montrant prêt à accepter le projet de Vienne avec les modifications susmentionnées, et la Sublime-Porte espère que ces mêmes puissances qui, dès l'origine de la question, ont reconnu son droit et n'ont cessé de lui témoigner un bienveillant intérêt, apprécieront cet incident et voudront bien agir en conséquence.

Sa Majesté Impériale ayant daigné m'ordonner de communiquer ce qui précède à Votre Excellence et à MM. les répresentants vos collègues, je saisis cette occasion pour vous renouveler, etc., etc.

Signé : Réchid.

15 zilcadé 1269 (20 août 1853).

XVI.

Circular by the Minister of Foreign Affairs to the different French Legations.

Paris, 30th December, 1853.

Sir,—The affairs of the East now assume a turn too serious for me not, at the moment when circumstances impose fresh duties on the Government of his Imperial Majesty, to remind you of the efforts which we have never ceased to make in order to prevent the complications with which Europe is so seriously threatened.

The question of the Holy Places, either badly presented or wrongly understood, had excited the alarms of the Cabinet of St. Petersburg; we endeavoured to quiet that uneasiness by complete explanations given in good faith. It had appeared to us that, while reserving the rights of the Porte, a discussion of this kind would better have taken place at a distance from the scene where it began. Our opinion was not shared in by Russia, and Prince Menschikoff received orders to proceed to Constantinople. I shall confine myself to remarking, that if we had entertained the exclusive views which were attributed to us, that if the vindication of our old and incontestible privileges had not been supported with so much moderation, the mission of that ambassador extraordinary would have been immediately the object of a conflict which we have known how to avoid. The affair of the sanctuaries of Jerusalem having been, according to the testimony of the Count de Nesselrode himself, settled in a satisfactory manner, another difficulty arose. Prince Menschikoff claimed guarantees for the maintenance of the privileges of the Greek Church. The Cabinet of St. Petersburg did not establish by any particular fact that these privileges had been violated, and the Porte, on the contrary, solemnly confirmed the religious immunities of its Christian subjects.

Animated with a desire to put an end to a difference which, if it on the one hand concerned the sovereign rights of the Sultan, on the other affected the conscience of the Emperor Nicholas, the Government of his Imperial Majesty, in concert with that of her Britannic Majesty, carefully sought for the means of reconciling the interests, at once so delicate and so complicated, which were engaged in it. The Cabinet of St. Petersburg cannot have forgotten the zeal and the good faith with which we endeavoured to fulfil this difficult task, nor can it deny that the resistance of the Porte to accede to a first plan of arrangement, emanating from the conference of Vienna, has not been the sole cause of our want of success.

In the course of these different negotiations grave facts occurred; a Russian army crossed the Pruth, and invaded in full peace two provinces of the Ottoman empire. The squadrons of France and England were made to approach the Dardanelles; and at that time, if the Government of his Imperial Majesty desired it, its naval forces would have anchored in the waters of Constantinople. However, if it thought it necessary to establish its right, it was only as it were to make its moderation more striking. The nature of the relations between Russia and the Sublime Porte had become such that it was necessary for the state of war to succeed the state of peace, or, to speak more correctly, it was necessary that things should take their veritable name, and that the aggression of which the Turkish territory was the object should produce its consequences. This change in the situation necessitated a new movement of our fleet, and on the demand of the Sultan the French flag appeared in the Bosphorus at the same time as the British flag. However, Monsieur ——, we had not abandoned the hope of arrangement; and in accord with Austria and Prussia, as we previously were with England, we continued to pursue a pacific object. New propositions, for the success of which we shall not cease to employ our efforts, have been addressed to the Porte by the representatives of the Four Powers.

No treaty concluded with Russia interdicted the navigation of the Black Sea to our vessels of war. The treaty of the 13th July, 1841, by closing in time of peace the passages of the Dardanelles and the Bosphorus, reserved to the Sultan the faculty of opening them in time of war, and from the day on which his Highness left us free access to the Straits, that of the Euxine was legally acquired to us. The same motives which had detained us in the Bay of Besika, detained our squadron in the roadstead of Beikos. The Government of his Imperial Majesty had at heart to testify to the end the sentiments of friendship which it professes for Russia, and to reject in the eyes of the world the responsibility of an aggravation of the state of things which all its circumspection (managements) had not succeeded in modifying. It took pleasure in believing, besides, from recent despatches of General de Castelbajac, that the Cabinet of St. Petersburg, satisfied with a taking of possession which it considered as a pledge, would not anywhere take the offensive in a conflict which has commenced so unfortunately for Turkey. It appeared to us sufficient that the presence of our flag in the waters of Constantinople should attest our firm intention to protect this capital from a sudden danger, and we did not wish that its premature appearance in a spot nearer to the Russian territory should run the risk of passing for a provocation.

The state of war rendered, no doubt, a collision possible on sea as well as on land between the belligerent parties; but we were warranted in believing that our reserve would be imitated by Russia, and that her Admirals would avoid, with the same care as ours, the occasions of a rencontre, by abstaining from proceeding to measures of aggression, within limits in which, if we could have supposed the Cabinet of St. Petersburg to be animated with different intentions, our fleet would certainly have exercised a more active surveillance.

The affair of Sinope, Monsieur ——, took place contrary to all previsions, and this deplorable fact also modifies the attitude which we should have desired to maintain.

The accord which has recently been effected at Vienna between France, Austria, England, and Prussia, has established the European character of the difference which existed between Russia and the Porte. The four Courts have solemnly recognized that the territorial integrity of the Ottoman empire is one of the conditions of their political equilibrium. The occupation of Moldavia and Wallachia constitutes a fresh attack on that integrity, and it is not doubtful but that the chances of war may lead to others.

Count de Nesselrode, some months since, represented the invasion of the Danubian Principalities as a necessary compensation for what he then called our maritime occupation. In our turn, Monsieur ——, we think that it has become indispensable to ourselves to measure the extent of the compensation to which we have a right, both from our title of a power interested in the existence of Turkey, and from the military positions already taken by the Russian army. It is necessary that we should have a pledge which will secure to us the re-establishment of peace in the East on conditions which shall not change the distribution of the respective strength of the great Satest of Europe.

The Government of his Imperial Majesty and that of her Britannic Majesty have in consequence decided that their squadrons shall enter into the Black Sea, and combine their movements in such a way as to prevent the Ottoman territory or the Ottoman flag from being the object of any fresh attack on the part of the naval forces of Russia.

Vice-Admirals Hamelin and Dundas will receive orders to communicate to whom it may concern the object of their mission, and we take pleasure in hoping that this straightforward proceeding will prevent conflicts, which we should see with the greatest regret. The Government of the Emperor, I repeat, has only one object, that of contributing to effect, on honourable conditions, a reconciliation (*rapprochement*) between the two belligerent parties; and if circumstances should oblige it to provide for redoubtable eventualities, it retains the confidence that the Cabinet of St. Petersburg, which has given such numerous examples of its prudence, will not expose Europe, scarcely yet recovered from the shocks it has experienced, to trials from which the lofty reason of Sovereigns has been able to preserve it for so many years.

I authorize you to read this despatch to M. ——.

DROUYN DE LHUYS.

APPENDIX II.

THE SECRET RUSSIAN CORRESPONDENCE.

COMPLETE.

Communication respecting Turkey, made to her Majesty's Government by the Emperor of Russia, with the Answers returned to them—January to April, 1853.

SIR G. H. SEYMOUR TO LORD JOHN RUSSELL.

No. 1.

[Received January 23.]

[Secret and confidential.]

ST. PETERSBURGH, January 11, 1853.

MY LORD—On the evening of the 9th inst. I had the honor of seeing the Emperor, at the palace of the Grand Duchess Helen, who, it appeared, had kindly requested permission to invite Lady Seymour and myself to meet the imperial family. The Emperor came up to me in the most gracious manner, to say that he had heard with great pleasure of her Majesty's government having been definitely formed—adding, that he trusted the ministry would be of long duration. His Imperial Majesty desired me particularly to convey this assurance to the Earl of Aberdeen, with whom, he said, he had been acquainted for nearly forty years, and for whom he entertained equal regard and esteem. His Majesty desired to be brought to the kind recollection of his lordship. "You know my feelings," the Emperor said, "with regard to England. What I have told you before, I say again: it was intended that the two countries should be upon terms of close amity, and I feel sure that this will continue to be the case. You have now been a certain time here, and, as you have seen, there have been a very few points upon which we have disagreed. Our interests, in fact, are upon all questions the same." I observed that I really was not aware that since I had been at St. Petersburgh there had been any actual disagreements whatever between us, except with regard to Louis Napoleon's No. III, a point respecting which each Government had its own opinion (*manière de voir*,) but a point, which, after all, was very immaterial. "The No. III," the Emperor replied, "would involve a long explanation; I will, therefore, not touch upon the subject at present. I should be glad, however, that you should hear what I have to say upon the question, and will beg of you to call upon me some morning when I am a little free from engagements." I, of course, requested that his Majesty would be good enough to lay his orders upon me. In the meantime, the Emperor went on to say: "I repeat, that it is very essential that the two governments—that is, the English government and I, and I and the English government—should be upon the best terms; and the necessity was never greater than at present. I beg you to convey these words to Lord John Russell. When we are agreed (*d'accord,*) I am quite without anxiety as to the west of Europe; it is immaterial what the others may think or do. As to Turkey, that is another question; that country is in a critical state, and may give us all a great deal of trouble. And now I will take my leave of you." Which his Majesty proceeded to do, by shaking hands with me very graciously. It instantly occurred to me, that the conversation was incomplete, and might never be renewed; and, as the Emperor still held my hand, I said, "Sir, with your gracious permission, I would desire to take a great liberty." "Certainly," his Majesty replied; "what is it? let me hear." "Sir," I observed, "your Majesty has been good enough to charge me with general assurances as to the identity of views between the two cabinets, which, assuredly, have given me the greatest pleasure, and will be received with equal satisfaction in England; but I should be particularly glad that your Majesty should add, in a few words, which may tend to calm the anxiety with regard to the affairs of Turkey which passing events are so calculated to excite on the part of her Majesty's government; perhaps you will be pleased to charge me with some additional assurances of this kind." The Emperor's words and manner, although still very kind, showed that his Majesty had no intention of speaking to me of the demonstration which he is about to make in the South. He said, however, at first with a little hesitation, but, as he proceeded, in an open and unhesitating manner, "The affairs of Turkey are in a very disorganized condition; *the country itself seems to be falling to pieces (menace ruine;)* the fall will be a great misfortune, and it is very important that *England and Russia should come to a perfectly good understanding upon these affairs, and that neither should take any decisive step of which the other is not apprised.*" I observed, in a few words, that I was rejoiced to hear that his Imperial Majesty held this language; that this was certainly the view I took of the manner in which the Turkish questions are to be treated. He said, as if proceeding with his remark, "Stay, we have on our hands a sick man—a very sick man; it will be, I tell you frankly, a great misfortune, if, one of these days, he should slip away from us, especially before all necessary arrangements are made. But, however, this is not the time to speak to you on that matter." It was clear that the Emperor did not intend to prolong the conversation. I therefore said, "Your Majesty is so gracious that you will allow me to make one further observation. Your Majesty says the man is sick; it is very true; but your Majesty will deign to excuse me if I remark, that it is the part of the generous and strong man to treat with gentleness the sick and feeble man." The Emperor then took leave of me in a manner which conveyed the impression of my having at least not given offence, and again expressed his intention of sending for me at some future day. Your lordship will pardon me if I remark, that, after reflecting attentively upon my conversation with the Emperor, it appears to me that this, and any overture of the kind which may be made, tends to establish a dilemma by which it is very desirable that her Majesty's government should not allow themselves to be fettered. The dilemma seems to be this : If her Majesty's government do not come to an understanding with Russia as to what is to happen in the event of the sudden downfall of Turkey, they will have the less reason for complaining if results displeasing to England should be prepared. If, on the contrary, her Majesty's government should enter into the consideration of such eventualities, they *make themselves, in some degree, consenting parties to a catastrophe which they have so much interest in warding off as long as possible.* The sum is probably this : that England has to desire a close concert with Russia, with the view to preventing the downfall of Turkey—while Russia would be well pleased that the concert should apply to the events by which the downfall is to be followed. Yours, &c.,

(Signed,) G. H. Seymour.

SIR G. H. SEYMOUR TO LORD JOHN RUSSELL.

No. 2.

[Received February 6.]

[Secret and confidential.]

St. Petersburgh, January 22, 1854.

My Lord—On the 14th instant, in consequence of a summons which I received from the Chancellor, I waited upon the emperor, and had the honor of holding with his Imperial Majesty the very interesting conversation of which it will be my duty to offer your lordship an account, which, if imperfect, will, at all events, not be incorrect. I found his Majesty alone; he received me with great kindness, saying, that I had appeared desirous to speak to him on Eastern affairs—that, on his side, there was no indisposition to do so, but that he must begin at a remote period. "You know," his Majesty said, "the dreams and plans in which the Empress Catharine was in the habit of indulging ; these were handed down to our time ; but while I inherited immense territorial possessions, I did not inherit those visions—those intentions, if you like to call them so. On the contrary, my country is so vast, so happily circumstanced in every way, that it would be unreasonable in me to desire more territory or more power than I possess ; on the contrary, I am the first to tell you, that our great, perhaps our only danger, is that which would arise from an extension given to an empire already too large. Close to us lies Turkey ; and in our present condition, nothing better for our interest can be desired. The times have gone by when we had anything to fear from the fanatical spirit or the military ardor of the Turks ; and yet the country is strong enough—or has hitherto been strong enough—to preserve its independence, and to insure respectful treatment from other countries.

"Well, in that empire there are several millions of Christians, whose interests I am called upon to watch over, (*surveiller,*) while the right of doing so is secured to me by treaty, I may truly say, that I make a moderate and sparing use of my right ; and I will freely confess, that it is one which is attended with obligations occasionally very inconvenient. But I cannot recede from the discharge of a distinct duty. Our religion, as established in this country, came to us from the East; and there are feelings, as well as obligations, which must never be lost sight of. Now Turkey, in the condition which I have described, has by degrees, fallen into such a state of decrepitude, that, as I told you the other night, eager as we all are for the prolonged existence of the man, (and that I am as desirous as you can be for the continuance of his life, I beg you to be, lieve,) he may suddenly die upon our hands *(nous rester sur le bras)*; we cannot recuscitate what is dead. If the Turkish Empire falls, it falls to rise no more. And I put it to you, therefore, *whether it is not better to be provided beforehand for a contingency, than to incur the chaos, confusion, and the certainty of a European war, all of which must attend the catastrophe if it should occur unexpectedly, and before some ulterior system has been sketched;* this is the point to which I am desirous that you should call the attention of the government. "Sir," I replied, "your Majesty is so frank with me, I am sure you will have the goodness to permit me to speak with the same spirit. I would, then, observe that deplorable as is the condition of Turkey, it is a country which has been plunged in difficulties supposed by many to be insurmountable. With regard to contingent arrangements, her Majesty's government, as your Majesty is well aware, objects, as a general rule, to taking engagements upon possible eventualities, and would, perhaps, be particularly disinclined to doing so in this instance. If I may be allowed to say so, a great disinclination *(repugnance)* might be expected in England to disposing by anticipation *(d'escompter)* of the succession of an old friend and ally." "The rule is a good one," the Emperor replied, "good at all times, especially in times of uncertainty and danger, like the present; still it is of the greatest importance that we should understand each other, and not allow events to take us by surprise. Now I desire to speak to you as a friend and gentleman. If England and I arrive at an understanding of this matter, as regards the rest, it matters little to me. Frankly, then, I tell you plainly, that if England thinks of establishing herself one of these days at Constantinople, I will not allow it. I do not attribute this intention to you, but it is better, on these occasions, to speak plainly. For my part, I am equally disposed to take the engagement not to establish myself there as proprietor, that is to say—for as occupier I do not say—it might happen, that circumstances, if no previous provision were made, if everything should be left to chance, might place me in the position of occupying Constantinople." I thanked his Majesty for the frankness of his declarations, and for the desire which he had expressed of acting cordially and openly with her Majesty's government, observing, at the same time, that such an understanding appeared the best security against the sudden danger to which his Majesty had alluded." I added, that "although unprepared to give a decided opinion upon questions of such magnitude and delicacy, it appeared to me possible that some such arrangement might be made between her Majesty's government and his Majesty as might guard, if not for, at least against, certain contingencies." To render my meaning more clear, I said further, "I can only repeat, sir, that in my opinion, her Majesty's government will be indisposed to make certain arrangements connected with the downfall of Turkey; but it is possible that they may be ready to pledge themselves against certain arrangements which might in that event be attempted." His Imperial Majesty then alluded to a conversation which he had held, the last time he was in England, with the Duke of Wellington, and to the motives which had compelled him to open himself to his Grace; then, as now, his Majesty was, he said, eager to provide against events, which, in the absence of any concert, might compel him to act in a manner opposed to the views of her Majesty's government. The conversation passed to the events of the day, when the Emperor briefly recapitulated his claims upon the Holy Places, claims recognised by the firman of last February, and confirmed by a sanction to which his Majesty said he attached much more importance—the word of a sovereign. The execution of promises so made, and so ratified, the Emperor said he must insist upon, but was willing to believe that this object would be attained by negotiation, the last advices from Constantinople being rather more satisfactory. I expressed my belief that negotiation, followed, as I supposed it had been, by the threats of military measures, would be found sufficient to secure a compliance with the just demands of Russia.

I added, that I desired to state to his Majesty what I had previously read from a written paper to his minister, viz., that what I feared for Turkey was not the intentions of his Majesty, but the actual result of the measures which appeared to be in contemplation. That I would repeat, that two consequences might be anticipated from the appearance of an imperial army on the frontiers of Turkey—the one the counter-demonstration which might be provoked on the part of France; the other, and the more serious, the rising on the part of the Christian population, against the Sultan's authority, already so much weakened by revolts, and by a severe financial crisis. The emperor assured me that no movement of his forces had yet taken place, (*n'ont pas bougé,*) and expressed his hope that no advance would be required. With regard to a French expedition to the Sultan's dominions, his Majesty intimated that such a step would bring affairs to an immediate crisis; that a sense of honor would compel him to *send his forces into Turkey without delay or hesitation;* that if the result of such an advance should prove to be the overthrow of the Great Turk, (*le Grand Turque,*) he should regret the event, but should feel that he had acted as he was compelled to do. To the above report I have only, I think, to add, that the Emperor desired to leave it to my discretion to communicate or not to his minister the particulars of our conversation; and that before I left the room, his Imperial Majesty said: "You will report what has passed between us to the Queen's government, and you will say that I shall be ready to receive any communication which it may be their wish to make to me on the subject." A noble triumph would be obtained by the civilization of the nineteenth century, if the void left by the extinction of Mohammedan rule in Europe, could be filled up without an interruption of the general peace, in consequence of the persecutions adopted by the two principal governments the most interested in the destinies of Turkey. I have, &c.,

(Signed,) G. H. Seymour.

SIR G. H. SEYMOUR TO LORD J. RUSSELL.

No. 3.

[Received February 6.]

[Secret and confidential.]

(Extract.) ST. PETERSBURGH, Jan. 22, 1853.

I have generally found straightforward conduct to be the best policy, and as it is peculiarly called for towards those who have acted by us in a similar manner, upon leaving the palace on the 4th inst., I drove to the Foreign Office, and gave Count Nesselrode a correct summary of the conversation I had just had the honor of holding with the Emperor.

LORD J. RUSSELL TO SIR G. H. SEYMOUR.

No. 4.

[Secret and confidential.]

FOREIGN OFFICE, Feb. 9, 1853.

SIR—I have received and laid before the Queen your secret and confidential despatch of the 22d of January.

Her Majesty, upon this as upon former occasions, is happy to acknowledge the moderation, the frankness, and the friendly disposition of his Imperial Majesty.

Her Majesty has directed me to reply in the same spirit of temperate, candid, and amicable discussion.

The question raised by his Imperial Majesty is a very serious one. It is, supposing the contingency of the dissolution of the Turkish Empire to be probable, or even imminent, "whether it is not better to be provided beforehand for a contingency than to incur the chaos, confusion, and the certainty of a European war, all of which must attend the catastrophe if it should occur unexpectedly, and before some ulterior system has been sketched; this is the point," said his Imperial Majesty, "to which I am desirous that you should call the attention of your government."

In considering this grave question, the first reflection which occurs to her Majesty's government is, that no actual crisis has occurred which renders necessary a solution of this vast European problem. Disputes have arisen respecting the Holy Places, but these are without the sphere of the internal government of Turkey, and concern Russia and France rather than the Sublime Porte. Some disturbance of the relations between Austria and the Porte has been caused by the Turkish attack on Montenegro; but this, again, relates rather to dangers affecting the frontier of Austria than the authority and safety of the Sultan; so that there is no sufficient cause for intimating to the Sultan that he cannot keep peace at home, or preserve friendly relations with his neighbors.

It occurs further to her Majesty's government to remark, that the event which is contemplated is not definitely fixed in point of time. When William III. and Louis XIV. disposed, by treaty, of the succession of Charles II. of Spain, they were providing for an event which could not be far off. The infirmaties of the sovereign of Spain and the certain end of any human life made the contingency in prospect both sure and near. The death of the Spanish King was in no way hastened by the treaty of partition. The same thing may be said of the provision made in the last century, for the disposal of Tuscany upon the decease of the last Prince of the house of Medici. But the contingency of the dissolution of the Ottoman Empire is of another kind. It may happen 20, 50, or 100 years hence.

In these circumstances it would hardly be consistent with the friendly feelings towards the Sultan which animate the Emperor of Russia, no less than the Queen of Great Britain, to dispose beforehand of the provinces under his dominion. Besides this consideration, however, it must be observed, that an agreement made in such a case tends very surely to hasten the contingency for which it is intended to provide. Austria and France could not, in fairness, be kept in ignorance of the transaction, nor would such concealment be consistent with the end of preventing an European war. Indeed, such concealment cannot be intended by his Imperial Majesty. It is to be inferred that, as soon as Great Britain and Russia should have agreed on the course to be pursued, and have determined to enforce it, they should communicate their intentions to the great Powers of Europe.

An agreement thus made, and thus communicated, would not be very long a secret; and while it would alarm and alienate the Sultan, the knowledge of its existence would stimulate all his enemies to increased violence and more obstinate conflict. They would fight with the conviction that they must ultimately triumph, while the Sultan's generals and troops would feel that no immediate success could save their cause from final overthrow. Thus would be produced and strengthened that very anarchy which is now feared, and the foresight of the friends of the patient would prove the cause of his death.

Her Majesty's government need scarcely enlarge on the dangers attendant on the execution of any similar convention. The example of the succession war is enough to show how little such agreements are respected when a pressing temptation urges their violation. The position of the Emperor of Russia as depositary, but not proprietor, of Constantinople, would be exposed to numberless hazards, both from the long cherished ambition of his own nation and the jealousies of Europe. The ultimate proprietor, whoever he might be, would hardly be satisfied with the inert, supine attitude of the heirs of Mohammed II. A great influence on the affairs of Europe seems naturally to belong to the Sovereign of Constantinople, holding the gates of the Mediterranean and the Black sea.

That influence might be used in favor of Russia; it might be used to control and curb her power.

His Imperial Majesty has justly and wisely said : " My country is so vast, so happily circumstanced in every way, that it would be unreasonable in me to desire more territory or more power than I possess. On the contrary," he observed, " our great, perhaps our only danger, is that which would arise from an extension given to an empire already too large." A vigorous and ambitious state, replacing the Sublime Porte, might, however, render war on the part of Russia a necessity for the Emperor or his successors.

Thus European conflict would arise from the very means taken to prevent it: for neither England nor France, nor probably Austria, would be content to see Constantinople permanently in the hands of Russia.

On the part of Great Britain, her Majesty's government at once declare, that they renounce all intention or wish to hold Constantinople. His Imperial Majesty may be quite secure upon this head. They are likewise ready to give an assurance, that they will enter into no agreement to provide for the contingency of the fall of Turkey without previous communication with the Emperor of Russia.

Upon the whole, then, her Majesty's government are persuaded that no course of policy can be adopted more wise, more disinterested, more beneficial to Europe, than that which his Imperial Majesty has so long followed, and which will render his name more illustrious than that of the most famous sovereigns who have sought immortality by unproked conquest and ephemeral glory.

With a view to the success of this policy, it is desirable that the utmost forbearance should be manifested towards Turkey; that any demands which the great powers of Europe may have to make should be made matter of friendly negotiation rather than of peremptory demand; that military and naval demonstrations to coerce the Sultan should as much as possible be avoided; that differences with respect to matters affecting Turkey, within the competence of the Sublime Porte, should be decided after mutual concert between the great powers, and not to be forced upon the weakness of the Turkish government.

To these cautions her Majesty's government wish to add, that in their view it is essential that the Sultan should be advised to treat his Christian subjects in conformity with the principles of equity and religious freedom which prevail generally among the enlightened nations of Europe. The more the Turkish government adopts the rules of impartial law and equal administration, the less will the Emperor of Russia find it necessary to apply that exceptional protection which his Imperial Majesty has found so burdensome and inconvenient, though no doubt prescribed by duty and sanctioned by treaty.

You may read this despatch to Count Nesselrode, and, if it is desired, you may yourself place a copy of it in the hands of the Emperor. In that case you will accompany its presentation with those assurances of friendship and confidence on the part of her Majesty the Queen, which the conduct of his Imperial Majesty was so sure to inspire.

I am, &c., J. Russell.

SIR G. H. SEYMOUR TO LORD J. RUSSELL.

No. 5.

[Received March 6.]

[Secret and confidential.]
(Extract.) St. Petersburgh, February 21, 1853.

The Emperor came up to me last night, at a party of the Grand Duchess Hereditary's, and in the most gracious manner took me apart, saying that he desired to speak to me. After expressing, in flattering terms, the confidence which he has in me, and his readiness to speak to me without reserve upon matters of the greatest moment, as, His Majesty observed, he had proved it in a late conversation, he said:—"And it is well it is so; for what I most desire is, that there should be the greatest intimacy between the two governments; it never was so necessary as at present. Well," the Emperor continued, "so you have got your answer, and you are to bring it to me to-morrow?"

"I am to have that honor, sir," I answered; "but your Majesty is aware that the nature of the reply is very exactly what I had led you to expect."

"So I was sorry to hear; but I think your government does not well understand my object. I am not so eager about what shall be done when the sick man dies, as I am to determine with England what shall not be done upon that event taking place."

"But, sir," I replied, "allow me to observe, that we have no reason to think that the sick man (to use your Majesty's expression) is dying. We are as much interested as we believe your Majesty to be in his continuing to live; while, for myself, I will venture to remark that experience shows me that countries do not die in such a hurry. Turkey will remain for many a year, unless some unforseen crisis should occur. It is precisely, sir, for the avoidance of all circumstances likely to produce such a crisis that her Majesty's government reckons upon your generous assistance."

"Then," rejoined the Emperor, "I will tell you that, if your government has been led to believe that Turkey retains any elements of existence, your government must have received incorrect information. I repeat to you, that the sick man is dying; and we can never allow such an event to take us by surprise. We must come to some understanding; and this we should do, I am convinced, if I could hold but ten minutes' conversation with your ministers—with Lord Aberdeen, for instance, who knows me so well, who has full confidence in me, as I have in him. And, remember, I do not ask for a treaty or a protocol; a general understanding is all I require—that, between gentlemen, is sufficient; and in this case I am certain that the confidence would be as great on the side of the Queen's ministers as on mine. So no more for the present; you will come to me to-morrow, and you will remember that as often as you think your conversing with me will promote a good understanding upon any point, you will send word that you wish to see me."

I thanked his Majesty very cordially, adding that I could assure him that her Majesty's government, I was convinced, considered his word, once given, as good as a bond.

It is hardly necessary that I should observe to your lordship that this short conversation, briefly but correctly reported, offers matter for most anxious reflection.

It can hardly be otherwise but that the sovereign who insists with such pertinacity upon the impending fall of a neighboring state, must have settled in his own mind that the hour, if not of its dissolution, at all events for its dissolution, must be at hand.

Then, as now, I reflected that this assumption would hardly be ventured upon unless some, perhaps general, but at all events, intimate understanding, existed between Russia and Austria.

Supposing my suspicion to be well founded, the Emperor's object is to engage her Majesty's government, in conjunction with his own cabinet and that of Vienna, in some scheme for the ultimate partition of Turkey, and for the exclusion of France from the arrangement.

SIR G. H. SEYMOUR TO LORD JOHN RUSSELL.

[No. 6.]

[Received March 6.]

[Secret and confidential.]

(Extract.) St. Petersburgh, February 22, 1853.

I had the honor of waiting yesterday upon the Emperor, and of holding with his Majesty one of the most interesting conversations in which I ever found myself engaged. My only regret is my inability to report full detail a dialogue which lasted an hour and twelve minutes.

The Emperor began by desiring me to read to him aloud your lordship's secret and confidential despatch of the 9th inst., saying that he should stop me occasionally, either to make an observation, or to call upon me for the translation of a passage.

Upon arriving at the fourth paragraph, the Emperor desired me to pause, and observed, that he was certainly most desirous that some understanding should be entered into with her Majesty's government for providing against a contingency so probable as the downfall of Turkey; that he was, perhaps, even more interested than England could be in preventing a Turkish catastrophe, but it was constantly impending; that it might be brought about at any moment, either by an external war, or by a feud between the old Turkish party and that of the "new superficial French reforms," or again, by a rising of the Christians, already known to be very impatient of shaking off the Mussulman's yoke (*joug*.) As regards the first cause, the Emperor said, that he had a good right to advert to it, inasmuch as, if he had not stopped the victorious progress of General Diebitsch in 1829, the Sultan's authority would have been at an end.

The Emperor likewise desired me to remember, that he, and he only, had hastened to the assistance of the Sultan, when his dominions were threatened by the Pacha of Egypt.

I proceeded to read, and was again stopped at the sentence beginning, "In these circumstances it would hardly be consistent with the friendly feelings"—when the Emperor observed, that her Majesty's government did not appear to be aware that his chief object was to obtain from her Majesty's government some declaration, or even opinion, of what ought not to be permitted in the event of the sudden downfall of Turkey. I said, "Perhaps your Majesty would be good enough to explain your own ideas upon this negative policy." This his Majesty for some time declined doing; he ended, however, by saying, "Well, there are several things which I never will tolerate; I will begin by ourselves. I will not tolerate the permanent occupation of Constantinople by the Russians; having said this, I will say that it never shall be held by the English, or French, or any other great nation. Again, I never will permit an attempt at the reconstruction of a Byzantine empire, or such an extension of Greece as would render her a powerful state; still less will I permit the breaking up of Turkey into little republics, asylums for the Kossuths and Mazzinis, and other revolutionists of Europe; rather than submit to any of these arrangements I would go to war, and as long as I have a man and a musket left, would carry it on. These," the Emperor said, "are at once some ideas; now give me some in return."

I remarked upon the assurance which would be found respecting the English resolution of never attempting to possess Constantinople, and upon the disinclination of her Majesty's government to enter into eventual arrangements; but upon being still pressed by his Imperial Majesty, I said, "Well, sir, the idea may not suit your Majesty—may not suit her Majesty's government, but what is good between man and man is often a good system between one state and another; how would it be if, in the event of any catastrophe occurring in Turkey, Russia and England were to declare that no power should be allowed to take possession of its provinces; that the property should remain, as it were, under seals, until amicable arrangements could be made as to its adjudication?"

"I will not say," the Emperor observed, "that such a course would be impossible, but, at least, it would be very difficult; there are no elements of provincial or communal government in Turkey; you would have Turks attacking Christians, Christians falling upon Turks, Christians of different sects quarreling with each other; in short, chaos and anarchy."

"Sir," I then observed, "if your Majesty will allow me to speak plainly, I would say that the great difference between us is this—that you continue to dwell upon the fall of Turkey, and the arrangements requisite before and after the fall; and that we, on the contrary, look to Turkey remaining where she is, and to the precautions which are necessary for preventing her condition from becoming worse."

"Ah!" replied the Emperor, "that is what the Chancellor is perpetually telling me; but the catastrophe will occur some day, and will take us all unawares."

His Imperial Majesty spoke of France. "God forbid," he said, "that I should accuse any one wrongfully, but there are circumstances both at Constantinople and Montenegro which are extremely suspicious; it looks very much as if the French government were endeavoring to embroil us all in the East, hoping in this way the better to arrive at their own objects, one of which, no doubt, is the possession of Tunis."

The Emperor proceeded to say, that, for his own part, he cared very little what line the French might think proper to take in Eastern affairs, and that little more than a month ago he had apprised the Sultan that if his assistance was required for resisting the menaces of the French, it was entirely at the service of the Sultan.

In a word, the Emperor went on to observe, "As I before told you, all I want is a good understanding with England, and this not as to what shall, but as to what shall not be done; this point arrived at, the English government and I, I and the English government, having entire confidence in one another's views, I care nothing about the rest."

I remarked that I felt confident that her Majesty's government could be as little disposed as his Imperial Majesty to tolerate the presence of the French at Constantinople; and being desirous, if possible, of ascertaining whether there was any understanding between the cabinets of St. Petersburgh and Vienna, I added, "But your Majesty has forgotten Austria; now all these Eastern questions affect her very nearly; she, of course, would expect to be consulted."

"Oh!" replied the Emperor, greatly to my surprise, "but you must understand that when I speak of Russia I speak of Austria as well; what suits the one suits the other; our interests as regards Turkey are perfectly identical." I should have been glad to make another inquiry or two upon this subject, but I did not venture to do so.

I ought to have stated, that in a preceding part of the conversation, his Majesty although without any appearance of anger, evinced some surprise at an expression in your lordship's despatch, "the long-cherished ambition of his (the Emperor's) own nation;" he would ask what that phrase meant?

It appears that I was prepared for the surprise expressed, any ready to answer any reflection which it might call forth.

"Sir," I said, "Lord John Russell is not speaking of your ambition, he speaks of that entertained by your people."

The Emperor could not at first admit that the phrase was applicable to the Russian nation any more than to himself; when I said, "Your Majesty will permit me to remark, that Lord John Russell only repeats what was said thirty years ago by your brother, of glorious memory. In writing confidentially to Lord Castlereagh, in the year 1822, the Emperor Alexander spoke of being the only Russian who resisted the views of his subjects upon Turkey, and of the loss of popularity which he had sustained by this antagonism."

This quotation, which, by accident, I could make almost in the words of the letter, seemed to change the current of the Emperor's ideas.

"You are quite right," he said; "I remember the events to which my late brother alluded. Now it is perfectly true, that the Empress Catharine indulged in all sorts of visions of ambition, but it is not less so that these ideas are not all shared by her descendants. You see how I am behaving towards the Sultan. This gentleman (*ce Monsieur*) breaks his written word to me, and acts in a manner extremely displeasing to me, and I have contented myself with despatching an ambassador to Constantinople to demand reparation. Certainly, I could send an army there if I chose—there is nothing to stop them; but I have contented myself with such a show of force as will prove that I have no intention of being trifled with."

"And, sir," I said, "you were quite right in refraining from violence; and I hope, upon future occasions, you will act with the same moderation; for your Majesty must be sensible that any fresh concessions which may have been obtained by the Latins are not referable to ill-will towards you, but to the excessive apprehensions of the French entertained by the unfortunate Turks; besides, sir," I observed, "the danger, I will venture to say, of the present moment is not Turkey, but the revolutionary spirit which broke out four years ago, and which in many countries still burns underground; there is the danger, and no doubt the war in Turkey would be the signal for fresh explosions in Italy, Hungary, and elsewhere. We see what is passing at Milan."

His Imperial Majesty spoke of Montenegro, observing that he approved the attitude taken by the Austrian cabinet, and that in these days it could not be permitted that the Turks should ill-treat and even murder a Christian population.

I ventured to remark, that upon this point the wrongs were at least divided between the Turks and Montenegrins, and that I had full reason for believing that the provocation came from the latter. The Emperor, with more impartiality than I had expected, admitted that there had been wrongs on both sides; that certainly the mountaineers were rather addicted to brigandage; and that the taking of Djblak had caused him great indignation. At the same time, His Majesty said, "It is impossible not to feel great interest in a population warmly attached to their religion, who have so long kept their ground against the Turks;" and the Emperor continued, "It may be fair to tell you, that if any attempts at exterminating those people should be made by Omer Pacha, and should a general rising of the Christians take place in consequence, the Sultan will, in all probability, lose his throne; but in this case he falls to rise no more. I wish to support his authority, but if he loses it, it is gone for ever. The Turkish empire is a thing to be tolerated, not to be reconstructed. In such a cause, I protest to you I will not allow a pistol to be fired."

The Emperor went on to say that, in the event of the dissolution of the Ottoman empire, he thought it might be less difficult to arrive at a satisfactory territorial arrangement than was commonly believed. "The principalities are," he said, "in fact, an independent state under my protection; this might so continue. Servia might receive the same form of government. So again with Bulgaria. There seems to be no reason why this province should not form an independent state. As to Egypt, I quite understand the importance to England of that territory. I can only say, that if, in the event of a distribution of the Ottoman succession upon the fall of the empire, you should take possession of Egypt, I shall have no objections to offer. I would say the same thing of Candia; that island might suit you, and I do not know why it should not become an English possession."

As I did not wish that the Emperor should imagine that an English public servant was caught by this sort of overture, I simply answered that I had always understood that the English views upon Egypt did not go beyond the point of securing a safe and ready communication between British India and the mother country.

The conversation now drawing towards an end, the Emperor expressed his warm attachment to the Queen, our gracious sovereign, and his respect for her Majesty's present advisers. The declarations contained in your lordship's despatch had been, he said, very satisfactory; he could only desire that they should be a little amplified. The terms in which your lordship had spoken of his conduct were, the Emperor said, very flattering to him.

In dismissing me, his Imperial Majesty said: "Well, induce your government to write again upon these subjects—to write more fully, and to do so without hesitation. I have confidence in the English government. Ce n'est point un engagement, une convention que je leur demande; c'est un libre échange d'idées, et, au besoin, une parole de gentleman; entre nous cela suffit."

I might venture to suggest, that some expressions might be used in the despatch to be addressed to me, which might have the effect of putting an end to the further consideration, or, at all events, discussion of points which it is highly desirable should not be regarded as offering subject for debate.

I may only add, apologetically, that I may possibly have failed in reporting some parts of his Majesty's conversation, and that I am conscious of having forgotten the precise terms employed by him with respect to the commercial policy to be observed at Constantinople when no longer held by the Turks.

The purport of the observation was, that England and Russia had a common interest in providing for the readiest access to the Black sea and the Mediterranean.

A copy of your lordship's despatch was left in the Emperor's hands.

SIR G. H. SEYMOUR TO THE EARL OF CLARENDON.

No. 7.

[Received March 19.]

[Secret and confidential.]

(Extract.) ST. PETERSBURGH, March, 9, 1853.

When I waited upon Count Nesselrode on the 7th inst., his excellency said that, in pursuance of orders which he had received from the Emperor, he had to place in my hands a very confidential memorandum which his Imperial Majesty had caused to be drawn up, and which was intended as an answer to, or a comment upon, the communication which I had made to his Imperial Majesty on the 21st ult.

At first Count Nesselrode invited me to read the paper; he subsequently observed that if, instead of reading it that time, I chose to take it away, I was at liberty to do so; that, in fact, the paper was intended for my use *(sic.)*

Very little conversation upon the subject passed between the Chancellor and me. He observed that I should find in the memorandum indications of the Emperor's wish to be further informed of the feelings of her Majesty's government as to what should not be permitted to take place in the event of any great catastrophe in Turkey; and I, on my side, remarked that, as there is danger in handling hot coals, it appeared to me desirable that communications upon a subject so delicate should not long be kept up.

I have the honor of inclosing to your lordship a copy of what, under the circumstances which have attended its drawing up and delivery, cannot fail of being considered as one of the most remarkable papers which have been issued, I do not say from the Russian "chancellor," but from the Emperor's secret cabinet.

It would not be difficult either to controvert some of the facts which the memorandum advances, or to show that the impression under which it has been framed is an incorrect one; that impression being evidently that, in the disputes carried on between Russia and France, her Majesty's government has leant partially to the latter power.

Three points appear to me to be fully established by the imperial memorandum—the existence of some distinct understanding between the two imperial courts upon the subject of Turkey, and the engagement taken by the Emperor Nicholas neither to possess nor establish himself at Constantinople, nor to enter into arrangements respecting the measures to be taken in the event of the fall of the Ottoman empire without previous concert with her Majesty's government.

The wording of this engagement, coupled with the conversation which I had the honor of holding with the Emperor, leaves upon my mind the impression, that, while willing to undertake not to make himself the permanent master of Constantinople, his Majesty is intentionally inexplicit as to its temporary occupation.

Assuming, as a certain and now acknowledged fact, the existence of an understanding or compact between the two emperors, as to Turkish affairs, it becomes of the deepest importance to know the extent of the engagements entered into between them. As to the manner in which it has been concluded, I conjecture that little doubt is to be entertained.

Its basis was, no doubt, laid at some of the meetings between the sovereigns which took place in the autumn; and the scheme has probably been worked out since, under the management of Baron Meyendorff, the Russian envoy at the Austrian court, who has been passing the winter at St. Petersburgh, and is still here.

—

[Translation.]

February 21, 1853.

The Emperor has, with the liveliest interest and real satisfaction, made himself acquainted with the secret and confidential despatch which Sir Hamilton Seymour communicated to him. He duly appreciates the frankness which has dictated it. He has found therein a fresh proof of the friendly sentiments which her Majesty the Queen entertains for him.

In conversing familiarly with the British envoy on the causes which, from one day to another, may bring on the fall of the Ottoman empire, it had by no means entered into the Emperor's thoughts to propose for this contingency a plan by which Russia and England should dispose beforehand of the provinces ruled by the Sultan—a system altogether arranged; still less a formal agreement to be concluded between the two cabinets. It was purely and simply the Emperor's notion, that each party should confidentially state to the other less what it wishes than what it does not wish; what would be contrary to English interests, what would be contrary to Russian interests; in order that, the case occurring, they might avoid acting in opposition to each other.

There is in this neither plans of partition, nor convention to be binding on the other courts. It is merely an interchange of opinions, and the Emperor sees no necessity of talking about it before the time. It is precisely for that reason that he took especial care not to make it the object of an official communication from one cabinet to another. By confining himself to speaking of it himself, in the shape of familiar conversation, to the Queen's representative, he selected the most friendly and confidential form of opening himself with frankness to her Britannic Majesty, being desirous that the result, whatsoever it might be, of these communications, should remain, as it ought to be, a secret between the two severeigns.

Consequently, the objections which Lord John Russell raises to any concealment as regards the other powers, in the event of a formal agreement being entered into—of which there is at present no question—fall to the ground; and consequently, also, the inconveniences disappear, which he points out as calculated to contribute to hasten the occurrence of the very event which Russia and England are desirous of averting, if the existence of such an agreement should become prematurely known to Europe and to the subjects of the Sultan.

As regards the object of this wholly confidential interchange of opinions (the possible downfall of the Ottoman empire), doubtless that is but an uncertain and remote contingency. Unquestionably, the period of it cannot be fixed, and no real crisis has arisen to render the realization of it imminent. But, after all, it may happen; happen even unexpectedly. Without mentioning the ever-increasing causes of dissolution which are presented by the moral, financial, and administrative condition of the Porte, it may proceed gradually from one, at least, of the two questions mentioned by the English Ministry in its secret despatch. In truth, it perceives in those questions only mere disputes, which would not differ in their bearing from difficulties which form the ordinary business of diplomacy. But, that kind of dispute may, nevertheless, bring on war, and, with war, the consequences which the Emperor apprehends from it: if, for instance, in the affair of the Holy Places, the *amour-propre* and the menaces of France, continuing to press upon the Porte, should compel it to refuse us all satisfaction, and if, on the other hand, the religious sentiments of the orthodox Greeks, offended by the concessions made to the Latins, should raise the immense majority of his subjects against the Sultan. As regards the affair of Montenegro, that, according to the late accounts, may happily be looked upon as settled. But at the time that the Emperor had his interview with Sir Hamilton Seymour, it might be apprehended that the question would take a most serious turn. Neither ourselves nor Austria could have allowed a protracted devastation or forced submission to Montenegro, a country which, up to the present time, has continued actually independent of the Porte, a country over which our protection has been extended for more than a century. The horrors which are committed there, those which, by the Ottoman fanaticism, have a short time since been extended over Bulgaria, Bosinia, and the Herzegovina, gave the other Christian provinces of the Porte only too much reason to anticipate that the same fate awaited them. They were calculated to provoke the general rising of the Christians who live under the sceptre of the Turkish empire, and to hasten its ruin. It is not, then, by any means an idle and imaginary question, a contingency too remote, to which the anxiety of the Emperor has called the attention of the Queen, his ally.

In the face of the uncertainty and decay of the existing state of things in Turkey, the Emglish cabinet expresses the desire that the greatest forbearance should be shown towards the Porte. The Emperor is conscious of never having acted otherwise. The English cabinet itself admits it. It addresses to the Emperor, with reference to the numerous proofs of moderation which he has given up to the present time, praises which his Majesty will not accept, because in that he has only listened to his own overbearing conviction. But, in order that the Emperor may continue to concur in that system of forbearance, to abstain from any demonstrations—from any peremptory language—it would be necessary that this system should be equally observed by all the powers at once. France has adopted another. By menace she obtained, in opposition to the letter of the treaties, the admission of a ship-of-the-line into the Dardanelles. At the cannon's mouth she twice presented her claims, and her demands for indemnity at Tripoli, and afterwards at Constantinople. Again, in the contest respecting the Holy Places, by menace she effected the abrogation of the firman and that of the solemn promises which the Sultan had given the Emperor. With regard to all these acts of violence, England observed a complete silence. She neither offered support to the Porte nor addressed remonstrances to the French government. The consequence is very evident. The Porte necessarily concluded from this that from France alone it has everything to hope as well as everything to fear, and that it can evade with impunity the demands of Austria and Russia. It is thus that Austria and Russia, in order to obtain justice, have seen themselves compelled in turn, against their will, to act by intimidation, since they have to do with a government which only yields to a peremptory attitude; and it is thus that by its own fault, or rather by that of those who have weakened it in the first instance, the Porte is urged on in a course which enfeebles it still more. Let England, then employ herself in making it listen to reason. Instead of uniting herself with France against the just demands of Russia, let her avoid supporting, or even appearing to support, the resistance of the Ottoman government. Let her be the first to invite the latter, as she herself considers it essential, to treat its Christian subjects with more equity and humanity. That will be the surest means of relieving the Emperor from the obligation of availing himself in Turkey of those rights of traditional protection to which he never has recourse but against his will, and of postponing indefinitely the crisis which the Emperor and her Majesty the Queen are equally anxious to avert.

In short, the Emperor cannot but congratulate himself at having given occasion for this intimate interchange of confidential communications between her Majesty and himself. He has found therein valuable assurances, of which he takes note with a lively satisfaction. The two sovereigns have frankly explained to each other what, in the extreme case of which they have been treating, their respective interests cannot endure. England understands that Russia cannot suffer the establishment at Constantinople of a Christian power sufficiently strong to control and disquiet her. She declares that, for herself, she renounces any intention or desire to possess Constantinople. The Emperor equally disclaims any wish or design of establishing himself there. England promises that she will enter into no arrangement for determining the measures to be taken in the event of the fall of the Turkish empire, without a previous understanding with the Emperor. The Emperor, on his side, willingly contracts the same engagement. As he is aware that in such a case he can equally reckon upon Austria, who is bound by her promises to concert with him, he regards with less apprehension the catastrophe which he still desires to prevent and avert, as much as it shall depend on him to do so.

No less precious to him are the proofs of friendship and personal confidence on the part of her Majesty the Queen, which Sir Hamilton Seymour has been directed on this occasion to impart to him. He sees in them the surest guaranty against the contingency which his foresight had deemed it right to point out to that of the English government.

SIR G. H. SEYMOUR TO THE EARL OF CLARENDON.

[No. 8.]

[Received March 19.]

[Secret and confidential.]

St. Petersburgh, March 9, 1853.

My Lord—As it appears very evident that the secret memorial which, by a despatch of this day, I have the honor of bringing to your lordship's knowledge, has been drawn up under a complete misapprehension (real or assumed) of the part taken by her Majesty's government in the late Turkish affairs, I have thought it my duty to address to Count Nesselrode the private and confidential letter of which I beg to enclose a copy to your lordship. I have, &c., G. H. Seymour.

SIR G. H. SEYMOUR TO COUNT NESSELRODE.

[Enclosure in No. 8.]

[Private and confidential.]

St. Petersburgh, Feb. 24, (March 8,) 1853.

My dear Count Nesselrode—There is an observation respecting the very important memorandum placed yesterday by your excellency in my hands, which I feel obliged to make.

I am most anxious to observe, that this paper must have been drawn up under the impression of English policy at Constantinople having been very different from what in reality it has been.

I can affirm, conscientiously and distinctly, that the object proposed to themselves, as well by the late as by her Majesty's present government, has been to act as a common friend in the contests between the allied governments; and that, far from having inclined, as has been stated, to

France in the late critical transactions, it has been the desire of the Queen's advisers, (to the full extent permitted to a government compelled to observe a neutral attitude,) that ample satisfaction should be given to the demands which his Imperial Majesty's government were justified in making.

This assertion I should have no difficulty in substantiating by written evidence; and I will add, that in any just demand which England may have to make upon a foreign cabinet, I only desire that the conduct of a friendly power towards us may be that which, quietly and unostentatiously, the English government has pursued in the complicated question of the Holy Places with regard to the claims of Russia.

I request your Excellency's good offices for causing this, the real state of the case, to be rightly understood; at all events, from preventing a contrary belief from being adopted until it shall be clearly ascertained whether or not my statement is correct. I have, &c.,

G. H. SEYMOUR.

SIR G. H. SEYMOUR TO THE EARL OF CLARENDON.

No. 9.

[Received March, 19.]

[Secret and confidential.]

ST. PETERSBURGH, March 10, 1853.

MY LORD—I have just had a very amicable and satisfactory conversation with the Chancellor, who, under the impression of my letter of the 8th inst. having originated in a misconception with regard to the Emperor's memorandum, had desired to see me.

We read over the memorandum together, and Count Nesselrode observed that all that was desired here was, that, while appealing to the Emperor's magnanimity and feelings of justice, her Majesty's government should employ some effort towards opening the eyes of the French ministers as to the false course into which they have been led by M. de Lavalette.

To this I replied that such had been the conduct pursued by her Majesty's government, not on one occasion, but on various occasions: and that, as a specimen of the language held by your lordship's predecessor to the French government, I would beg to read to him an extract from one of Lord John Russell's despatches.

I read, accordingly, the five or six lines of Lord John Russell's despatch to Lord Cowley of January 28, beginning, "But her Majesty's government cannot avoid perceiving," and concluding with "the relations of friendly powers," which passage I had copied out and taken with me.

Count Nesselrode expressed his warm satisfaction at finding that her Majesty's government had given such excellent advice to the French government; and only regretted that he had not long ago been put in possession of evidence so conclusive as to the part taken upon the question of the Holy Places by her Majesty's principal Secretary of State for Foreign Affairs.

In conclusion, the Chancellor requested that I would consider the passage in the imperial memorandum commencing with the words: "Que l'Angleterre s'emploie donc," as expressing a hope, and not as implying a reproach—as referrible to the course which it was desired should be taken by her Majesty's government, and not as alluding to that which had been pursued.

I have, &c. G. H. SEYMOUR.

THE EARL OF CLARENDON TO SIR G. H. SEYMOUR.

No. 10.

[Secret and confidential.]

FOREIGN OFFICE, March 23, 1853.

SIR—Your despatches of the 21st and 22d ult. have been laid before the Queen, and I am commanded to express her Majesty's entire approval of the discretion and judgment displayed by you in the conversation which you had the honor to hold with the Emperor.

I need not assure you that the opinions of his Imperial Majesty have received from her Majesty's government the anxious and deliberate consideration that their importance demands; and, although her Majesty's government feel compelled to adhere to the principles and the policy laid down in Lord John Russell's despatch of the 9th of February, yet they gladly comply with the Emperor's wish, that the subject should be further and frankly discussed. The generous confidence exhibited by the Emperor entitles his Imperial Majesty to the most cordial declaration of opinion on the part of her Majesty's government, who are fully aware that, in the event of an understanding with reference to future contingencies being expedient, or, indeed, possible, the word of his Imperial Majesty would be preferable to any convention that could be framed.

Her Majesty's government persevere in the belief that Turkey *still possesses the elements of existence*, and they consider that recent events have proved the correctness of the opinion expressed in the despatch of my predecessor, that there was no sufficient cause for intimating to the Sultan that he cannot keep peace at home or preserve friendly relations with his neighbors.

Her Majesty's government have, accordingly, learnt with sincere satisfaction that the Emperor considers himself even more interested than England in preventing a Turkish catastrophe; bacause they are convinced that, upon the policy pursued by his Imperial Majesty towards Turkey will mainly depend the hastening or the indefinite postponement of an event which every power in Europe is concerned in averting. Her Majesty's government are convinced that nothing is more calculated to precipitate that event than the constant prediction of its being near at hand; that nothing can be more fatal to the vitality of Turkey than the assumption of its rapid and inevitable decay; and that, if the opinion of the Emperor, that the days of the Turkish empire were numbered, became notorious, its downfall must occur even sooner than his Imperial Majesty now appears to expect.

But, on the supposition that, from unavoidable causes, the catastrophe did take place, her Majesty's government entirely share the opinion of the Emperor, that the occupation of Constantinople by either of the great powers would be incompatible with the present balance of power and the maintenance of peace in Europe, and must at once be regarded as impossible; that there are no elements for the reconstruction of the Byzantine empire; that the systematic misgovernment of Greece offers no encouragement to extend its territorial dominion; and that, as there are no materials for provincial or communal government, anarchy would be the result of leaving the provinces of Turkey to themselves, or permitting them to form separate republics.

The Emperor has announced that, sooner than permit a settlement of the question by any one of these methods, he will be prepared for war at every hazard; and however much her Majesty's government may be disposed to agree in the soundness of the views taken by his Imperial Majesty, yet they consider that the simple predetermination of what shall not be tolerated does little towards solving the real difficulties, or settling in what manner it would be practicable, or even desirable, to deal with the heterogeneous materials of which the Turkish empire is composed.

England desires no territorial aggrandizement, and could be no party to a previous arrangement from which she was to derive any such benefit. England could be no party to any understanding, however general, that was to be kept secret from other powers; but her Majesty's government believe that no arrangements could control events, and that no understanding could be kept secret. They would, in the opinion of her Majesty's government, be the signal for preparation for intrigues of every description, and for revolts among the Christian subjects of the Porte. Each power and each party would endeavor to secure its future interests, and the dissolution of the Turkish empire would be preceded by a state of anarchy which must aggravate every difficulty, if it did not render a peaceful solution of the question impossible.

The only mode by which such a solution could be attempted would be that of a European Congress, but that only affords an additional reason for desiring that the present order of things in Turkey should be maintained, as her Majesty's government cannot, without alarm, reflect on the jealousies that would then be evoked, the impossibility of reconciling the different ambitions and the divergent interests that would be called into play, and the certainties that the treaties of 1815 must then be open to revision, when France might be prepared to risk the chances of a European war to get rid of the obligations which she considers injurious to her national honor, and which, having been imposed by victorious enemies, are a constant source of irritation to her.

The main object of her Majesty's government—that to which their efforts have been and always will be directed—is the preservation of peace; and they desire to uphold the Turkish empire, from their conviction that no great question can be agitated in the East without becoming a source of discord in the West, and that every great question in the West, will assume a revolutionary character, and embrace a revision of the entire social system, for which the continental governments are certainly in no state of preparation.

The Emperor is fully cognizant of the materials that are in constant fermentation beneath the surface of society, and their readiness to burst forth even in times of peace; and his Imperial Majesty will probably, therefore, not dissent from the opinion, that the first cannon shot may be the signal for a state of things more disastrous even than those calamities which war inevitably brings in its train.

But such a war would be the result of the dissolution and dismemberment of the Turkish empire; and hence the anxiety of her Majesty's government to avert the catastrophe. Nor can they admit, that the signs of Turkish decay are now either more evident or more rapid than of late years. There is still great energy and great wealth in Turkey; a disposition to improve the system of government is not wanting; corruption, though unfortunately great, is still not of a charater nor carried to an extent that threatens the existence of the state; the treatment of Christians is not harsh, and the toleration exhibited by the Porte towards this portion of its subjects, might serve as an example to some governments who look with contempt upon Turkey as a barberous power.

Her Majesty's government believe that Turkey only requires forbearance on the part of its allies, and a determination not to press their claims in a manner humiliating to the dignity and independence of the Sultan, that friendly support, in short, that, with states as with individuals, the weak are entitled to expect from the strong—in order not only to prolong its existence, but to remove all cause of alarm respecting its dissolution.

It is in this work of benevolence and sound European policy that her Majesty's government are desirous of co-operating with the Emperor. They feel entire confidence in the rectitude of his Imperial Majesty's intentions, and, as they have the satisfaction of thinking that the interests of Russia and England in the East are completely identical, they entertain an earnest hope that a similar policy there will prevail, and tend to strengthen the alliance between the two countries, which it is alike the object of her Majesty and her Majesty's government to promote.

You will give a copy of this despatch to the Chancellor, or to the Emperor, in the event of your again having the honor to be received by his Imperial Majesty. I am, &c.,

CLARENDON.

SIR G. H. SEYMOUR TO THE EARL OF CLARENDON.

No. 11.

[Received March 26.]

[Secret and confidential.]

ST. PETERSBURGH, March 12, 1853.

MY LORD—The Chancellor sent for me this morning, when he placed in my hands a copy of the memorandum which was brought to your lordship's knowledge by my despatch of the 9th inst.

Upon this copy the Emperor had written in pencil, that he was sorry to find that Sir Hamilton Seymour had considered a passage in the paper as reflecting upon the conduct of her Majesty's government; that no reproach had been intended, and that the Chancellor would do well to see me, and to state that, if it should be my wish, the paper might be taken back and altered.

After a few moments' reflection, it occurred to me that the explanations which I had received were sufficient, so that a record could be obtained of the Emperor's amicable intentions, and that the paper, if taken back, might be altered in more than one of its passages; I therefore stated that, instead of changing the memorandum, I would suggest that his Excellency should write me a few lines explanatory of the purport of the passage which I had considered objectionable.

To this the Chancellor at once acceded, and it only remained for me to request that his Excellency would be kind enough to express to the Emperor how sensibly I felt his gracious solicitude to efface a disagreeable impression. I have, &c.,

G. H. SEYMOUR.

SIR G. H. SEYMOUR TO THE EARL OF CLARENDON.

No. 12.

[Received April 4.]

[Secret and confidential.]

ST. PETERSBURGH, March 16, 1853.

MY LORD—With reference to the despatch marked "secret and confidential," which I had the honor of addressing to your lordship on the 12th instant, I beg to transmit, in original, the letter which Count Nesselrode undertook to write to me, expressive of the Emperor's willingness to change the passage in his memorandum, which I had considered open to some misinterpretation. I have, &c.,

G. H. SEYMOUR.

COUNT NESSELRODE TO SIR G. H. SEYMOUR.

[Enclosed in No. 12.]

3 (15) Mars, 1853.

A l'explication que j'ai eu l'honneur de vous offrir verbalement, mon cher Sir Hamilton, je me fais un plaisir d'ajouter, qu'ayant porté vos doutes à la connaissance de l'Empereur, sa Majesté m'a authorisé à modifier le passage qui les a fait naitre dans votre esprit, si toutefois vous le jugiez nécessaire. L'Empereur desire avant tout écarter d'une communication tout personelle et amicale avec le gouvernement de sa Majesté la Reine ce qui porrait donner lieu à une interprétation même erronée, qui serait contraire aux intentions qui l'ont dictée, comme au but que sa Majesté se propose. Veuillez, &c.,

NESSELRODE.

[Translation.]

March 3 (15), 1853.

I have the pleasure, my dear Sir Hamilton, to add to the explanation which I had the honor to offer to you verbally, that, having communicated your doubts to the Emperor, his Majesty has authorized me to modify the passage which had caused you to entertain them, at least if you should consider it necessary. The Emperor is, above all things, desirous of removing from a communication altogether personal and friendly with the government of her Majesty the Queen, what might give occasion even to an erroneous interpretation, which would be contrary to the intentions by which it was dictated, as also to the object which his Majesty proposes to himself. Be pleased, &c.,

NESSELRODE.

THE EARL OF CLARENDON TO SIR G. H. SEYMOUR.

No. 13.

[Secret and confidential.]

FOREIGN OFFICE, April 5, 1853.

SIR—Your despatches of the 9th, 10th, and 12th ultimo have been laid before the Queen.

My despatch of the 23d ultimo will have furnished you with answers upon all the principal points alluded to in the memorandum which Count Nesselrode placed in your hands; but it is my duty to inform you that that important and remarkable document was received by her Majesty's government with feelings of sincere satisfaction, as a renewed proof of the Emperor's confidence and friendly fellings; and her Majesty's government desire to convey their acknowledgments to his Imperial Majesty for having thus placed on record the opinions he expressed at the interview with which you were honored by his Imperial Majesty.

Her Majesty's government do not consider that any useful purpose would be served by prolonging a correspondence upon a question with respect to which a complete understanding has been established; and I have only, therefore, further to state, that her Majesty's government observe with pleasure that, in the opinion of the Emperor, the fall of the Turkish empire is looked upon as an uncertain and distant contingency, and that no real crisis has occurred to render its realization imminent.

Her Majesty's government have never any wish to disguise their policy, which they trust is honest and straight-forward towards all other countries; but on such a question they would particularly regret that any misapprehension existed on the mind of the Emperor, and they accordingly approve the confidential note which you addressed to Count Nesselrode, for the purpose of rectifying some ideas which reflected upon the course pursued by her Majesty's government.

On the subject of the Charlemagne coming up to the Bosphorus, a correspondence took place between the English and French governments, and, although the Porte gave its sanction unconditionally, the eventual solution of the question was in conformity with the opinion of her Majesty's goverement, and it was settled that the Charlemagne should convey M. de. Lavalette to Constantinople, under which circumstances it was stated that the passage of the French ship-of-war would not be further remonstrated against by her Majesty's government, but that it must not be drawn into a precedent.

As regards the Holy Places, you are aware of the instruction given to Colonel Rese for his guidance at the Porte, and of the despatch addressed to her Majesty's ambassador at Paris, which was communicated to the French government, and I have further to inform you that Viscount Stratford de Redcliffe was instructed to bear in mind that her Majesty's government, without professing to give an opinion on the subject, were not insensible to the superior claims of Russia, both as respected the treaty obligations of Turkey, and the loss of moral influence that the Emperor would sustain throughout his dominion, if, in the position occupied by his Imperial Majesty with reference to the Greek church, he has to yield any privileges it had hitherto enjoyed to the Latin church, of which the Emperor of the French claimed to be the protector.

With respect to the advice which the Emperor recommends should be given to the Porte by her Majesty's government, you will inform the Chancellor, that Viscount Stratford de Redcliffe was directed to return to his post, and a special character was given to his mission by an autograph letter from her Majesty, under the impression that the Porte would be better disposed to listen to moderate counsels when offered by one of Viscount Stratford de Redcliffe's high position and great knowledge and experience of Turkish affairs ; and he was particularly desired to advise the Porte to treat its Christian subjects with the utmost leniency.

Upon this latter point her Majesty's government are inclined to believe that the Turkish govenrment are at length awakened to a sense of their own true interests. At the beginning of this year we know that orders were sent to Kiamil Pacha to proceed instantly to Bosnia in order to redress Christian grievances, and to empower the Christian communities to build churches. About the same time, also, the Porte sent the strongest instructions to Omer Pacha to act with unvaried moderation and humanity towards his enemies, (the Montenegrins ;) and the English vice-consul at Scutari confirmed all the previous statements, that the inhabitants of Montenegro committed an unprovoked attack on the troops and subjects of the Porte ; while the accounts that have reached her Majesty's government respecting the atrocities said to have been committed by the Turks in Bosnia, Herzegovino and Montenegro are extracted from Austrian newspapers, and must necessarily, therefore, be received with caution.

I have only in conclusion to add that, as her Majesty and the Emperor have now mutually renewed the assurances of their intention to uphold the independence and integrity of the Turkish empire, it is the earnest desire of her Majesty's government that the representatives of the two powers may henceforward co-operate together in carrying out this intention by giving similar advice in the same friendly spirit to the Porte.

You are instructed to read this despatch to the Chancellor, and to furnish him with a copy, should he desire it.

I am, &c.,

CLARENDON.

SIR G. H. SEYMOUR TO THE EARL OF CLARENDON.

No. 14.

[Received May 2.]

[Secret and confidential.]

(Extract.) ST. PETERSBURGH, April 20, 1853.

The Emperor, on rising from the table when I had the honor of dining at the palace on the 18th instant, desired me to follow him into the next room.

His Majesty then said that he wished to state to me the real and sincere satisfaction which he received from your lordship's despatch, marked "secret and confidential," of the 23d ultimo.

It had been, his Majesty said, most agreeable to him to find that the overtures which he had addressed to her Majesty's government had been responded to in the same friendly spirit in which they were made; that, to use a former expression, there was nothing in which he placed so much reliance as "*la parole d'un gentilhomme;*" that he felt that the relations of the two courts stood upon a better basis, now that a clear understanding had been obtained as to points which, if left in doubt, might have been productive of misintelligence, and, as his Majesty was pleased to add, he felt obliged to me for having contributed towards bringing about this friendly *entente*.

And his Majesty said, "I beg you to understand that what I have pledged myself to do will be equally binding on my successor; there now exist memorandums of my intentions, and whatever I have promised, my son, if the changes alluded to should occur in his time, would be as ready to perform as his father would have been."

The Emperor proceeded to state that he would very frankly offer an observation or two—it might be a criticism—on your lordship's despatch.

The despatch spoke of the fall of the Turkish empire as an uncertain and distant event. He would remark that the one term excluded the other; uncertain it was, certainly, but, for that reason, not necessarily remote. He desired it might be, but he was not sure that it might so prove.

His Majesty desired further to observe, that he could not doubt that her Majesty's government had taken too favorable a view of the state of the Christian population in Turkey; the Sultan might have intended to better their condition, might have given orders in that sense, but he was quite certain that his commands had not been attended to.

Upon my remarking that her Majesty's government were understood to receive very accurate reports of what passes in Turkey, the Emperor replied, with considerable animation, that he called this fact in question; that he believed, on the contrary, that some of the English consular agents were incorrect in their reports. He would only refer to Bulgaria; the greatest discontent prevailed there, and his Majesty would affirm, that, were it not for his continued efforts to repress the manifestation of feelings of the sort, the Bulgarians would some time since have been in insurrection.

His Majesty proceeded to contrast the threatening attitude which had been assumed by Count Leiningen with the peaceable character of Prince

Menchikoff's mission; not, however, that he desired to blame the Emperor of Austria, a noble prince, whom he loved sincerely, and all of whose acts he approved; the difference existed in circumstances, and when Montenegro was threatened with utter devastation, the Emperor of Austria was obliged to act with energy. His Majesty would, he said, have acted in the same manner.

I am desirous of remarking here, that part of the Emperor's observaeions were, it was obvious, addressed to me personally, and were intended as a reply as well to an allusion which I had made as to religious intolerance in Tuscany, as to my comments to the Chancellor upon the conduct of the Austrian cabinet with regard to the late confiscatory measures in Lombardy.

His Majesty, after observing that, according to the accounts just received, (those of the 29th ult.,) little or no progress had been made towards an adjustment of difficulties at Constantinople, said, that as yet he had not moved a ship or a battalion; that he had not done so from motives of consideration for the Sultan and from economical motives; but that he would repeat, that he had no intention of being trifled with, and that, if the Turks did not yield to reason, they would have to give way to an approach of danger.

I ventured to remark to the Emperor, that it was only by the despatches just arrived that he had received intelligence of the landing at Pera of the French Ambassador, who was understood to be a party to the arrangements about to be concluded; the indirect answer, however, returned to me by his Majesty, and the expressions which he used, lead me to apprehend that this consideration did not receive the attention of which, in fairness, it appears to me deserving.

SIR G. H. SEYMOUR TO THE EARL OF CLARENDON.

[No. 15.]

[Received May 2.]

[Secret and confidential.]

St. Petersburgh, April 21, 1853.

My Lord—I have had the honor of receiving your lordship's despatch, marked "secret and confidential," of the 5th inst., which, in obedience to your lordship's orders, I communicated to Count Nesselrode on the 15th inst.

His excellency, before the arrrival of this messenger, had desired to see me for the purpose of communicating to me a paper which had been drawn up by the Emperor's desire, and which was to be considered as an answer to your lordship's despatch of the 23d ult.

This document, which I beg to transmit in original, was accordingly placed in my hands by the Chancellor, who observed that he had previously thought that it would close the correspondence, but it was possible that the fresh despatch which I had brought to his knowledge might, upon being laid before the Emperor, call for some fresh observations on the part of his Majesty.

The only passage in the inclosed paper to which Count Nesselrode was desirous of drawing my attention, was that in which an observation is made respecting the treatment of the Christian population, as described by English or by Russian agents.

I remarked, in reply, that the point was the less material, by her Majesty's government being (as his Excellency had been made aware,) as desirous as the Imperial cabinet could be, that no effort should be wanting on the part of the Porte, to remove any and every cause of complaint which could be made in justice by the Sultan's Christian subjects.

Your lordship will perhaps allow me to observe that, supposing the present crisis in Turkish affairs to pass over, an intimation is made in the enclosed paper which, if taken up and embodied in a joint resolution by all the great powers, might possibly be the means of long averting a catastrophe which, happen when it may, will probably have disastrous consequences even to those to whom it may be considered the most profitable.

Since the preceding part of this despatch was written, the Chancellor has intimated to me that the Emperor, being of opinion that the paper which I now enclose, followed up by the conversation which I had the honor of holding with his Majesty on the 18th, may be considered as replying to any points touched upon in your lordship's despatch, does not propose to offer any fresh observation upon the subjects which have been under discussion. His Excellency does not conceal from me his satisfaction at this resolution, these subjects being, as he remarked, of so delicate a nature that there are always objections to their being brought under discussion.

I have, &c., G. H. SEYMOUR.

[Translation]

The Emperor has, with lively satisfaction, made himself acquainted with Lord Clarendon's despath of the 23d of March. His Majesty congratulates himself on perceiving that his views and those of the English cabinet entirely coincide on the subject of the political combinations which it would be chiefly necessary to avoid in the extreme case of the contingency occurring in the East, which Russia and England have equally at heart to prevent, or, at all events to delay as long as possible. Sharing generally the opinions expressed by Lord Clarendon on the necessity of the prolonged maintenance of the existing state of things in Turkey, the Emperor, nevertheless, cannot abstain from adverting to a special point which leads him to suppose that the information received by the British government is not altogether in accordance with ours. It refers to the humanity and the toleration to be shown by Turkey in her manner of treating her Christian subjects.

Putting aside many other examples to the contrary of an old date, it is, for all that, notorious, that recently the cruelties committed by the Turks, in Bosnia, forced hundreds of Christian families to seek refuge in Austria. In other respects, without wishing on this occasion to enter upon a discussion as to the symptoms of decay, more or less evident, presented by the Ottoman power, or the greater or less degree of vitality which its internal constitution may retain, the Emperor will readily agree that the best means of upholding the duration of the Turkish government is not to harass it by overbearing demands, supported in a manner humiliating to its independence and its dignity. His Majesty is disposed, as he has ever been, to act upon this system, with the clear understanding, however, that the same rule of conduct shall be observed, without distinction and unanimously, by each of the great powers, and that none of them shall take advantage of the weakness of the Porte, to obtain from it concessions which might turn to the prejudice of the others. This principle being laid down, the Emperor declares that he is ready to labor, in concert with England, at the common work of prolonging the existence of the Turkish empire, setting aside all cause of alarm on the subject of its dissolution. He readily accepts the evidence offered by the British cabinet of entire confidence in the uprightness of his sentiments, and the hope that, on this basis, his alliance with England cannot fail to become stronger.

St. Petersburgh, April 3, (15,) 1853.

The following is the memorandum by Count Nesselrode delivered to her Majesty's government, and founded on communications received from the Emperor of Russia subsequently to his Imperial Majesty's visit to England in June, 1844 :

[Translation.]

Russia and England are mutually penetrated with the conviction, that it is for their common interest that the Ottoman Porte should maintain itself in the state of independence and territorial possession which at present constitute that empire, as that political combination is the one which is most compatible with the general interest of the maintenance of peace.

Being agreed on this principle, Russia and England have an equal interest in uniting their efforts in order to keep up the existence of the Ottoman empire, and to avert all the dangers which can place in jeopardy its safety.

With this object, the essential point is to suffer the Porte to live in repose, without needlessly disturbing it by diplomatic bickerings, and without interfering, unless with absolute necessity, in its internal affairs.

In order to carry out skilfully this system of forbearance, with a view to the well-understood interest of the Porte, two things must not be lost sight of. They are these :

In the first place, the Porte has a constant tendency to extricate itself from the engagements imposed upon it by the treaties which it has concluded with the other powers. It hopes to do so with impunity, because it reckons on the mutual jealousy of the cabinets. It thinks that if it fails in its engagements towards one of them, the rest will espouse its quarrel, and will screen it from all responsibility.

It is essential not to confirm the Porte in this delusion. Every time that it fails in its obligations towards one of the great powers, it is the interest of all the rest to make it sensible of its error, and seriously to exhort it to act rightly towards the cabinet which demands just reparation.

As soon as the Porte shall perceive that it is not supported by the other cabinets, it will give way, and the differences which have arisen will be aranged in a conciliatory manner, without any conflict resulting from them.

There is a second cause of complication, which is inherent in the situation of the Porte: it is the difficulty which exists in reconciling the respect due to the sovereign authority of the Sultan, founded on the Mussulman law, with the forbearance required by the interests of the Christian population of that empire.

This difficulty is real. In the present state of feeling in Europe the cabinets cannot see with indifference the Christian population in Turkey exposed to flagrant acts of oppression and religious intolerance.

It is necessary constantly to make the Ottoman ministry sensible of this truth, and to persuade them that they can only reckon on the friendship and on the support of the great powers on the condition that they treat the Christian subjects of the Porte with toleration and with mildness.

While insisting on this truth, it will be the duty of the foreign representatives, on the other hand, to exert all their influence to maintain the Christian subjects of the Porte in submission to the sovereign authority.

It will be the duty of the foreign representatives, guided by these principles, to act among themselves in a perfect spirit of agreement. If they address remonstrances to the Porte, those remonstrances must bear a real character of unanimity, though divested of one of exclusive dictation.

By persevering in this system with calmness and moderation, the representatives of the great cabinets of Europe will have the best chance of succeeding in the steps which they may take, without giving occasion for complications which might affect the tranquility of the Ottoman empire. If all the great powers frankly adopt this line of conduct, they will have a well-founded expectation of preserving the existence of Turkey.

However, they must not conceal from themselves how many elements of dissolution that empire contains within itself. Unforeseen circumstances may hasten its fall without its being in the power of the friendly cabinets to prevent it.

As it is not given to human foresight to settle beforehand a plan of action for such unlooked-for case, it would be premature to discuss eventualities which may never be realized.

In the uncertainty which hovers over the future, a single fundamental idea seems to admit of a really practical application; it is, that the danger which may result from a catastrophe in Turkey will be much diminished, if, in the extent of its occurring, Russia and England have come to an understanding as to the course to be taken by them in common.

That understanding will be the more beneficial, inasmuch as it will have the full assent of Austria. Between her and Russia there exists already an entire conformity of principles in regard to the affairs of Turkey, in a common interest of conservatism and of peace.

In order to render their union more efficacious, there would remain nothing to be desired, but that England should be seen to associate herself thereto with the same view.

The reason which recommends the establishment of this agreement is very simple.

On land Russia exercises in regard to Turkey a preponderant action.

On sea England occupies the same position.

Isolated, the action of these two powers might do much mischief. United, it can produce a real benefit; thence the advantage of coming to a previous understanding before having recourse to action.

This notion was in principle agreed upon during the Emperor's last residence in London. The result was the eventual engagement, that if anything unforeseen occurred in Turkey, Russia and England should previously concert together as to the course which they should pursue in common.

The object for which Russia and England will have to come to an understanding may be expressed in the following manner:

1. To seek to maintain the existence of the Ottoman empire in its present state, so long as that political combination shall be possible.

2. If we foresee that it must crumble to pieces, to enter into previous concert as to everything relating to the establishment of a new order of things, intended to replace that which now exists, and, in conjunction with each other, to see that the change which may have occurred in the internal situation of that empire shall not injuriously affect either the security of their own states and the rights which the treaties assure to them respectively, or the maintenance of the balance of power in Europe.

For the purpose thus stated, the policy of Russia and of Austria, as we have already said, is closely united by the principle of perfect identity. If England, as the principal maratime power, acts in concert with them, it is to be supposed that France will find herself obliged to act in conformity with the course agreed upon between St. Petersburgh, London and Vienna.

Conflict between the great powers being thus obviated, it is to be hoped that the peace of Europe will be maintained even in the midst of such serious circumstances. It is to secure this object of common interest, if the case occurs, that, as the Emperor agreed with her Britannic Majesty's ministers during his residence in England, the previous understanding which Russia and England shall establish between themselves must be directed.

THE END.

PHILOSOPHERS AND ACTRESSES

By Arsene Houssaye. With beautifully-engraved Portraits of Voltaire and Mad. Parabère. Two vols., 12mo, price $2.50.

"We have here the most charming book we have read these many days,—so powerful in its fascination that we have been held for hours from our imperious labors or needful slumbers, by the entrancing influence of its pages. One of the most desirable fruits of the prolific field of literature of the present season."—*Portland Eclectic.*

"Two brilliant and fascinating—we had almost said, bewitching—volumes, combining information and amusement, the lightest gossip, with solid and serviceable wisdom."—*Yankee Blade.*

"It is a most admirable book, full of originality, wit, information and philosophy Indeed, the vividness of the book is extraordinary. The scenes and descriptions are absolutely life-like."—*Southern Literary Gazette.*

"The works of the present writer are the only ones the spirit of whose rhetoric does justice to those times, and in fascination of description and style equal the fascinations they descant upon."—*New Orleans Commercial Bulletin.*

"The author is a brilliant writer, and serves up his sketches in a sparkling manner" *Christian Freeman.*

ANCIENT EGYPT UNDER THE PHARAOHS.

By John Kendrick, M. A. In 2 vols., 12mo, price $2.50.

"No work has heretofore appeared suited to the wants of the historical student, which combined the labors of artists, travellers, interpreters and critics, during the periods from the earliest records of the monarchy to its final absorption in the empire of Alexander. This work supplies this deficiency."—*Olive Branch.*

"Not only the geography and political history of Egypt under the Pharaohs are given, but we are furnished with a minute account of the domestic manners and customs of the inhabitants, their language, laws, science, religion, agriculture, navigation and commerce."—*Commercial Advertiser.*

"These volumes present a comprehensive view of the results of the combined labors of travellers, artists, and scientific explorers, which have effected so much during the present century toward the development of Egyptian archæology and history."—*Journal of Commerce.*

"The descriptions are very vivid and one wanders, delighted with the author, through the land of Egypt, gathering at every step, new phases of her wondrous history, and ends with a more intelligent knowledge than he ever before had, of the land of the Pharaohs."—*American Spectator.*

COMPARATIVE PHYSIOGNOMY;

Or Resemblances between Men and Animals. By J. W. Redfield, M. D. In one vol., 8vo, with several hundred illustrations. price, $2.00.

"Dr. Redfield has produced a very curious, amusing, and instructive book, curious in its originality and illustrations, amusing in the comparisons and analyses, and instructive because it contains very much useful information on a too much neglected subject. It will be eagerly read and quickly appreciated."—*National Ægis.*

"The whole work exhibits a good deal of scientific research, intelligent observation, and ingenuity."—*Daily Union.*

"Highly entertaining even to those who have little time to study the science."—*Detroit Daily Advertiser.*

"This is a remarkable volume and will be read by two classes, those who study for information, and those who read for amusement. For its originality and entertaining character, we commend it to our readers."—*Albany Express.*

"It is overflowing with wit, humor, and originality, and profusely illustrated. The whole work is distinguished by vast research and knowledge."—*Knickerbocker.*

"The plan is a novel one; the proofs striking, and must challenge the attention of the curious."—*Daily Advertiser*

NOTES AND EMENDATIONS OF SHAKESPEARE.

Notes and Emendations to the Text of Shakespeare's Plays, from the Early Manuscript Corrections in a copy of the folio of 1632, in the possession of JOHN PAYNE COLLIER, Esq., F.S.A. Third edition, with a fac-simile of the Manuscript Corrections. 1 vol 12mo, cloth, $1 50.

"It is not for a moment to be doubted, we think, that in this volume a contribution has been made to the clearness and accuracy of Shakespeare's text, by far the most important of any offered or attempted since Shakespeare lived and wrote."—*Lond. Exam*

"The corrections which Mr. Collier has here given to the world are, we venture to think, of more value than the labors of nearly all the critics on Shakespeare's text put together."—*London Literary Gazette.*

"It is a rare gem in the history of literature, and can not fail to command the attention of all the amateurs of the writings of the immortal dramatic poet."—*Ch'ston Cour*

"It is a book absolutely indispensable to every admirer of Shakespeare who wishes to read him understandingly."—*Louisville Courier.*

"It is clear from internal evidence, that for the most part they are genuine restorations of the original plays. They carry conviction with them."—*Home Journal.*

"This volume is an almost indispensable companion to any of the editions of Shakespeare, so numerous and often important are many of the corrections."—*Register Philadelphia.*

THE HISTORY OF THE CRUSADES.

By JOSEPH FRANÇOIS MICHAUD. Translated by W. Robson, 3 vols. 12mo., maps, $3 75.

"It is comprehensive and accurate in the detail of facts, methodical and lucid in arrangement, with a lively and flowing narrative."—*Journal of Commerce.*

"We need not say that the work of Michaud has superseded all other histories of the Crusades. This history has long been the standard work with all who could read it in its original language. Another work on the same subject is as improbable as a new history of the 'Decline and Fall of the Roman Empire.'"—*Salem Freeman.*

"The most faithful and masterly history ever written of the wild wars for the Holy Land."—*Philadelphia American Courier.*

"The ability, diligence, and faithfulness, with which Michaud has executed his great task, are undisputed; and it is to his well-filled volumes that the historical student must now resort for copious and authentic facts, and luminous views respecting this most romantic and wonderful period in the annals of the Old World."—*Boston Daily Courier.*

MARMADUKE WYVIL.

An Historical Romance of 1651, by HENRY W. HERBERT, author of the "Cavaliers of England," &c., &c. Fourteenth Edition. Revised and Corrected.

"This is one of the best works of the kind we have ever read—full of thrilling incidents and adventures in the stirring times of Cromwell, and in that style which has made the works of Mr. Herbert so popular."—*Christian Freeman, Boston.*

"The work is distinguished by the same historical knowledge, thrilling incident, and pictorial beauty of style, which have characterized all Mr. Herbert's fictions and imparted to them such a bewitching interest."—*Yankee Blade.*

"The author out of a simple plot and very few characters, has constructed a novel of deep interest and of considerable historical value. It will be found well worth reading"—*National Ægis, Worcester.*

SKETCHES OF THE IRISH BAR.

By the Right Hon. RICHARD LALOR SHEIL, M. P. Edited with a Memoir and Notes, by Dr. SHELTON MACKENZIE. Fourth Edition. In 2 vols. Price $2 00.

"They attracted universal attention by their brilliant and pointed style, and their liberality of sentiment. The Notes embody a great amount of biographical information, literary gossip, legal and political anecdote, and amusing reminiscences, and, in fact, omit nothing that is essential to the perfect elucidation of the text."—*New York Tribune.*

"They are the best edited books we have met for many a year. They form, with Mackenzie's notes, a complete biographical dictionary, containing succinct and clever sketches of all the famous people of England, and particularly of Ireland, to whom the slightest allusions are made in the text."—*The Citizen (John Mitchel).*

"Dr. Mackenzie deserves the thanks of men of letters, particularly of Irishmen, for his research and care. Altogether, the work is one we can recommend in the highest terms."—*Philadelphia City Item.*

"Such a repertory of wit, humor, anecdote, and out-gushing fun, mingled with the deepest pathos, when we reflect upon the sad fate of Ireland, as this book affords, it were hard to find written in any other pair of covers."—*Buffalo Daily Courier.*

"As a whole, a more sparkling lively series of portraits was hardly ever set in a single gallery It is Irish all over; the wit, the folly, the extravagance, and the fire are all alike characteristic of writer and subjects."—*New York Evangelist.*

"These volumes afford a rich treat to the lovers of literature."—*Hartford Christian Sec.*

CLASSIC AND HISTORIC PORTRAITS.

By JAMES BRUCE. 12mo, cloth, $1 00.

"A series of personal sketches of distinguished individuals of all ages, embracing pen and ink portraits of near sixty persons from Sappho down to Madame de Stael. They show much research, and possess that interest which attaches to the private life of those whose names are known to fame."—*New Haven Journal and Courier.*

"They are comprehensive, well-written, and judicious, both in the selection of subjects and the manner of treating them."—*Boston Atlas.*

"The author has painted in minute touches the characteristics of each with various personal details, all interesting, and all calculated to furnish to the mind's eye a complete portraiture of the individual described."—*Albany Knickerbocker.*

"The sketches are full and graphic, many authorities having evidently been consulted by the author in their preparation."—*Boston Journal.*

THE WORKINGMAN'S WAY IN THE WORLD.

Being the Autobiography of a Journeyman Printer. By CHARLES MANBY SMITH, author of "Curiosities of London Life." 12mo, cloth, $1 00.

"Written by a man of genius and of most extraordinary powers of description."—*Boston Traveller.*

"It will be read with no small degree of interest by the professional brethren of the author, as well as by all who find attractions in a well-told tale of a workingman."—*Boston Atlas.*

"An amusing as well as instructive book, telling how humble obscurity cuts its way through the world with energy, perseverance, and integrity."—*Albany Knickerbocker.*

"The book is the most entertaining we have met with for months."—*Philadelphia Evening Bulletin.*

"He has evidently moved through the world with his eyes open, and having a vein of humor in his nature, has written one of the most readable books of the season"—*Zion's Herald.*

MACAULAY'S SPEECHES.

Speeches by the Right Hon. T. B. MACAULAY, M. P., Author of "The History of England," "Lays of Ancient Rome," &c., &c. Two vols., 12mo, price $2.00.

"It is hard to say whether his poetry, his speeches in parliament, or his brilliant essays, are the most charming; each has raised him to very great eminence, and would be sufficient to constitute the reputation of any ordinary man."—*Sir Archibald Alison*

"It may be said that Great Britain has produced no statesman since Burke, who has united in so eminent a degree as Macaulay the lofty and cultivated genius, the eloquent orator, and the sagacious and far-reaching politician."—*Albany Argus.*

"We do not know of any living English orator, whose eloquence comes so near the ancient ideal—close, rapid, powerful, *practical* reasoning, animated by an intense earnestness of feeling."—*Courier & Enquirer.*

"Mr. Macaulay has lately acquired as great a reputation as an orator, as he had formerly won as an essayist and historian. He takes in his speeches the same wide and comprehensive grasp of his subject that he does in his essays, and treats it in the same elegant style."—*Philadelphia Evening Bulletin.*

"The same elaborate finish, sparkling antithesis, full sweep and copious flow of thought, and transparency of style, which made his essays so attractive, are found in his speeches. They are so perspicuous, so brilliantly studded with ornament and illustration, and so resistless in their current, that they appear at the time to be the wisest and greatest of human compositions."—*New York Evangelist.*

TRENCH ON PROVERBS.

On the Lessons in Proverbs, by RICHARD CHENEVIX TRENCH, B. D., Professor of Divinity in King's College, London, Author of the "Study of Words." 12mo, cloth, 50 cents.

"Another charming book by the author of the "Study of Words," on a subject which is so ingeniously treated, that we wonder no one has treated it before."—*Yankee Blade.*

"It is a book at once profoundly instructive, and at the same time deprived of all approach to dryness, by the charming manner in which the subject is treated."—*Arthur's Home Gazette.*

"It is a wide field, and one which the author has well cultivated, adding not only to his own reputation, but a valuable work to our literature."—*Albany Evening Transcript.*

"The work shows an acute perception, a genial appreciation of wit, and great research. It is a very rare and agreeable production, which may be read with profit and delight."—*New York Evangelist.*

"The style of the author is terse and vigorous—almost a model in its kind."—*Portland Eclectic.*

THE LION SKIN

And the Lover Hunt; by CHARLES DE BERNARD. 12mo, $1.00.

"It is not often the novel-reader can find on his bookseller's shelf a publication so full of incidents and good humor, and at the same time so provocative of honest thought."—*National* (Worcester, Mass.) *Ægis.*

"It is full of incidents; and the reader becomes so interested in the principal personages in the work, that he is unwilling to lay the book down until he has learned their whole history."—*Boston Olive Branch.*

"It is refreshing to meet occasionally with a well-published story which is written for a story, and for nothing else—which is not tipped with the snapper of a moral, or loaded in the handle with a pound of philanthropy, or an equal quantity of leaden philosophy."—*Springfield Republican.*

MOORE'S LIFE OF SHERIDAN.

Memoirs of the Life of the Rt. Hon. Richard Brinsley Sheridan, by THOMAS MOORE, with Portrait after Sir Joshua Reynolds. Two vols., 12mo, cloth, $2.00.

"One of the most brilliant biographies in English literature. It is the life of a wit written by a wit, and few of Tom Moore's most sparkling poems are more brilliant and fascinating than this biography."—*Boston Transcript.*

"This is at once a most valuable biography of the most celebrated wit of the times, and one of the most entertaining works of its gifted author."—*Springfield Republican.*

"The Life of Sheridan, the wit, contains as much food for serious thought as the best sermon that was ever penned."—*Arthur's Home Gazette.*

"The sketch of such a character and career as Sheridan's by such a hand as Moore's, can never cease to be attractive."—*N. Y. Courier and Enquirer.*

"The work is instructive and full of interest."—*Christian Intelligencer.*

"It is a gem of biography; full of incident, elegantly written, warmly appreciative, and on the whole candid and just. Sheridan was a rare and wonderful genius, and has in this work justice done to his surpassing merits."—*N. Y. Evangelist.*

BARRINGTON'S SKETCHES.

Personal Sketches of his own Time, by SIR JONAH BARRINGTON, Judge of the High Court of Admiralty in Ireland, with Illustrations by Darley. Third Edition, 12mo, cloth, $1 25.

"A more entertaining book than this is not often thrown in our way. His sketches of character are inimitable; and many of the prominent men of his time are hit off in the most striking and graceful outline."—*Albany Argus.*

"He was a very shrewd observer and eccentric writer, and his narrative of his own life, and sketches of society in Ireland during his times, are exceedingly humorous and interesting."—*N. Y. Commercial Advertiser.*

"It is one of those works which are conceived and written in so hearty a view, and brings before the reader so many palpable and amusing characters, that the entertainment and information are equally balanced."—*Boston Transcript.*

"This is one of the most entertaining books of the season."—*N. Y. Recorder.*

"It portrays in life-like colors the characters and daily habits of nearly all the English and Irish celebrities of that period."—*N. Y. Courier and Enquirer.*

JOMINI'S CAMPAIGN OF WATERLOO.

The Political and Military History of the Campaign of Waterloo from the French of Gen. Baron Jomini, by Lieut. S. V. BENET U. S. Ordnance, with a Map, 12mo, cloth, 75 cents.

"Of great value, both for its historical merit and its acknowledged impartiality."—*Christian Freeman, Boston.*

"It has long been regarded in Europe as a work of more than ordinary merit, while to military men his review of the tactics and manœuvres of the French Emperor during the few days which preceded his final and most disastrous defeat, is considered as instructive, as it is interesting."—*Arthur's Home Gazette.*

"It is a standard authority and illustrates a subject of permanent interest. With military students, and historical inquirers, it will be a favorite reference, and for the general reader it possesses great value and interest."—*Boston Transcript.*

"It throws much light on often mooted points respecting Napoleon's military and political genius. The translation is one of much vigor."—*Boston Commonwealth.*

"It supplies an important chapter in the most interesting and eventful period of Napoleon's military career."—*Savannah Daily News.*

"It is ably written and skilfully translated."—*Yankee Blade.*

LIFE IN THE MISSION.

Life in the Mission, the Camp, and the Zenana. By Mrs. COLIN MACKENZIE. 2 vols., 12mo. Cloth. $2 00.

"It is enlivened with countless pleasant anecdotes, and altogether is one of the most entertaining and valuable works of the kind that we have met with for many a day."—*Boston Traveller.*

"A more charming production has not issued from the press for years, than this journal of Mrs. Mackenzie."—*Arthur's Home Gazette.*

"She also gives us a clearer insight into the manners, position, climate, and way of life in general, in that distant land, than we have been able to obtain from any other work."—*Christian Herald.*

"Her observations illustrative of the religious state of things, and of the progress of Missions in the East, will be found specially valuable. It is on the whole a fascinating work, and withal is fitted to do good."—*Puritan Recorder.*

"She was familiarly acquainted with some of the excellent laborers sent out by the Presbyterian Board of Foreign Missions, of whom she speaks in the most favorable terms. The work is instructive and very readable."—*Presbyterian.*

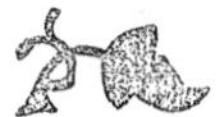

WESTERN CHARACTERS.

Western Characters; being Types of Border Life in the Western States. By J. L. M'CONNEL. Author of "Talbot and Vernon," "The Glenns," &c., &c. With Six Illustrations by Darley. 12mo. Cloth. $1 25.

"Ten different classes are sketched in this admirable book, and written by the hand of a master. The author is an expert limner, and makes his portraits striking."—*Buffalo Express.*

"Never has Darley's pencil been more effectively used. The writer and sketcher have made a unique and most attractive American book."—*Boston Transcript.*

"When we say that the book before us is calm in style as it is forcible in matter, we have indicated a sufficiency of good qualities to secure the attention of the reader, who would extend his sympathies and secure himself a due degree of amusement, without —what is not uncommon in books with similar titles—a shock to his taste, or insult to his judgment. There is nothing equal to them in the book illustrations of the day. A special paragraph should be given to the illustrations by Darley."—*Literary World.*

A THANKSGIVING STORY.

Chanticleer: A Story of the Peabody Family. By CORNELIUS MATHEWS. With Illustrations by Darley, Walcutt, and Dallas. 12mo. 75 cents.

"Its success is already a fixed fact in our literature. 'Chanticleer' is one of those simple and interesting tales which, like the 'Vicar of Wakefield' and Zchokke's 'Poor Pastor,' win their way to the reader's heart and dwell there. It is full of sunshine: a hearty and a genial book."—*New York Daily Times.*

"'Chanticleer' is scarcely inferior in a literary point of view to any of the Christmas stories of Charles Dickens, and is more interesting to Americans because of its allusions to the peculiar customs of this country."—*N. Y. Com. Advertiser.*

"'Chanticleer' has won the public heart, both by the felicity of its subject, and the grace, wit, and goodness, displayed in its execution."—*Southern Literary Gazette.*

"It possesses literary merit of the highest order, and will live in the affections of all readers of good taste and good morals, not only while Thanksgiving dinners are remembered, but while genius is appreciated."—*Morning News, Savannah.*

THE BLACKWATER CHRONICLE;

A Narrative of an Expedition into the Land of Canaan, in Randolph County, Virginia, a Country flowing with Wild Animals, such as Panthers, Bears, Wolves, Elk, Deer, Otter, Badger, &c., &c., with innumerable Trout, by Five Adventurous Gentlemen, without any Aid of Government, and solely by their Own Resources, in the Summer of 1851. By "THE CLERKE OF OXENFORDE." With Illustrations from Life, by Strother.

"This is a handsomely-printed and beautifully-illustrated volume. Those who have a taste for field sports will be delighted with this cleverly-written narrative of the achievements and experiences of a hunting party in the hunting-grounds of the Old Dominion."—*Savannah Daily News.*

"A queer, quaint, amusingly-written book, brimful of drollery and dare-devil humor. The work overflows with amusement, and has a vignette-title and other beautiful illustrations, by Strother."—*Yankee Blade.*

"A pleasant book of American character and adventure, of interest geographically, sportively, and poetically. The authorship is of a good intellectual race; the "Clerke of Oxenforde," who figures in the title-page, being own brother to the author of "Swallow Barn," which, as everybody knows, is the "Sketch-Book" of that land of gentlemen and humorists."—*Literary World.*

MINNESOTA AND ITS RESOURCES;

To which are Appended Camp-Fire Sketches, or Notes of a Trip from St. Paul to Pembina and Selkirk Settlements on the Red River of the North. By J. WESLEY BOND. With a New Map of the Territory, a View of St. Paul, and One of the Falls of St. Anthony. In One Volume, 12mo. Cloth. $1 00.

"To the immigrant to the northwest, and to the tourist in search of pleasure it is worthy of being commended for the valuable and interesting knowledge it contains."—*Chicago Daily Tribune.*

"The work will surprise many, as it opens to us a new land, shows its vast resources, and treats its history with all the accuracy that could be acquired by diligent research and careful observation, during a three years' residence."—*Boston Gazette.*

"It contains notices of the early history of the country, of its geographical features, its agricultural advantages, its manufactures, commerce, facilities for travelling, the character of its inhabitants—everything, indeed, to illustrate its resources and its prospects." -*Puritan Recorder.*

"We have seen no work respecting the northwest of equal value to this."—*Christian Intelligencer.*

THE YEMASSEE.

A Romance of South Carolina. By WILLIAM GILMORE SIMMS Author of "The Partisan," "Guy Rivers," &c., &c. New and Revised Edition. With Illustrations by Darley. 12mo Cloth. $1 25.

"A picture of the early border life of the Huguenot settlers in South Carolina. Like Scott's novels, it is a mixture of history and romance."—*Hartford Christian Secretary.*

"It is written in an uncommonly glowing style, and hits off the Indian character with uncommon grace and power."—*Albany Argus.*

"The whole work is truly American, much of the material being of that character which can be furnished by no other country."—*Daily Times.*

"The delineations of the red men of the south are admirably sketched while the historical events upon which the work is founded are vouched for by the author as strictly true."—*New Bedford Mercury*

ART AND INDUSTRY,

As Represented in the Exhibition at the Crystal Palace, New York. Showing the Progress and State of the Various Useful and Esthetic Pursuits. From the *New York Tribune.* Revised and Edited by HORACE GREELEY. 12mo., Cloth. Fine Paper, $1 00. Paper Covers, 50 Cents.

"The articles comprised in this work are thirty-six in number, on various subjects; they are elaborately and vigorously written, and contain much desirable information." —*Savannah Republican.*

"It will be read extensively and with interest by all who are engaged in any department of the useful or graceful arts."—*Lowell Journal and Courier.*

"Everybody interested in the state of American art or industry should have a copy." *Register, Phila.*

"Evidently written with a great deal of care, and presents in a small compass a very large amount of information, in relation to the latest improvements in science and art." —*Arthur's Home Gazette.*

"In each department of industry there is a rapid view of the history of the art or arts involved in its production, so that the work is much more than a mere descriptive account of the contents of the Crystal Palace. It deserves to be studied for the information it contains, and to be preserved as a book of reference."—*Puritan Recorder, Boston.*

"Especially to the mechanic and the manufacturer, this book will prove highly acceptable."—*Christian Secretary, Hartford.*

A MONTH IN ENGLAND.

By HENRY T. TUCKERMAN. Author of "Sicily, a Pilgrimage," "The Optimist," &c. 12mo., Cloth. 75 Cents.

"Commend us to this, for the pleasantest book on England we ever read, always excepting Macaulay's history."—*Springfield Evening Post.*

"His sketches are complete pictures of the history and life of English literature; condensed yet full, chaste yet glowing with beauty."—*N. Y. Independent.*

"This is really a delightful book. The author is well known as an original and vigorous writer and keen observer."—*Christian Freeman.*

"A lively, racy volume of travels, in which the author gives us his impressions of the castles, books, artists, authors, and other et cetera which came in his way."—*Zion's Herald.*

"Mr. Tuckerman is one of the purest and most elegant writers that adorn American literature."—*Knickerbocker, Albany.*

VASCONSELOS.

A Romance of the New World. By FRANK COOPER. 12mo., Cloth. $1 25.

"The scenes are laid in Spain and the New World, and the skill with which the pomp and circumstance of chivalry are presented, make Vasconselos one of the most interesting works of American fiction."—*N. Y. Evening Post.*

"It is well written, full of spirit, interesting historical facts, beautiful local descriptions, and well-sustained characters. Cuban associations abound in it, and there is a fine southern glow over the whole."—*Boston Transcript.*

"It is freely written, full of sparkle and freshness, and must interest any one whose appreciation is at all vigorous." *Buffalo Express.*

"The story is an interesting one, while the style is most refreshingly good for these days of easy writing."—*Arthur's Home Gazette.*

"This is an American romance, and to such as are fond of this order of literature, it will be found intensely interesting."—*Hartford Christian Secretary.*

A STRAY YANKEE IN TEXAS.

A Stray Yankee in Texas. By PHILIP PAXTON. With Illustrations by Darley. Second Edition, 12mo., cloth. $1 25.

"The work is a *chef d'œuvre* in a style of literature in which our country has no rival, and we commend it to all who are afflicted with the blues or *ennui*, as an effectual means of tickling their diaphragms, and giving their cheeks a holyday."—*Boston Yankee Blade.*

"We find, on a perusal of it, that Mr. Paxton has not only produced a readable, but a valuable book, as regards reliable information on Texan affairs.—*Hartford Christian Secretary.*

"The book is strange, wild, humorous, and yet truthful. It will be found admirably descriptive of a state of society which is fast losing its distinctive peculiarities in the rapid increase of population."—*Arthur's Home Gazette.*

"One of the richest, most entertaining, and, at the same time, instructive works one could well desire."—*Syracuse Daily Journal.*

"The book is a perfect picture of western manners and Texan adventures, and will occasion many a hearty laugh in the reader."—*Albany Daily State Register.*

NICK OF THE WOODS.

Nick of the Woods, or the Jibbenainosay; a Tale of Kentucky. By ROBERT M. BIRD, M. D., Author of "Calavar," "The Infidel," &c. New and Revised Edition, with Illustrations by Darley. 1 volume, 12mo., cloth, $1 25.

"One of those singular tales which impress themselves in ineradicable characters upon the memory of every imaginative reader."—*Arthur's Home Gazette.*

"Notwithstanding it takes the form of a novel, it is understood to be substantial truth in the dress of fiction; and nothing is related but which has its prototype in actual reality."—*Albany Argus.*

"It is a tale of frontier life and Indian warfare, written by a masterly pen, with its scenes so graphically depicted that they amount to a well-executed painting, at once striking and thrilling."—*Buffalo Express.*

WHITE, RED, AND BLACK.

Sketches of American Society, during the Visits of their Guests, by FRANCIS and THERESA PULSZKY. Two vols., 12mo., cloth, $2.

"Mr. Pulszky and his accomplished wife have produced an eminently candid and judicious book, which will be read with pleasure and profit on both sides of the Atlantic."—*New York Daily Times.*

"The authors have here furnished a narrative of decided interest and value. They have given us a view of the Hungarian war, a description of the Hungarian passage to this country, and a sketch of Hungarian travels over the country."—*Philad. Christian Chronicle.*

"Of all the recent books on America by foreign travellers, this is at once the most fair and the most correct."—*Philad. Saturday Gazette.*

"Unlike most foreign tourists in the United States, they speak of our institutions, manners, customs, &c., with marked candor, and at the same time evince a pretty thorough knowledge of our history."—*Hartford Christian Secretary.*

"This is a valuable book, when we consider the amount and variety of the information it contains, and when we estimate the accuracy with which the facts are detailed. —*Worcester Spy*

DISCOVERY AND EXPLORATION

Of the Mississippi Valley. With the Original Narratives of Marquette, Allouez, Membré, Hennepin, and Anastase Douay. By JOHN GILMARY SHEA. With a fac-simile of the Original Map of Marquette. 1 vol., 8vo, ; Cloth. Antique. $2.00.

"A volume of great and curious interest to all concerned to know the early history of this great Western land."—*Cincinnati Christian Herald.*

"We believe that this is altogether the most thorough work that has appeared on the subject to which it relates. It is the result of long-continued and diligent research, and no legitimate source of information has been left unexplored. The work combines the interest of romance with the authenticity of history."—*Puritan Recorder.*

"Mr. Shea has rendered a service to the cause of historical literature worthy of all praise by the excellent manner in which he has prepared this important publication for the press."—*Boston Traveller.*

NEWMAN'S REGAL ROME.

An Introduction to Roman History. By FRANCIS W. NEWMAN, Professor of Latin in the University College, London. 12mo, Cloth. 63 cents.

"The book, though small in compass, is evidently the work of great research and reflection, and is a valuable acquisition to historical literature."—*Courier and Enquirer.*

"A work of great erudition and power, vividly reproducing the wonderful era of Roman history under the kings. We greet it as a work of profound scholarship, genial art, and eminent interest—a work that will attract the scholar and please the general reader."—*N. Y. Evangelist.*

"Nearly all the histories in the schools should be banished, and such as this should take their places."—*Boston Journal.*

"Professor Newman's work will be found full of interest, from the light it throws on the formation of the language, the races, and the history, of ancient Rome."—*Wall-street Journal.*

THE CHEVALIERS OF FRANCE,

From the Crusaders to the Mareschals of Louis XIV. By HENRY W. HERBERT, author of "The Cavaliers of England," "Cromwell," "The Brothers," &c., &c. 1 vol. 12mo. $1.25.

"Mr. Herbert is one of the best writers of historical tales and legends in this or any other country."—*Christian Freeman.*

"This is a work of great power of thought and vividness of picturing. It is a moving panorama of the inner life of the French empire in the days of chivalry."—*Albany Spec*

"The series of works by this author, illustrative of the romance of history, is deservedly popular. They serve, indeed, to impart and impress on the mind a great deal of valuable information; for the facts of history are impartially exhibited, and the fiction presents a vivid picture of the manners and sentiments of the times."—*Journal of Commerce.*

"The work contains four historical tales or novelettes, marked by that vigor of style and beauty of description which have found so many admirers among the readers of the author's numerous romanaes."—*Lowell Journal.*

THE MASTER BUILDER;

Or, Life at a Trade. By DAY KELLOGG LEE, author of "Summerfield, or Life on the Farm." One vol., 12mo, price $1.00.

"He is a powerful and graphic writer, and from what we have seen of the pages of the 'Master Builder,' it is a romance of excellent aim and success."—*State Register.*

"The 'Master Builder' is the master production. It is romance into which is instilled the reality of life: and incentives are put forth to noble exertion and virtue. The story is pleasing—almost fascinating; the moral is pure and undefiled."—*Daily Times.*

"Its descriptions are, many of them, strikingly beautiful; commingling in good proportions, the witty, the grotesque, the pathetic, and the heroic. It may be read with profit as well as pleasure."—*Argus.*

"The work before us will commend itself to the masses, depicting as it does most graphically the struggles and privations which await the unknown and uncared-for Mechanic in his journey through life. It is what might be called a romance, but not of love, jealousy and revenge order."—*Lockport Courier.*

"The whole scheme of the story is well worked up and very instructive."—*Albany Express.*

GRISCOM ON VENTILATION.

The Uses and Abuses of Air: showing its Influence in Sustaining Life, and Producing Disease, with Remarks on the Ventilation of Houses, and the best Methods of Securing a Pure and Wholesome Atmosphere inside of Dwellings, Churches, Workshops, &c By JOHN H. GRISCOM, M. D. One vol. 12mo, $1.00.

"This comprehensive treatise should be read by all who wish to secure health, and especially by those constructing churches, lecture-rooms, school-houses, &c.—It is undoubted, that many diseases are created and spread in consequence of the little attention paid to proper ventilation. Dr. G. writes knowingly and plainly upon this all-important topic."—*Newark Advertiser.*

"The whole book is a complete manual of the subject of which it treats; and we venture to say that the builder or contriver of a dwelling, school-house, church, theatre, ship, or steamboat, who neglects to inform himself of the momentous truths it asserts, commits virtually a crime against society."—*N. Y. Metropolis.*

"When shall we learn to estimate at their proper value, pure water and pure air, which God provided for man before he made man, and a very long time before he permitted the existence of a doctor? We commend the Uses and Abuses of Air to our readers, assuring them that they will find it to contain directions for the ventilation of dwellings, which every one who values health and comfort should put in practice."—*N. Y. Dispatch.*

HAGAR, A STORY OF TO-DAY.

By ALICE CAREY, author of "Clovernook," "Lyra, and Other Poems," &c. One vol., 12mo, price $1.00.

"A story of rural and domestic life, abounding in humor, pathos, and that naturalness in character and conduct which made 'Clovernook' so great a favorite last season. Passages in 'Hagar' are written with extraordinary power, its moral is striking and just, and the book will inevitably be one of the most popular productions of the season."

"She has a fine, rich, and purely original genius. Her country stories are almost unequaled."—*Knickerbocker Magazine.*

"The Times speaks of Alice Carey as standing at the head of the living female writers of America. We go even farther in our favorable judgment, and express the opinion that among those living or dead, she has had no equal in this country; and we know of few in the annals of English literature who have exhibited superior gifts of real poetic genius."—*The (Portland, Me.) Eclectic.*

POETICAL WORKS OF FITZ-GREENE HALLECK

New and only Complete Edition, containing several New Poems, together with many now first collected. One vol., 12mo., price one dollar.

"Halleck is one of the brightest stars in our American literature, and his name is like a household word wherever the English language is spoken."—*Albany Express.*

"There are few poems to be found, in any language, that surpass, in beauty of thought and structure, some of these."—*Boston Commonwealth.*

"To the numerous admirers of Mr. Halleck, this will be a welcome book; for it is a characteristic desire in human nature to have the productions of our favorite authors in an elegant and substantial form."—*Christian Freeman.*

"Mr. Halleck never appeared in a better dress, and few poets ever deserved a better one."—*Christian Intelligencer.*

THE STUDY OF WORDS.

By Archdeacon R. C. Trench. One vol., 12mo., price 75 cts.

"He discourses in a truly learned and lively manner upon the original unity of language, and the origin, derivation, and history of words, with their morality and separate spheres of meaning."—*Evening Post*

"This is a noble tribute to the divine faculty of speech. Popularly written, for use as lectures, exact in its learning, and poetic in its vision, it is a book at once for the scholar and the general reader."—*New York Evangelist.*

"It is one of the most striking and original publications of the day, with nothing of hardness, dullness, or dryness about it, but altogether fresh, lively, and entertaining." —*Boston Evening Traveller.*

BRONCHITIS, AND KINDRED DISEASES.

In language adapted to common readers. By W. W. Hall, M. D One vol., 12 mo, price $1.00.

"It is written in a plain, direct, common-sense style, and is free from the quackery which marks many of the popular medical books of the day. It will prove useful to those who need it."—*Central Ch. Herald.*

"Those who are clergymen, or who are preparing for the sacred calling, and public speakers generally, should not fail of securing this work."—*Ch. Ambassador.*

"It is full of hints on the nature of the vital organs, and does away with much superstitious dread in regard to consumption."—*Greene County Whig.*

"This work gives some valuable instruction in regard to food and hygienic influences."—*Nashua Oasis.*

KNIGHTS OF ENGLAND, FRANCE, AND SCOTLAND.

By Henry William Herbert. One vol., 12mo., price $1.25.

"They are partly the romance of history and partly fiction, forming, when blended, portraitures, valuable from the correct drawing of the times they illustrate, and interesting from their romance."—*Albany Knickerbocker.*

"They are spirit-stirring productions, which will be read and admired by all who are pleased with historical tales written in a vigorous, bold, and dashing style."—*Boston Journal.*

"These legends of love and chivalry contain some of the finest tales which the graphic and powerful pen of Herbert has yet given to the lighter literature of the day" —*Detroit Free Press.*

CLOVERNOOK;

Or, Recollections of our Neighborhood in the West. By ALICE CAREY. Illustrated by DARLEY. One vol., 12mo., price $1.00. (Fourth edition.)

"In this volume there is a freshness which perpetually charms the reader. You seem to be made free of western homes at once."—*Old Colony Memorial.*

"They bear the true stamp of genius—simple, natural, truthful—and evince a keen sense of the humor and pathos, of the comedy and tragedy, of life in the country."—*J G Whittier.*

DREAM-LAND BY DAY-LIGHT:

A Panorama of Romance. By CAROLINE CHESEBRO'. Illustrated by DARLEY. One vol., 12mo., price $1.25. (Second edition.)

"These simple and beautiful stories are all highly endued with an exquisite perception of natural beauty, with which is combined an appreciative sense of its relation to the highest moral emotions."—*Albany State Register.*

"Gladly do we greet this floweret in the field of our literature, for it is fragrant with sweet and bright with hues that mark it to be of Heaven's own planting."—*Courier and Enquirer.*

"There is a depth of sentiment and feeling not ordinarily met with, and some of the noblest faculties and affections of man's nature are depicted and illustrated by the skilful pen of the authoress."—*Churchman.*

LAYS OF THE SCOTTISH CAVALIERS.

By WILLIAM E. AYTOUN, Professor of Literature and Belles-Lettres in the University of Edinburgh and Editor of Blackwood's Magazine. One vol., 12mo. cloth, price $1.00.

"Since Lockhart and Macaulay's ballads, we have had no metrical work to be compared in spirit, vigor, and rhythm with this. These ballads imbody and embalm the chief historical incidents of Scottish history—literally in 'thoughts that breathe and words that burn.' They are full of lyric energy, graphic description, and genuine feeling."—*Home Journal.*

"The fine ballad of 'Montrose' in this collection is alone worth the price of the book.' *Boston Transcript.*

THE BOOK OF BALLADS.

By BON GAULTIER. One volume, 12mo., cloth, price 75 cents.

"Here is a book for everybody who loves classic fun. It is made up of ballads of all sorts, each a capital parody upon the style of some one of the best lyric writers of the time, from the thundering versification of Lockhart and Macaulay to the sweetest and simplest strains of Wordsworth and Tennyson. The author is one of the first scholars, and one of the most finished writers of the day, and this production is but the frolic of his genius in play-time."—*Courier and Enquirer.*

"We do not know to whom belongs this *nom de plume*, but he is certainly a humorist of no common power."—*Providence Journal.*

NAPOLEON IN EXILE;

Or, a Voice from St. Helena. Being the opinions and reflections of Napoleon, on the most important events in his Life and Government, in his own words. By BARRY E. O'MEARA, his late Surgeon, with a Portrait of Napoleon, after the celebrated picture of Delaroche, and a view of St. Helena, both beautifully engraved on steel. 2 vols. 12mo, cloth, $2.

"Nothing can exceed the graphic truthfulness with which these volumes record the words and habits of Napoleon at St. Helena, and its pages are endowed with a charm far transcending that of romance."—*Albany State Register.*

"Every one who desires to obtain a thorough knowledge of the character of Napoleon, should possess himself of this book of O'Meara's."—*Arthur's Home Gazette.*

"It is something indeed to know Napoleon's opinion of the men and events of the thirty years preceding his fall, and his comments throw more light upon history than anything we have read."—*Albany Express.*

"The two volumes before us are worthy supplements to any history of France."—*Boston Evening Gazette.*

MEAGHER'S SPEECHES.

Speeches on the Legislative Independence of Ireland, with Introductory Notes. By FRANCIS THOMAS MEAGHER. 1 vol. 12mo, Cloth. Portrait. $1.

"The volume before us embodies some of the noblest specimens of Irish eloquence; not florid, bombastic, nor acrimonious, but direct, manly, and convincing."—*New York Tribune.*

"There is a glowing, a burning eloquence, in these speeches, which prove the author a man of extraordinary intellect."—*Boston Olive Branch.*

"As a brilliant and effective orator, Meagher stands unrivalled."—*Portland Eclectic.*

"All desiring to obtain a good idea of the political history of Ireland and the movements of her people, will be greatly assisted by reading these speeches."—*Syracuse Daily Star.*

"It is copiously illustrated by explanatory notes, so that the reader will have no difficulty in understanding the exact state of affairs when each speech was delivered."—*Boston Traveller.*

THE PRETTY PLATE,

A new and beautiful juvenile. By JOHN VINCENT. Illustrated by DARLEY. 1 vol. 16mo, Cloth, gilt, 63 cts. Extra gilt edges, 88 cts.

"We venture to say that no reader, great or small, who takes up this book, will lay it down unfinished."—*Courier and Enquirer.*

"This is an elegant little volume for a juvenile gift-book. The story is one of peculiar instruction and interest to the young, and is illustrated with beautiful engravings."—*Boston Christian Freeman.*

"One of the very best told and sweetest juvenile stories that has been issued from the press this season. It has a most excellent moral."—*Detroit Daily Advertiser.*

"A nice little book for a holyday present. Our little girl has read it through, and pronounces it first rate."—*Hartford Christian Secretary.*

"It is a pleasant child's book, well told, handsomely published, and illustrated in Darley's best style."—*Albany Express*

SIMMS' REVOLUTIONARY TALES.

UNIFORM SERIES.

New and entirely Revised Edition of WILLIAM GILMORE SIMMS' Romances of the Revolution, with Illustrations by DARLEY. Each complete in one vol., 12mo, cloth; price $1.25.

I. THE PARTISAN. **III. KATHARINE WALTON.** (In press.)
II. MELLICHAMPE. **IV. THE SCOUT.** (In press.)
V. WOODCRAFT. (In press.)

"The field of Revolutionary Romance was a rich one, and Mr. Simms has worked it admirably."—*Louisville Journal.*

"But few novelists of the age evince more power in the conception of a story, more artistic skill in its management, or more naturalness in the final *denouĕment* than Mr. Simms."—*Mobile Daily Advertiser.*

"Not only *par excellence the* literary man of the South, but next to no romance writer in America."—*Albany Knickerbocker.*

"Simms is a popular writer, and his romances are highly creditable to American literature."—*Boston Olive Branch.*

"These books are replete with daring and thrilling adventures, principally drawn from history."—*Boston Christian Freeman.*

"We take pleasure in noticing another of the series which Redfield is presenting to the country of the brilliant productions of one of the very ablest of our American authors—of one indeed who, in his peculiar sphere, is inimitable. This volume is a continuation of 'The Partisan.'"—*Philadelphia American Courier.*

ALSO UNIFORM WITH THE ABOVE

THE YEMASSEE,

A Romance of South Carolina. By WM. GILMORE SIMMS. New and entirely Revised Edition, with Illustrations by DARLEY. 12mo, cloth; price $1.25.

"In interest, it is second to but few romances in the language; in power, it holds a high rank; in healthfulness of style, it furnishes an example worthy of emulation."—*Greene County Whig.*

SIMMS' POETICAL WORKS.

Poems: Descriptive, Dramatic, Legendary, and Contemplative. By WM. GILMORE SIMMS. With a portrait on steel. 2 vols., 12mo, cloth; price $2.50.

CONTENTS: Norman Maurice; a Tragedy.—Atalantis; a Tale of the Sea.—Tales and Traditions of the South.—The City of the Silent—Southern Passages and Pictures.—Historical and Dramatic Sketches.—Scripture Legends.—Francesca da Rimini, etc.

"We are glad to see the poems of our best Southern author collected in two handsome volumes. Here we have embalmed in graphic and melodious verse the scenic wonders and charms of the South; and this feature of the work alone gives it a permanent and special value. None can read 'Southern Passages and Pictures' without feeling that therein the poetic aspects, association, and sentiment of Southern life and scenery are vitally enshrined. 'Norman Maurice' is a dramatic poem of peculiar scope and unusual interest; and 'Atalantis,' a poem upon which some of the author's finest powers of thought and expression are richly lavished. None of our poets offer so great a variety of style or a more original choice of subjects."—*Boston Traveller.*

"His versification is fluent and mellifluous, yet not lacking in point of vigor when an energetic style is requisite to the subject."—*N. Y. Commercial Advertiser.*

"Mr. Simms ranks among the first poets of our country, and these well-printed volumes contain poetical productions of rare merit."—*Washington (D. C.) Star.*

www.ingramcontent.com/pod-product-compliance
Lightning Source LLC
LaVergne TN
LVHW010137110826
845151LV00002B/373

* 9 7 8 1 4 2 5 5 4 0 2 3 4 *